Explaining Growth: A Global Research Project

This is IEA conference volume no. 137

International Economic Association
Series Standing Order ISBN 0–333–71242–0 hardback
Series Standing Order ISBN 0–333–80330–2 paperback
(*outside North America only*)

You can receive future titles in this series as they are published by placing a standing order. Please contact your bookseller or, in case of difficulty, write to us at the address below with your name and address, the title of the series and the ISBN quoted above.

Customer Services Department, Macmillan Distribution Ltd, Houndmills, Basingstoke, Hampshire RG21 6XS, England

Explaining Growth
A Global Research Project

Edited by

Gary McMahon and Lyn Squire
The Global Development Network

with a Foreword by Robert M. Solow

in association with the
International Economic Association

First published 2003 by
PALGRAVE MACMILLAN
Houndmills, Basingstoke, Hampshire RG21 6XS and
175 Fifth Avenue, New York, N. Y. 10010
Companies and representatives throughout the world

PALGRAVE MACMILLAN is the global academic imprint of the Palgrave
Macmillan division of St. Martin's Press, LLC and of Palgrave Macmillan Ltd.
Macmillan® is a registered trademark in the United States, United Kingdom
and other countries. Palgrave is a registered trademark in the European
Union and other countries.

ISBN 1–4039–1254–8 hardback
ISBN 1–4039–1746–9 paperback

This book is printed on paper suitable for recycling and made from fully
managed and sustained forest sources.

A catalogue record for this book is available from the British Library.

Library of Congress Cataloging-in-Publication Data
Explaining growth:a global research project / edited by Gary McMahon and
Lyn Squire; with a foreword by Robert Solow.
      p. cm.
   Includes bibliographical references and indexes.
   ISBN 1–4039–1254–8 – ISBN 1–4039–1746–9 (pbk.)
   1. Economic development. 2. Economic development–Case studies.
3. Developing countries–Economic policy–Case studies. 4. Developing
countries–Commercial policy–Case studies. 5. Globalization–Economic
aspects–Developing countries. I. McMahon, Gary. II. Squire, Lyn, 1946–
III. International Economic Association.
HD75.E97 2003
338.9–dc21   2003040527

10   9   8   7   6   5   4   3   2   1
12   11   10   09   08   07   06   05   04   03

Printed and bound in Great Britain by
Antony Rowe Ltd, Chippenham and Eastbourne

Contents

The International Economic Association

A non-profit organization with purely scientific aims, the International Economic Association (IEA) was founded in 1950. It is a federation of some 60 national economic associations in all parts of the world. Its basic purpose is the development of economics as an intellectual discipline, recognizing a diversity of problems, systems and values in the world and taking note of methodological diversities.

The IEA has, since its creation, sought to fulfil that purpose by promoting mutual understanding among economists through the organization of scientific meetings and common research programmes, and by means of publications on problems of fundamental as well as current importance. Deriving from its long concern to assure professional contacts between East and West and North and South, the IEA pays special attention to issues of economies in systemic transition and in the course of development. During its 50 years of existence, it has organized more than 100 round-table conferences for specialists on topics ranging from fundamental theories to methods and tools of analysis and major problems of the present-day world. Participation in round tables is at the invitation of a specialist programme committee, but 13 triennial World Congresses have regularly attracted the participation of individual economists from all over the world.

The Association is governed by a Council, comprising representatives of all member associations, and by a 15-member Executive Committee which is elected by the Council. The Executive Committee (2002–05) at the time of the publication of this volume was:

President:	Professor Janos Kornai, Hungary
President-elect:	Professor Guillermo Calvo, Chile
Vice-President:	Professor Bina Agarwal, India
Treasurer:	Professor Jacob Frenkel, Israel
Past President:	Professor Robert Solow, USA
Other members:	Professor Maria Augusztinovics, Hungary
	Professor Eliana Cardoso, Brazil
	Professor Eduardo Engel, USA
	Professor Heba Handoussa, Egypt
	Professor Michael Hoel, Norway
	Professor Jean-Jacques Laffont, France

	Professor Andreu Mas Colell, Spain
	Professor Kotaro Suzumura, Japan
	Professor Alessandro Vercelli, Italy
Advisers:	Professor Fiorella Padoa Schioppa, Italy
	Professor Vitor Constancio, Portugal
Secretary-General:	Professor Jean-Paul Fitoussi, France
General Editor:	Professor Michael Kaser, UK

Sir Austin Robinson was an active Adviser on the publication of IEA Conference proceedings from 1954 until his final short illness in 1993.

The Association has also been fortunate in having secured many outstanding economists to serve as President:

Gottfried Haberler (1950–53), Howard S. Ellis (1953–56), Erik Lindahl (1956–59), E.A.G. Robinson (1959–62), Ugo Papi (1962–65), Paul A. Samuelson (1965–68). Erik Lundberg (1968–71), Fritz Machlup (1971–74), Edmund Malinvaud (1974–77), Shigeto Tsuru (1977–80), Victor L. Urquidi (1980–83), Kenneth J. Arrow (1983–86), Amartya Sen (1986–89), Anthony B. Atkinson (1989–92), Michael Bruno (1992–95), Jacques Drèze (1995–99) and Robert Solow (1999–2002).

The activities of the Association are mainly funded from the subscriptions of members and grants from a number of organizations, including continuing support from UNESCO, through the International Social Science Council.

The Global Development Network

The Global Development Network (GDN) was inaugurated at the First Annual Global Development Conference held in Bonn in December 1999 with the objective of generating, sharing, and applying multidisciplinary knowledge for the purpose of development. GDN is an evolving network of research and policy institutes working together to address problems of national and regional development. Launched in 1999 by the World Bank, GDN became independent in 2001.

GDN is global:

- Supports multidisciplinary research in social sciences and mobilizes resources worldwide
- Produces policy-relevant knowledge on a global scale
- Promotes application of global knowledge through its local 'reinvention'

GDN is a network:

- Links research institutes from more than 100 countries and 10 regions of the world
- Coordinates research and strengthens partnerships worldwide
- Facilitates knowledge-sharing among researchers and policy-makers
- Promotes multidisciplinary collaboration

GDN is for development:

- Builds research capacity for development and alleviation of poverty
- Fosters research in developing/transitional countries
- Disseminates development knowledge to the public and policy-makers
- Bridges the gap between ideas and policies

Governance

Since December 2000, GDN has had its own governance statement and governing body, consisting of 17 members from around the world. The members represent the research community in different regions of the world, various social science disciplines, and professional international associations. Lal Jayawardena, the South Asian representative from Sri

Lanka, chairs the governing body. GDN activities are open to practitioners in all social sciences. Governing body members are:

Lal Jayawardena (Chair)	Social Scientists Association, Colombo, Sri Lanka
Bina Agarwal	International Economic Association, New Delhi, India
Richard Cooper	Harvard University, Cambridge, USA
Vittorio Corbo	Universidad Catolica de Chile, Santiago, Chile
Ulrich Hiemenz	OECD Development Centre, Paris, France
Inge Kaul	United Nations Development Programme, New York, USA
Jan Kmenta	Charles University, Prague, Czech Republic
Kyung Tae Lee	Korea Institute for International Economic Policy, Seoul, Korea
Samir Makdisi	American University of Beirut, Beirut, Lebanon
Krzysztof Palecki	International Political Science Association, Kraków, Poland
Sujata Patel	International Sociological Association, Pune, India
Guillermo Perry	World Bank, Bogota, Colombia
Victor Polterovich	Russian Academy of Sciences, Moscow, Russia
Hoda Rashad	Social Research Center, American University in Cairo, Cairo, Egypt
Akilagpa Sawyerr	Association of African Universities, Accra, Ghana
Diane Stone	University of Warwick, Coventry, UK
Shujiro Urata	Waseda University, Tokyo, Japan
Lyn Squire	Director, Global Development Network

Regional partners

Region	Network	Location
Asia/Pacific	GDN-Japan	Tokyo, Japan
East Asia	East Asian Development Network (EADN)	Singapore

Region	Network	Location
Eastern Europe	Center for Economic Research and Graduate Education (CERGE-EI)	Prague, Czech Republic
Europe	European Union Development Network (EUDN)	Bonn, Germany
Former Soviet Union	Economics and Education Research Consortium (EERC)	Moscow, Russia
Latin America and the Caribbean	Latin American and Caribbean Economic Association (LACEA)	Buenos Aires, Argentina
Middle East and North Africa	Economic Research Forum for Arab Countries, Iran and Turkey (ERF)	Cairo, Egypt
North America	GDN-North America (GDN-NA)	Washington, USA
South Asia	South Asian Network of Economic Institutes (SANEI)	New Delhi, India
Sub-Saharan Africa	African Economic Research Consortium (AERC)	Nairobi, Kenya

List of Contributors

Micael Castanheira, Université Libre de Bruxelles, Belgium.

Hadi Salehi Esfahani, University of Illinois at Urbana-Champagne, USA.

Sergei Guriev, New Economic School, Moscow, Russia.

Štěpán Jurajda, CERGE-EI, Prague, Czech Republic.

Jongil Kim, Dongguk University, Seoul, Korea.

Janet Mitchell, Facultés Universitaires Saint-Louis, Brussels.

Gary McMahon, Global Development Network, Washington, DC, USA.

Lant Pritchett, Harvard University, USA.

Djavad Salehi-Isfahani, Virginia Polytechnical Institute, Blacksburg, VA, USA.

Robert M. Solow, Massachusetts Institute of Technology, USA.

Charles C. Soludo, African Institute for Applied Economics, Enugu, and University of Nigeria, Nsukka, Nigeria.

Lyn Squire, Global Development Network, Washington, DC, USA.

List of Abbreviations

BMA	Bayesian model averaging
BMT	Becker, Murphy and Tamura
CEE	Central and Eastern Europe
CEPR	Centre for Economic Policy Research
CIS	Commonwealth of Independent States
CMEA	Council for Mutual Economic Assistance
EAP	East Asia and Pacific
EBRD	European Bank for Reconstruction and Development
ECA	Eastern Europe and Central Asia
ECARES	European Centre for Advanced Research in Economics
ESA	extreme bounds analysis
FDI	foreign direct investment
FSU	Former Soviet Union
GDN	Global Development Network
GDP	gross domestic product
GMM	generalized method of moments
GNP	gross national product
GRP	Global Research Project
HC	human capital
IADB	Interamerican Development Bank
ICOR	incremental capital–output ratio
ICRG	International Country Risk Guide
ILO	International Labour Office
IMF	International Monetary Fund
INDU	industrialised countries
IV	independent variable
LAC	Latin America and the Caribbean
MENA	Middle East and North Africa
MOOI	measure of our ignorance
NBER	National Bureau of Economic Research
NIE	newly-industrialized economy
NTB	non-tariff barrier
OECD	Organization for Economic Cooperation and Development
OLS	ordinary least squares
PE	public enterprise
PM	policy-maker

PMS	policy message sender
RHS	right-hand side
SAS	South Asia
s.d.	standard deviation
s.e.	standard error
SSA	Sub-Saharan Africa
SUR	seemingly-unrelated regression
SW	Sachs–Warner
TFP	total factor productivity
TFR	total fertility rate
UMNO	United Malays National Organization
UNCTAD	United Nations Conference on Trade and Development
VAR	vector auto-regression

Foreword

Anyone who has ever given or attended a public lecture knows that the statement 'X needs no introduction' is invariably followed by an introduction. My problem here is rather different. This potentially important book could use any one of several kinds of introduction. The question is which kind should I try to provide?

The main chapters are themselves summaries, so trying to summarize each of them would verge on pointlessness. Lyn Squire and Gary McMahon already describe the much larger project of which this book is a partial record, so there is no need to go over that ground either. I can afford to be idiosyncratic. So I shall offer a handful of comments inspired by the project and the book, the sort of thoughts that might naturally come from an economist who has participated peripherally in the project, through the International Economic Association, and whose professional interests are related to economic development though certainly not centred there.

It is worth emphasizing that the project is a coordinated enterprise of the Global Development Network, which is itself a sort of federation of Regional Development Networks, which are themselves much like federations of independent research institutes in many countries. Many serious economists in the development world are focusing their combined and organized efforts on what is pretty clearly the most important economic issue facing us all, everywhere: how to understand the poverty of poor countries, and by implication how to improve what is not a pretty situation. Nor is that situation getting better by itself: in Lant Pritchett's pungent phase, when you compare the poor countries with OECD countries, what you see is 'divergence, big time'. Understanding comes first, because logically it should come first, and also because the authors of the study are research economists first and foremost.

That shows itself right away in the particular set of headings under which the work was organized: the macroeconomic sources of growth, the microeconomics of growth, markets, and political economy. That classification rests on an analytical structure that is missing from most popular and political discussion.

The treatment of the sources of economic growth uses a standard common framework. To my way of thinking, however, this choice should not be viewed as intending to shoehorn all poor, developing countries into a single, tight model (and least of all into a model that was originally devised to apply to an advanced capitalist industrial economy). In this context, the standard approach represents an accounting framework rather than an equilibrium model.

The accounting-framework view has the merit of directing attention to the underlying data, especially those on physical and human capital. No doubt there are issues of 'measurement' to be settled, but there are even more important conceptual matters to be straightened out. Physical capital can be wasted in foolish uses, or rendered unproductive by the absence of complementary inputs. In the case of human capital, almost universally we measure schooling or school expenditures. Both of these are inputs into the production of human capital, rather than human capital itself. Most of us know from personal experience that some hours of schooling produce less human capital than others. Some more direct measure of the accumulation of productive human capital, if it were available, might resolve some puzzles about the role of education and training in the economic growth of poor countries.

The accounting framework has the additional advantage that it facilitates the process of looking at similarities and differences across regions and, eventually, across individual countries. The logic of such comparisons does not lead inevitably to routine cross-country regressions. It seems reasonable to me to look for whatever intuitively relevant characteristics fast-growing countries have in common, and similarly for slow-growing countries. (It might be better to think of rich and poor countries instead.) However, either kind of descriptive exercise falls short of regarding each country as a point on a function, differing from other countries only in the values of a small number of variables (including 0–1 variables of course). This project proposes to use comparisons in a better way through more extensive and intensive country-by-country analysis.

It is important to take anomalies seriously. If one or two countries have all the variables right (or wrong) and still grow slowly (or rapidly), it is a mistake just to say: Oh well, this must be a bad (or good) draw from some distribution of luck. National economies observed over decades are not a sample from some meaningful probability distribution. Careful study of an anomaly can lead to real insight about development. If you assemble a Christmas toy according to the instructions and still it does not work, yes, it may merely be a defective item. Yet, we all know from experience that it is a good idea to go over the process carefully, trying to discover just why the toy does not work.

One function of 'sources of growth' analysis for a single country is to give some estimate of what is physically-technically feasible, as a benchmark against which to consider what has been politically-economically achieved or achievable. In interpreting the results, one should keep in mind that poor countries are usually not at the known technological frontier, even leaving aside questions of allocative inefficiency.

Poor countries are not usually in the position of an OECD country, not knowing what technological possibilities will be available 10 years from now. The poor country is more likely plotting a path toward an already thinkable state of affairs. This will require the adoption of more advanced but existing technology, the acquisition of the physical and human capital required to exploit it, and perhaps the creation of necessary social and institutional infrastructure.

I think it may be a wasteful detour to frame this problem in terms of 'growth'. The poor country is trying to get from an observable here to a clearly imaginable there, from a lower to a higher level of technology and productivity. Of course, if it succeeds it will grow in the course of getting from here to there, but this is not at all steady-state growth, and not even quite what academic growth theory is about. Clarity might be served if there were more talk about growth in this context.

In logical order, the next step is probably the microeconomics of growth. Economists are trained to be methodological individualists. The emphasis here is on 'methodological'. I am talking about the presumption that whatever happens in an economy happens because some individual agents take some specific actions, and therefore a full understanding rests on understanding why those persons or families or firms or governments did those things. This has nothing to do with the quite different belief that individual agents either act or should act for narrow private motives, constrained only by technology and enforced laws (that is, to maximize a personal utility subject only to a budget constraint). A methodological individualist is free to believe that what agents do is in some respects socially determined and departs from mere individualistic self-interest.

Microeconomic institutions represent another dimension along which regional or national (or local) economies can differ from one another. Probably the key question here is the nature of the incentives provided to individual agents by various legal, customary or other rules of the game. Since it is the actions of individual agents that generate national economic outcomes, it is important to know how their perceived environment leads individual agents to act. This is not necessarily a simple, straightforward matter. Here are a couple of examples that occur to a non-specialist economist.

One would not be surprised to find that imperfections and asymmetries of information are as significant in developing economies as they are in developed ones. It also seems likely that the variety of institutions and customs could imply that such imperfections appear in different contexts and function in different ways in economies at differing stages of development. Hence, they may give rise to different strategies for adapting to information failures, and therefore to different incentives.

Analogously, exposure to risk is ubiquitous, and possibly more dangerous in poor societies than in rich ones. Context and history provide a wide variety of institutions and transactions for insuring against risk or otherwise dealing with it. Once again the incentives presented to agents will depend on the possibilities available to them and on the attitudes they have learned.

The presence of corruption – public and private – and the ways in which it operates will also affect incentives and therefore actions. Outside economic observers usually praise 'entrepreneurship' and those who exercise it as agents of development, but under some circumstances entrepreneurship may tend to be directed toward swindling, extortion and violently enforced monopoly. Presumably it is a matter of the incentives presented by local institutions and historically determined attitudes. Is criminal entrepreneurship better than no entrepreneurship at all? One hopes that there are other alternatives, at any stage of development. The point that I am trying to make is that the microeconomics of growth and development is much more than the application of lessons learned in Marshall.

The importance of foreign direct investment and the role of multinational corporations play a role here as well as in any calculation of the sources of growth. The question of incentives is two-sided. One has to ask: what are the incentives that local institutions and regulations provide for multinational corporations and other foreign investors? But one also has to ask: what do the incentives that local institutions and regulations provide for multinational corporations and other foreign investors and corporations do to the incentives of local agents?

Markets are not the only mechanism by which individual agents interact, but they are probably the most important. The nature of those markets – intensity of competition, ubiquity of information, disparities of power, enforcement of rules – is an important source of incentives to the individual agents themselves. The same factors govern the efficiency with which markets transmit individual incentives into outcomes, and into incentives from other agents; hence the importance of distortions, delays and biases.

The possible variety of market arrangements is staggering. There are retail markets to analyse, labour markets, markets for intermediate inputs, credit markets, housing markets, the market for land, each capable of different institutional arrangements with different implications for incentives, behaviour and outcomes. A market may be characterized by more than just the conditions of entry and the degree of monopoly. Market institutions create certain shared expectations about behaviour, which have to be taken into account in understanding the relation between institutions and outcomes: efficiency, equity, linkage with other markets.

Apart from this interplay among markets, incentives and outcomes, any plan of reform in the interests of development will need to figure out how to proceed through interrelated markets, and how to use the institutions that are already there.

The last broad topic is the *political economy* of development and growth. There is more than one possible interpretation of the ancient phase 'political economy'. I take it that we want to study such questions as: what groups in a particular country will gain most from development and can probably be counted on to support it? What groups are likely to be damaged, at least in the short run and maybe longer, and will probably oppose it? In other words, what are the main constituencies for and against development? What might be done to compensate the losers without endangering development itself? Which reforms are politically feasible at the start of the process, and which might become feasible later on? The answers to questions like these will surely depend on preexisting history and institutions in each country and region, so the country studies will play the essential role.

It is not the task of this book to design and urge development programmes, but it could mark the beginning of an important discussion of economically and politically feasible development programmes (or at least of useful steps toward development). It is an important and special characteristic of this project that it is in the hands of trained research economists, mainly from the developing countries themselves. The hope is that the network structure will encourage and foster both international comparisons and international collaboration in research with consequent exchange of ideas, methods and results. This is only the first of what we all hope will be a series of collaborative studies of development economics in all its variety. It is a privilege for me and for the International Economic Association to be connected with it.

Massachusetts Institute of Technology   ROBERT M. SOLOW

1
Explaining Growth: A Global Research Project

Gary McMahon and Lyn Squire

1   Introduction

The Global Research Project 'Explaining Growth' is an attempt to compile the most comprehensive assessment of growth in developing and transition countries. Supported by the Global Development Network (GDN) – an independent association of research and policy institutes whose goal is to generate, share, and apply to policy multi-disciplinary knowledge for the purpose of development – it is an integrated yet decentralized project, designed by and for people from every corner of the globe.[1]

The focus on growth does not imply the old mistake of seeing economic wealth as the ultimate measure of well-being. Rather, the project takes the view that growth provides the opportunity to use resources well – while stagnation or deterioration robs countries of the power to act. The project also recognizes that there are many paths toward growth, some leading to dead-ends and others ever onwards to sustainable prosperity for all. A thorough understanding of the history of growth points the way forward.

Designed in two phases, the first phase has sought to review and discover broad similarities and comparable experiences in each of six regions spanning the developing world.[2] These reviews provide the framework for the second phase of the project, in-depth country case studies of growth. This volume bridges the two phases. It summarizes the main results of the regional analyses and in doing so sets the stage for the country studies.

Similar to the entire volume, this introductory chapter has two main objectives. In a very summary form, it reaches back to bring out the most important results of the first phase of the project. At the same time it points the way forward to the country studies in the second phase of the project. However, rather than simply summarize the results of the other chapters, a simple discriminant analysis (described in detail in section 4) is used to illustrate and emphasize two main lessons of the regional thematic studies. First, although cross-country sources of growth studies can point the way to important determinants of growth, they are not very adept at catching the key interactions between variables that can be critical for sustained growth to occur. Second, and consequently, countries with similar values of key variables often have quite different growth records. The regional thematic studies show that there are stories at the level of micro behaviour, markets and political economy that can help explain these divergent results. However, the precise nature and relative importance of the underlying relationships can only be determined at the level of the individual countries.

The organization of this chapter is as follows. The next section contains a description of the project and the organization of this volume. Section 3 highlights the key results of the other chapters, and in section 4 the discriminant analysis and the data are described with the empirical results being presented in section 5. The last section contains conclusions and lessons for the country studies in the second phase of the project arising from the regional thematic studies and this volume.

2   Project description and organization of the volume

As noted above, there are two phases to this project, with this volume being the bridge between them. The first (completed) phase consisted of thematic papers undertaken at the regional level; the second, which began in early 2001, consists of approximately 70 country studies.

Phase 1: regional reviews

Each of the regional reviews encompassed four themes. The first focused on sources and determinants of *aggregate growth* and sought to deliver to country case study authors a summary of cross-country growth analysis. The second turned to the role of *markets* in influencing economic growth. Authors explored the functioning of key markets – especially those for labour and capital – and assessed the he extent to which they have hampered or contributed to growth performance. The third examined the performance of *microeconomic agents* in the growth process, focusing particularly on households and enterprises, and covering such issues as household saving and spending on education, and firm and farm investment and productivity growth. The fourth looked at the *political economy* of growth. Certain policies undoubtedly constitute an important source of variation in growth experiences, and the papers on the political economy of growth investigated why countries pursued the particular policies that they did, sometimes even in the face of evidence of their failure.

With the objective of providing a framework for the country studies, the regional thematic research drew heavily on the existing empirical literature to support findings and, depending on data, used a long historical perspective of 30 to 50 years to inform a close look at more recent events and prospects for the future. A considerable effort went into interpretation, providing vehicles that help the country authors to explain growth in the context of specific countries by pointing to areas warranting additional work, as well as indicating countries that in some respect present a unique issue or problem that warrants separate analysis.

Over 40 authors drawn from all six regions participated in the first phase of the project. The authors worked together and with eminent economists as resource persons designated to provide technical assistance to the researchers.[3] The final step for the thematic papers took place in June 2000 in Prague when the International Economic Association undertook an independent review of the thematic papers prior to publication.

Phase 2: country studies

Phase two of the project turns from broad regional themes to the in-depth analysis of the particular experiences of about 70 countries. Given the four themes of the regional reviews, the authors of the country studies will explore how each theme played out over a nation's history. Thus, the authors will substantiate general conclusions with real instances, while adding a necessary degree of nuance. In some cases, authors will explore circumstances that led to experiences substantially different from prevailing regional events. This sharper look at particular examples will inform a fresh look at the regional themes.

The authors divide the years from approximately 1950–2000 into different periods, each of which is distinguished by an important turning point in the country's growth history. For example, a major policy shift or large natural resource discovery may have set a country off on to a different growth pattern, both quantitatively and qualitatively. For each period, the authors will present the initial conditions, including the institutional and policy heritage and political interest groups. Then they will undertake an analysis of: the behaviour of agents and their behaviour with respect to any exogenous or endogenous shocks; the interaction between the behaviour of agents and policy and institutional changes; the growth outcome of each period and any important changes in institutions, policies and political interest groups; and any important changes in other indicators of development, such as poverty, income distribution, health, education and the environment.

Authors then outline the main conclusions of the results of the period analysis, emphasizing the factors of production that were most important for explaining aggregate growth, and the policies and institutions that helped or hindered the accumulation or efficient use of these factors of production. Prospects for aggregate growth in the country and policy and institutional recommendations will be discussed. Finally, authors will explain how their results shed light on the issues highlighted in the thematic overview studies, as discussed in this volume. From the conclusions of the 70 or so country studies will emerge a new synthesis that revisits and deepens the comparative assessment of growth begun by the thematic papers. Such a synthesis will greatly enrich an already comprehensive global account of economic growth.

Organization of this volume

This volume takes stock of the project at its mid-point. Each of the four central chapters deals with one of the four themes covered in the regional studies. Their purpose is to look at the results of the first phase by theme *across regions*. As such they make an independent contribution in their own right by drawing out cross-regional similarities and differences. The final chapter is an attempt to alert the country authors to issues that may have been missed or underemphasized in phase 1.

3　Key results of thematic chapters

As noted above, studies were undertaken in each region on four different aspects of growth. Chapters 2 to 5 in this volume analyse sources of growth, microeconomic agents and growth, markets and growth, and the political economy of growth, respectively, both by reference to the general literature on the subject and by placing the results of the regional thematic papers in the context of this literature. Chapter 6 then steps back and raises fundamental questions about current thinking regarding growth and about some of the empirical methods used in the literature in general and in some of the thematic papers prepared for this project. The questions lend further justification to both the effort in the thematic studies to go beyond simple cross-country regressions and growth accounting, and to the focus in phase 2 on country studies. In this section the key arguments and results of each of these chapters will be presented. These are not meant to be a summary of the chapters but only a guide to readers on the nature of the discussions to be encountered.

Sources of growth

The authors (Soludo and Kim) of this chapter begin by noting:

> The goal of this chapter is to illuminate the state of play by summarizing what we know, what we don't know and what we should know about the sources of growth in developing regions in the last 40 years. ... Our key finding is that the literature has come a long way to underscore some of the growth fundamentals consistent with our educated guesses. However, we admit that the largely unresolved issues tend to raise more questions than answers. (p. 33)

In much of the rest of the chapter they give evidence supporting this statement.

In the next section on growth accounting, they examine the debate of capital accumulation versus total factor productivity (TFP) growth as driving long-run growth. While they give evidence for both views, they emphasize that the data and methodological problems are generally too serious to give too much credence to the results. They do note that there is evidence supporting the fact that regions with higher capital accumulation also had higher TFP growth, a finding which if generally true could put an end to an increasingly contentious debate.

Next, they evaluate the cross-country 'regression-based' approaches to decomposing the sources of growth. On the positive side, they find that the same things tend to matter in different regions – initial conditions, savings and investment in human and physical capital, population growth, adequate macroeconomic policy, openness to trade, private-sector orientation, adequate governance and institutional quality, and size and composition of government expenditure. Moreover, after liberalization the same variables tend to be important for transition economies as for developing countries. The problem is that there is a sense that everything is important, which is not very useful to the policy-maker. Finally, with respect to methodological issues, they say: 'A huge research agenda on the methodology of cross-national regressions is yet to begin' (p. 67).

In their conclusions they point towards the importance of context-specific analysis and country case studies. Sources of growth analysis can only take us so far, and this type of analysis may well have already reached the point of strong diminishing returns.

Microeconomic agents and growth

The focus of this chapter is the micro behaviour of two types of agents – households and firms. The authors Guriev and Salehi-Isfahani discuss behavioural differences across regions and countries in the way that micro agents save, invest, innovate and accumulate human capital.

The strongest result arising from the analysis of households is that the movement from a strategy based on high fertility and low human capital accumulation to one centred on low fertility and high levels of human capital is crucial for economic growth. The authors analyse different aspects of this problem, with the key result that households will continue with a high fertility, low human-capital strategy as long as either the risks of its alternatives are perceived to be too high or the returns to risk management are too low. Moreover, the structures of the markets and institutions in which the households must function will often determine the types of risks that can be avoided or adequately managed. In sum, very different strategies are followed in different regions and countries due to different risk–reward trade-offs.

The discussion of firm behaviour also focuses on strategies to reduce risk, many of which seem inefficient without a clear understanding of the market and institutional structure in which firms find themselves. However, the importance of rent-seeking – both by firms and the predatory actions of others on firms' profits – takes centre-stage in the analysis. Small firms are often unable to prosper and grow due to the payments owners must make to bureaucrats and criminals. Large firms are often resistant to restructuring as they are loath to give up the subsidies, cheap credit and other advantages that they have become dependent on. As is clear from the case of the transition countries, society gains little or nothing from privatization if soft budget constraints exist. There must be incentives to restructure, and strategies that have centred on openness and foreign competition seem the most useful, as long as they are accompanied by a functioning infrastructure.

An important question left open in this chapter is whether micro agents cause markets to change in response to their behaviour, or is it that changing market (or institutional) structures cause micro behaviour to change. Of course, if markets and institutions lead the way, it usually means that there must be changes in the micro behaviour of a third group of agents – that is, politicians and government officials.

Markets and growth

Analytically, this chapter is divided into two parts. In the first part the authors Jurajda and Mitchell discuss the effects of various types of markets – financial, labour, natural resource, and product – on growth. The analysis of each market is undertaken in three dimensions: infrastructure (including factors such as laws and courts); price wedges or distortions; and participants. In the second part of the chapter, the authors summarize the findings of the regional papers by presenting four stylized growth scenarios, each relevant for some regions of the world: (1) importance of openness policies; (2) market flexibility in response to major shocks; (3) influence of high natural-resource endowments; and (4) consistently low growth.

A strong message coming from this chapter is that reforming a distorted market will usually not lead to increased efficiency and growth if the supporting infrastructure does not exist or if the distortions created strong rent-collecting interests. For example, opening up the economy to international trade is unlikely to attract significant investment if the physical infrastructure, such as roads and electric power, or the legal infrastructure, such as contract enforcement and general law and order, are highly deficient. The varied experience of the transition economies – most of which opened up significantly – strongly supports this argument.

Similarly, if the market distortion has existed for some time, the holders of the rents that it generated are going to be very reluctant to give them up and are likely to behave in a manner to thwart the intentions of the reform. The latter result is particularly true if the distortion, as is often the case, was put in place to protect a state-owned enterprise. Moreover, reform in one market can face indirect vested interests when its success depends on flexibility in another market. For example, the opening up of a product market to increase efficiency will generally have unsatisfactory results if existing laws and regulations make it very difficult to shed or reallocate labour. In general, it is important to analyse who the rent-seeking participants are, how their rent-seeking behaviour manifests itself, and how they are likely to react if challenged with reforms.

The importance of factor reallocation is emphasized strongly in the chapter. Economies that do well over the long term are usually those that can reallocate factors in the face of major or minor shocks, and it is essential to understand what allows a system to do so. Of course, the ability to reallocate factors is often strongly linked to the inability of various groups of participants to protect themselves from shocks at the expense of society as a whole. Moreover, reallocation will often depend on the supporting infrastructure. For example, in many transition countries the reallocation of labour has been made considerably more difficult by the lack of a mortgage market in housing. More generally, the authors believe that the ability of the labour market to efficiently allocate human capital is often as important as the ability of society to create human capital. One of the strongest empirical points of the regional studies is that many countries that have devoted large amounts of resources to creating human capital have had poor or mediocre growth performances. However, there is a dearth of research on how labour markets allocate this human capital.

Finally, in many cases it is not clear whether it is lack of market development or poor initial conditions that is the primary brake on growth. For example, the initial conditions in much of Sub-Saharan Africa may have been so poor as to make market development extremely difficult. Hence, the low growth found in many of these countries may be due more to the profoundly difficult conditions in which these economies found themselves as much as to inadequate market development.

Political economy of growth

The key question addressed in this chapter by Castanheira and Esfahani is why governments undertake and persist with policies that are inefficient for long-run growth. While ruling politicians usually want control over larger rents, some seem to totally ignore the negative externalities that they can have on growth, but others place a greater emphasis on increasing the size of the pie. The authors try to explain these different results, but even more so they stress how little there is that we are sure of, and how much more work needs to be done. They present a methodology whose core idea is that:

> Sub-optimal growth outcomes are the results of contracting problems among the players in an economy. Inefficiency may arise when policy-makers represent only narrow interests, cannot commit the government to constrained sets of future actions, or fail to coordinate themselves and the groups that they represent. (p. 201)

Their work focuses on the institutions necessary for effective reform and the reasons that these institutions do not develop. While they do not ignore the importance of interest groups on the existence and persistence of inefficient policies, they put as much stress on (a) the types of interest groups that form in different situations, (b) the persistence of inefficient policies due to institutional structures that do not permit effective reform, and (c) the persistence of inefficient institutions.

Similarly, when the authors examine the relationship between different forms of government and growth or inequality and growth, they find that there are few generalities that can be made. It is necessary to look at the underlying institutions in the democracy or in the country trying to undertake redistribution. They note the need for much more work on how political and economic inequality interact, and why redistribution works in some countries but not in others.

Finally, the authors note the wide variation across countries. They indicate the results of some country studies but note that except in a couple of cases there is little comparability across countries. Hence, there is a need for more studies in which similar methodologies are used. In their chapter they give guidance on the ingredients of such a methodology.

Concluding chapter

The author of the concluding chapter does not attempt to summarize the other chapters in this volume but rather to point out possible ways that the country studies in phase 2 could move forward. He breaks up his presentation into two sections. In the first he examines the validity of a number of answers that economists think they know about growth. In the second he warns about areas where the country-study researchers may focus their attention on the object rather than the reason it is as it is (which he colourfully depicts as examining the place where the tyre is flat rather than trying to find the hole).

In both sections a constant theme is that generalities about growth – especially those based on cross-country regressions – are not going to bring us very far. More in-depth studies of the experiences of individual countries are necessary for understanding the growth process as well as making realistic policy recommendations. For example, in the section on 'received wisdom', the author points out that there is nothing new in the new growth theory's emphasis on education and human capital. Development economists had seen education as a key to economic growth since at least the 1950s. However, he points out that what is new is that no-one can statistically find a strong link between investments in education and the growth records of countries. Nevertheless, he does not give up on education; what is needed is a new type of analysis, one that can only be done at the country level:

> The country case studies need to go beyond 'education is good' to understand how quality of learning, demand for educated labour, and government policies (including hiring policies) interact to determine the impact of education on growth. (p. 217)

Similarly, the author stresses the need for country case studies when looking at diverse topics such as political economy, institutions and policies themselves. Researchers have a strong tendency to look at institutions or at policies as if they mattered in themselves. However, he points out that it is the performance of institutions and how policies become actions that are the key issues. A researcher will be able to say little about a country's growth history simply by looking at the existing set of institutions and economic policies in a country. The reality is that countries with very similar institutions and very similar policies have very different experiences and results.

In the conclusion he notes that every country study will not be able to deal with all of the outstanding issues on growth. Nevertheless, by focusing on a subset of these concerns, each one will help to advance our understanding of the complexities of the growth process.

4   Discriminant analysis: methodology and data

The analysis employed in this chapter demonstrates the central message of this research: growth is a complex process that can occur in different ways at different times. Attempts to identify 'the' factors leading to growth, useful though they may be, can never tell the full story for all or even most countries. To show this we use simple discriminant analysis to identify the factors that *on average* distinguish high-growth countries from low-growth countries. This mirrors the approach of the regional reviews in that it focuses on groups of countries, though not necessarily geographic regions. At the same time, it identifies countries that have many of the factors associated with high growth and yet do not manage to achieve it. It also identifies countries that have many of the factors associated with low growth and yet achieve high growth. These errors of classification raise questions that can only be answered through the country studies.

Rules, exceptions and interdependencies

As Lucas (1988) argued in his Marshall Lectures, explaining growth must be an important priority. The power of compound growth and the observed variation in growth rates have tremendous consequences:

for example, Botswana's GDP per capita grew at an annual rate of 6.8 per cent a year for the 30 years 1969 to 1998 and as a result, average incomes increased sevenfold. In nearby Zimbabwe, the per capita growth rate was only 0.4 per cent implying a negligible increase of 13 per cent in average incomes over the entire period. The difference is startling. Moreover, well over 20 countries in the developing world actually saw GDP per capita decline. In the worst case, the Democratic Republic of Congo saw GDP per capita decline at an annual rate of 3.9 per cent, and the citizens of that country saw their incomes decline by over 75 per cent from the beginning to the end of the period. Explaining these differences commands our attention.

The economics profession has responded with a major empirical assault. Excellent surveys of the by-now vast empirical literature on the determinants of growth include Barro (1997), Sala-i-Martin (1997) and Aghion and Howitt (1998). Much of this work employs two techniques: growth accounting and cross-country regressions. Given this vast effort, why have we undertaken yet another project on the same issue? The answer comes in two parts. First, while our project does make use of growth accounting and cross-country regressions, the thematic papers of the first phase take other approaches as well in an attempt to provide a richer understanding of growth. For example, growth accounting and cross-country regressions say nothing about the political environment governing the choice of policies that in turn influence growth rates. Yet this was the focus of one of our four themes. Second, phase 2 of the project will take us into the details of specific countries, something that growth accounting and cross-country regressions typically fail to address. This chapter focuses on the importance of conducting analysis at the level of individual countries.

To begin, consider one of the 'rules' that typically emerges from both growth accounting and cross-country regressions. A common finding in the literature is the importance of factor accumulation, in particular physical capital accumulation.[4] The same result emerged from the regional reviews conducted for this study. For instance, in Hahn and Kim (2000), physical capital accumulation, openness and institutional quality seem to play a major role in economic growth in East Asia. Though not as important as in East Asia, results for South Asia in Guha-Khasnobis and Bari (2000) also highlighted capital accumulation. In searching for an explanation of the relatively slower African growth, O'Connell and Ndulu (2000) point to the relatively slow accumulation of capital, low growth in total factor productivity and pressures from high population growth rates.

This and similar evidence, then, points to the accumulation of physical capital as one of the key determinants of growth. Nevertheless, it is very easy to point to well-known exceptions to this 'rule'. For example, Gabon's investment rate has averaged 35.5 per cent of GDP for the same 30 years examined above, and yet its GDP per capita has increased at the extraordinarily low level of 0.2 per cent a year. Pakistan, on the other hand, with a relatively modest investment rate of 17.7 per cent has seen its GDP per capita increase at a very respectable 2.8 per cent a year. This is of course an obvious point, but its implications have not been actively pursued. Here we consider an explanation based on interdependencies and thresholds. Growth may require the simultaneous presence of several factors because of powerful interdependencies among determinants, and the power of any single determinant then becomes context-specific. And growth may require that key determinants exceed certain critical levels or thresholds before the interdependencies exert a powerful influence on growth.

A great deal happens between the act of investing and the moment that new output is created. Investment has to be allocated to different purposes, other factors of production have to be combined with capital, and the environment must be sufficiently stable and free of disruption, external shocks, war, and so on. In other words, the output yielded by a unit of investment depends on a whole slew of factors. Investment interacts with these other factors and it is the interaction that determines the final outcome. Thus, any assessment has to allow for the interdependencies that determine whether investment promotes rapid growth or a waste of resources. In the extreme, investment's yield is context-specific. Indeed, different sets of interdependent variables might be perfectly capable of generating growth. The regional reviews can be viewed as a partial attempt to place the analysis in a more uniform context precisely by analysing each region separately. The use of regions as the domain of analysis presumably helps control for a range of institutional and cultural factors that differ sharply across regions. Whether this is a useful device is an issue to which we will return.

While cross-country regressions can deal with context-dependence or interdependencies through the use of interactive terms, the scope for doing so is limited. Typically, the standard growth studies assume that the marginal impact of an explanatory variable is independent of the value of other variables. This assumption abstracts from context-dependence. In addition, these studies also assume that the marginal impact of an explanatory variable is independent of the value of that variable.

Thus, they also ignore the possibility of non-linearities in the growth relationships. Yet a factor's ability to generate significant interdependencies might depend entirely on reaching a critical level. For example, a high degree of literacy and a well-developed legal system may be necessary before the full potential benefit of a given level of investment is realized. Furthermore, the benefit may only manifest itself when investment also exceeds a certain threshold.

To provide a straightforward link between the regionally based analysis of the thematic papers and the country studies, this chapter employs a simple discriminant analysis that identifies interdependencies and thresholds. It simultaneously points to common patterns and highlights outliers. Some recent work covering these concepts – thresholds and interdependencies – includes Ghosh and Wolf (1998), Easterly (1994), and Azariadis and Drazen (1990).

Growth performance

We seek to explain the long-run growth performance of as many developing countries as possible, and to that end we categorize 83 developing countries according to their long-run growth experience. We use the least-squares growth rate to represent the average per capita GDP growth rate measured in local currency units for each country for the 31-year period 1968–1998.[5] Using these rates relative to the average growth rate for high-income OECD countries (2.1 per cent for the 31 years), we identify three types of growth experience – high, medium and low. Table 1.1 shows the categories of countries sorted by their least-square growth rates.

The high-growth category consists of countries whose average growth rate is at least equal to the mean of the OECD countries. The observed period average growth rates for these countries range between 2.1 and 6.9 per cent with a group average growth rate of 4 per cent for the 31 years. Countries whose mean growth rate lies farthest below that of the OECD countries form the low-growth performance category. Their average growth rates fall within the range of –3.9 to 0.2 per cent with a group average growth rate of –0.9 per cent for the 31 years. The rest, with average growth rates ranging between 0.3 and 2.0 per cent, constitute the medium-growth performance countries. Their group average is 1.1 per cent.

Analytical method

The analytical method employed is the classification tree analysis *à la* Breiman *et al.* (1984). This approach, as mentioned earlier, is a subtle

Table 1.1 Country categorization by per capita GDP growth performance

High-growth performance		Medium-growth performance		Low-growth performance	
Country	*Average growth rate*	*Country*	*Average growth rate*	*Country*	*Average growth rate*
China	6.9	Colombia	2.0	Argentina	0.2
Botswana	6.8	Paraguay	2.0	Gabon	0.2
Taiwan, China	6.7	Brazil	2.0	Benin	0.2
Korea, Rep.	6.6	Morocco	1.8	Guinea-Bissau	0.1
Malta	6.0	Congo, Rep.	1.8	Mali	-0.2
Singapore	6.0	Ecuador	1.7	South Africa	-0.3
Hong Kong, China	5.5	Trinidad and Tobago	1.6	Nigeria	-0.3
Thailand	5.3	Bangladesh	1.6	Rwanda	-0.4
Indonesia	4.9	Barbados	1.4	Mauritania	-0.4
Mauritius	4.2	Uruguay	1.4	Jamaica	-0.4
Malaysia	4.2	Mexico	1.3	Senegal	-0.4
Egypt, Arab Rep.	3.4	Nepal	1.3	El Salvador	-0.4
Seychelles	3.3	Fiji	1.1	Chad	-0.5
Oman	3.2	Burkina Faso	1.1	Peru	-0.5
Sri Lanka	3.1	Costa Rica	1.1	Guyana	-0.5
Belize	3.0	Cameroon	1.0	Togo	-0.8
Lesotho	2.9	Bahamas, The	1.0	Ghana	-0.8
Pakistan	2.8	Kenya	0.9	Venezuela	-0.9
Chile	2.8	Panama	0.8	Saudi Arabia	-0.9
India	2.6	Algeria	0.7	Haiti	-1.0
Tunisia	2.5	Philippines	0.6	Cote d'Ivoire	-1.1
Solomon Islands	2.4	Honduras	0.5	Central African Rep.	-1.3
Israel	2.2	Guatemala	0.5	Sierra Leone	-1.4

Table 1.1 Country categorization by per capita GDP growth performance–*continued*

High-growth performance		Medium-growth performance		Low-growth performance	
Country	Average growth rate	Country	Average growth rate	Country	Average growth rate
Dominican Republic	2.1	Zimbabwe	0.4	Madagascar	-2.0
Swaziland	2.1	Papua New Guinea	0.4	Zambia	-2.0
Syrian Arab Republic	2.1	Burundi	0.4	Niger	-2.3
		Sudan	0.4	Nicaragua	-3.4
		Gambia, The	0.4	Congo, Dem. Rep.	-3.9
		Malawi	0.4		
Total 26		Total 29		Total 28	

form of discriminant analysis that sets a sequence of rules for classifying a binary dependent variable on the basis of a set of explanatory variables. The objective of the method is to determine the set of rules that captures a discriminant variable and a threshold, permitting the best sorting of the dependent variable into its two constituent groups, high and low-growth.

There are two stages to the classification tree procedure – growing and pruning. In the growing stage, the algorithm splits the sample of observations into two sub-samples at each branch of the tree. Each split of the sample is predicated on a threshold value of one of the explanatory variables. Suppose, for example, that in all countries falling into the high-growth group, the average investment rate is above 22 per cent, while in all countries falling in the low-growth group, the average investment is below 22 per cent. In this case, *average investment rates below 22 per cent imply low growth* becomes the rule that discriminates between the two groups and the resulting decision tree would have a single branching with two nodes. The algorithm chooses the explanatory variable and the threshold that best divides the sample.

In practice, such discriminating rules are rarely perfect and most have associated errors. For instance, if a tree splits on investment, there may be some low-growth countries with high investment rates and some high-growth countries with low investment rates. Hence, the algorithm must search for the variable and its associated threshold value that minimize the weighted sum of the two types of errors and thus best distinguishes between the high and low-growth observations. In growing trees, weights are assigned to these errors a *priori*. In this analysis, the two types of errors are assigned equal weights. By design, as the tree grows, any additional sub-branch reduces the overall classification error.

In the pruning stage, a cost is imposed on the splits as the tree grows. This cost serves as a penalty that helps promote parsimony in the process. The algorithm prunes away a branch if the reduction in the error rate becomes less than the penalty imposed at that branch. This process resembles the adjusted R-squared criterion that penalizes for additional variables used to try and improve the explanatory power of a multiple regression model. In general, the classification tree method will result in sub-samples of countries being categorized by different variables. In the context of this study, these various categorizations (and mis-categorizations) will help to show the context-specificity of the growth path of individual countries.

Data

The data used in the analysis are obtained primarily from the growth database compiled by the World Bank. The dependent variable is a binary variable set equal to 1 for countries identified as high-growth performing, and 0 for those that are identified as low-growth performing. The explanatory variables are broadly categorized into four groups: exogenous variables, intermediate inputs, policy variables, and institutional variables.[6] Some of these are further sorted into sub-categories; for instance, exogenous factors are variables that proxy for initial conditions, demographic characteristics and external shocks. Policy variables are those that illustrate macroeconomic and trade openness policies. See Table 1.2 for a detailed description of the data. All of these variables are observed commonly in the thematic papers and are broadly in consonance with those widely employed in the growth literature. The benchmark case (Figure 1.1) focuses on high- and low-growth performing countries, using 31-year average data for the variables. Institutional variables are initially omitted from the analysis because they are available only in the latter half of the period but are included in the sensitivity analysis.

The discriminant analysis identifies the investment share of GDP as the explanatory variable that has the highest discriminatory power, a result that is similar to the findings of the thematic papers as well as other growth studies. The threshold value of investment that separates high and low growth is 22 per cent.[7] According to the analysis, the probability of obtaining high growth is far greater for countries that meet the threshold value of investment (81 per cent) compared to countries that do not (13 per cent). However, high investment by itself does not necessarily lead to superior growth, and low investment does not necessarily condemn a country to low growth. For example, unless there is low inflation (which could be interpreted as a proxy for good macroeconomic management), high investment often does not result in high growth. Conversely, a high growth rate in the labour force compensates for low investment. These results demonstrate the importance of the coexistence of certain explanatory variables that meet threshold criteria in achieving a status of high-growth performance.[8]

Thus, the analysis yields four groups of countries and three thresholds. In one group of high-growth countries, the critical interdependency is between investment, with a threshold of 22 per cent, and inflation, with a threshold of 18.5 per cent. The other group of high-growth countries does not achieve the threshold for investment but this is compensated by growth in the labour force above the threshold

Table 1.2 Description of explanatory variables

Variables	Data description	Source
I Exogenous variables		
a *Initial conditions*		
1 Initial income	1968 GDP per capita in local currency	WDI 99 (SIMA)
2 Initial life expectancy	Years of life expectancy at birth in 1967	WDI 99 (SIMA)
3 Initial human capital stock	Average secondary years of schooling in total population aged 25 or over in 1970	Barro and Lee (1994)
b *Demographics*		
4 Age-dependency ratio	Ratio of population below 15 or above 65 to population between 15 and 65	WDI 99 (SIMA)
5 Growth in potential labour force	Difference between average growth rate of population of labour force aged 15–65 and average growth rate of total population	WDI 99 (SIMA)
c *External shocks*		
6 Terms-of-trade shock	Terms of trade volatility – 5 years standard deviation of terms of trade	Growth data base
7 Trading partner growth	Average weighted growth of GDP per capita for country trading partners – weights defined as partner's share in total (import + export)	Growth database
II Immediate inputs		
8 Physical capital accumulation	Average ratio of gross domestic investment to GDP	WDI 99 (SIMA)
9 Human capital	Average secondary years of schooling in total population aged 25 or over	Barro and Lee (1994)
III Policy variables		
a *Macroeconomic policy*		
10 Inflation rate	Average change in the CPI index	Growth database
11 Black-market premium	Ratio of parallel exchange rate to official exchange rate	Growth database
12 Exchange-rate overvaluation	Ratio of real exchange rate to overvaluation index	Growth database

Table 1.2 Description of explanatory variables–*continued*

Variables	Data description	Source
13 External debt position	Ratio of total external debt outstanding to GDP	Growth database
14 Financial deepening	Ratio of M2 to GDP	Growth database
b *Openness*		
15 Trade/GDP	Ratio of total exports and imports to GDP	Growth database
16 Sachs and Warner's openness	Index of dummy variables set to 1 if country is open to trade and 0 otherwise	Sachs and Warner (1995)
IV Institutional variables		ICRG dataset, Knack and Keefer (1996)
17 Government corruption index	Measured on scale (0–6), lower values implying high level of corruption	
18 Bureaucratic quality index	Measured on scale (0–6), lower values implying poor quality	
19 Rule of law index	Measured on scale (0–6), lower values implying low regards for rule of law	
20 Risk of repudiation of contracts index	Measured on scale (0–10), lower values implying high risk	
21 Risk of expropriation index	Measured on scale (0–10), lower values implying high risk	

of 0.23 per cent. Of the two groups of low-growth countries, one fails to meet the threshold for investment and the threshold for growth in the labour force. And the other, although meeting the threshold for investment, is plagued by inflation above the critical level of 18.5 per cent.

These three variables successfully classify 25 of the 26 high-growth countries and 23 of the 28 low-growth countries. This of course reflects our focus on two clearly separated groups. Later, we will examine how these few variables fare when we apply them to the medium-growth countries. Nevertheless, even with the current focus, further investigation is required for the six misclassified countries. For example, among the high-growth countries, Israel meets the investment threshold but is well-above the threshold for inflation. Israel is apparently able to grow

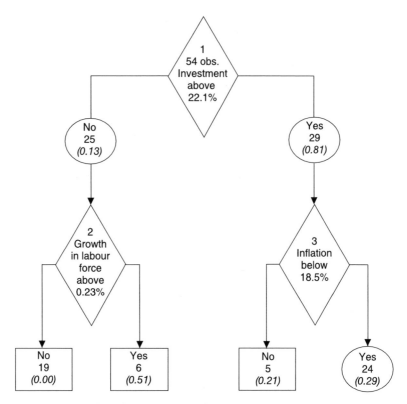

Figure 1.1   Benchmark case: high vs low-growth performance (institutional variables excluded)

Note: Values in parenthesis are probability of high growth, conditional on being at the current node.

rapidly despite a high rate of inflation. And among the low-growth countries, Gabon meets the investment threshold as well as the inflation threshold and yet experienced low growth. These 'outliers' clearly indicate the importance of country-specific analysis.

Sensitivity analysis

We subject the benchmark results to two sensitivity tests. The first uses decades as the unit of observation rather than 31 years. Investment and inflation still emerge as the key variables discriminating high-growth countries from low-growth ones. The only new variable of importance is growth of trading partners. Several countries that failed on the investment criterion in this medium-run analysis have high growth rates over the decade if their main trading partners had high growth.

In the second test we introduce the institutional variables. Recall that these variables only cover the second half of the 31 years. We are assuming therefore that the values observed in the second half of the period hold for the entire period. Proceeding on this basis, risk of expropriation emerges as the key discriminant between high and low growth. Risk of expropriation may be interpreted as a prerequisite for a high rate of investment, and indeed the two variables are highly corre- lated with a correlation coefficient of 0.7. In fact, 70 per cent of the countries overlap when the sample is divided along either investment or risk of expropriation.

In addition, investment and inflation rates remain important explanatory variables even with institutional variables included. That is, for countries that failed the risk of expropriation threshold, if they met the investment and inflation thresholds they still had a 91 per cent chance of being in the high-growth group (see Figure 1.2).

Investment and growth mismatches

One of the main themes of this chapter is that while cross-country analysis can help point to the right direction when trying to under- stand determinants of growth, for many countries it is necessary to take a more in-depth look at its history and experience. In this section we elaborate on this point by examining more closely two of the mis- matches found among the high- and low-growth countries that have been the focus of this chapter. Then we turn to the medium-growth countries and see whether their collective experience throws any addi- tional light on the issues.

High-growth and low-growth countries

Clearly countries can have high growth with relatively low investment if there is an abundance of something else or a number of other things. For example, from 1968–98, Pakistan averaged per capita GDP growth of 2.8 per cent despite an investment share of only 17.7 per cent of GDP. However, the productivity of investment over this period was high at about 15.7 per cent. Of course, the important question is why was this productivity so high. Part of the answer to this question can be found by looking at distinct sub-periods. For example, GDP per capita growth for Pakistan was only 0.4 per cent from 1971–77, but 4.5 per cent from 1980–85 and 2.1 per cent from 1991–98. In fact, greater economic growth took place in precisely the periods when the

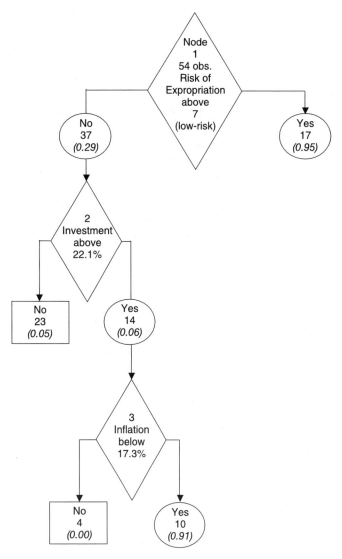

Figure 1.2   High vs low-growth performance (institutional variables included)
Note: Values in parenthesis are probability of high growth, conditional on being at the current node. Node 1 – risk of expropriation is measured on scale (0–10), lower values imply high risk.

Government of Pakistan undertook reforms to encourage the private sector and foreign investment. Of course, other governments have done the same with less successful growth results or, in the case of many East Asian countries, with much more investment. More in-depth analysis is needed to understand why the investment response of the reforms in Pakistan was so tepid in quantity but outstanding in quality.

At the other extreme is a country such as Jamaica, which experienced negative per capita GDP growth for the period 1968–98, despite a high level of investment averaging 26 per cent of GDP. Again, it is helpful to look at sub-periods. From 1961–72, annual per capita GDP growth in Jamaica was 4.6 per cent. The oil shock came in 1973, along with a series of policy responses, from which Jamaica has never really recovered. The immediate response to the shock was to shift large parts of the economy to the public sector, the result of which was average annual per capita GDP growth of –4.4 per cent from 1973–80. Then, very similar to Pakistan, the (new) government undertook a series of reforms in the early and mid-1980s to encourage the private sector and foreign investment. However, despite an annual increase of per capita GDP of 4.1 per cent from 1985–90, in the 1990s the economy once more slid into recession, despite very high levels of investment. An important question that needs to be addressed in the case of Jamaica is whether the reforms were inadequate or whether important complementary 'inputs' for growth were lacking. Indeed, it is not clear why the level of investment continued to be so high despite its low productivity. There are likely issues of both composition and quality that need to be examined here.

Medium-growth countries

How does the analysis above and in the preceding section fit the medium-growth group? If we apply the preceding results to the medium-growth countries, we find that 10 of them – Algeria, Congo Republic, Costa Rica, Honduras, Mexico, Morocco, Papua New Guinea, Paraguay, Philippines, and Trinidad and Tobago – achieve the threshold value for investment that should put them in the high-growth category. Moreover, except for Mexico, they all meet the threshold criterion for inflation. Despite their stable macroeconomic environment, as evidenced by low inflation, relatively high levels of investment are not being translated into rapid growth in these nine countries. Also, among the 10 countries, only two – Algeria and the Congo Republic – fail to meet the threshold for the terms-of-trade shock, while none fail that for the black-market premium. In seven countries, therefore, there is little evidence of macroeconomic mismanagement and external shocks in addition to low inflation, yet high investment is not transformed into high growth.

Similarly, but conversely, eight countries – Burkina Faso, Burundi, Cameroon, Gambia, Guatemala, Malawi, Nepal and Uruguay – fail to meet the threshold criteria for both investment and growth in the labour force and should therefore have been placed firmly in the low-growth category. Burundi, Gambia and Malawi, each with a growth rate of 0.4 per cent, are in fact very close to falling into the low-growth group. Uruguay, on the other hand, maintains a growth rate of 1.4 per cent even in the presence of features identified to be growth-impeding.

The difficulty in relating a general story of growth is, once again, highlighted. Generalizations about the nature of growth to be obtained from cross-country analyses seem to fit the medium-growth group even more poorly than the high-growth and low-growth countries. Understanding discrepancies in the above observations indeed warrants further investigations on an individual country basis.

Level and productivity of investment

We have described a share of investment in GDP of 22 per cent as a threshold. This is obviously true in the sense that it is the value that best divides the sample. We now want to see if it also indicates a different relationship between investment and growth above the threshold from that below the threshold. In other words, is there any evidence of a nonlinear relationship between growth and investment. To test this, we run the following regression:

$$\text{Growth} = A + B.INV + C \qquad (\text{dummy equal to 1 if } INV > 22 \text{ per cent})$$

The results strongly support the view that the productivity of investment is significantly higher in countries where the rate of investment exceeds the threshold. The estimated equation is:

$$\text{Growth} = -3.3 + 0.16 \ (INV/Y) + 1.99 \qquad (\text{dummy} = 1, \text{ if } INV/Y > 22 \text{ per cent})$$
$$\phantom{\text{Growth} = } (-2.9) \quad (2.5) \qquad\qquad (2.2)$$

where INV = investment, Y = gross domestic product

Thus, for countries with an investment share above the threshold, growth in GDP per capita is 2 percentage points higher than would be predicted given the average relationship between growth and investment for all countries in the sample. High-investment countries benefit twice – once from the high investment itself and once from the higher productivity of that investment. We return to this finding below.

Grouping countries by investment and productivity levels

Although investment, the key determinant in the benchmark case, is treated as an explanatory variable that is exogenous to the model, it could be that causality is from growth to investment rather than the opposite case. This endogeneity problem of investment is discussed extensively in the existing growth literature. In addition, one strand of the literature argues that total factor productivity is as important in determining growth as levels of physical investment, if not more so. We do not tackle these problems here, but instead make use of a simple decomposition of growth to explore, first, some of the factors that directly discriminate high-investment countries from low-investment ones and, second, some of the factors that discriminate countries where the productivity of investment is high from those where the productivity of investment is low.

The growth rate *G* of GDP per capita may be decomposed as follows:

$$G = \Delta Y/Y = (\Delta Y/INV).(INV/Y)$$

where *INV/Y* is the rate of investment and $\Delta Y/INV$ in the incremental capital–output ratio or the productivity of investment. (Note that the productivity of investment is not the same as total factor productivity because the latter makes explicit allowance for the contribution of other factors.) Thus, without becoming embroiled in issues of causality, we can still explore the factors associated with high levels of investment. Furthermore, since the aggregate of the decomposition is growth in income per capita, we can use this technique to look at the two components of growth and investigate whether or not the interdependencies associated with high levels of investment are the same as those associated with high productivity of investment. We have already seen that the productivity of investment is clearly different for countries with levels of investment above the threshold of 22 per cent, suggesting that similar factors may be driving both. Nevertheless, the group of countries with high levels of investment is not the same as the group with high productivity. In fact, only 15 of the 28 countries in the high investment group are in the high productivity of investment group.

Therefore, we apply the classification analysis separately to countries ranked first by their investment shares, and then by the productivity of investment, to determine the key interdependencies and threshold values.

The objective, as with growth, is to identify those factors which best distinguish high-investment countries from low-investment and those factors which best distinguish high-productivity countries from low-productivity ones. We use the same array of explanatory variables on the top-third and bottom-third of countries sorted by their investment levels and by their productivity of investment and report as our benchmark case the results when institutional variables are excluded (Figure 1.3).

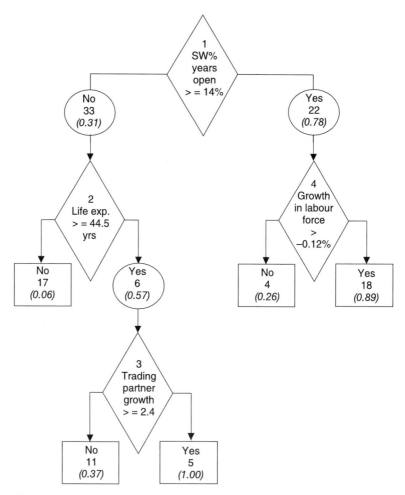

Figure 1.3 Level of investment: benchmark case
Note: Values in parenthesis refer to probability of high investment level, conditional on being at the current node.

Trade openness emerges as the most important variable distinguishing countries with high rates of investment from those with low rates (Figure 1.3). The analysis suggests that the key interdependency is between openness and labour-force growth. For a country with the combination of an open trading regime and rapid growth in the labour force, the probability of a high investment rate is 89 per cent. For a country that does not have an open trading regime, other factors come into play: for these countries the combination of a life-expectancy in excess of 44.5 years and trade with a rapidly growing partner is associated with a high rate of investment.[9] Turning to the determinants of the productivity of investment (Figure 1.4), the result emphasizes the importance of policy variables in providing the enabling environment to enhance the productivity of investment. The most important variable discriminating between countries with high and low productivity of investment is the real exchange-rate overvaluation. In addition to the exchange rate, the key set of interdependencies also includes low levels of external debt/GDP and strong financial deepening (measured by M2/GDP). The probability of high-productivity investment for these countries is 86 per cent.[10,11]

When the analysis of rate of investment and productivity of investment are combined, we can begin to see why some countries with high investment levels failed to achieve high growth, and why some countries with low levels of investment nevertheless grew rapidly. In our original classification, five low-growth countries were misclassified as well as one high-growth country. As can be seen in Table 1.3, three of the misclassified low-growth countries – Peru, Gabon and Guinea-Bissau – did poorly on all these determinants of productivity for which there are data. On the other hand, Israel, the only misclassified high-growth country had relatively modest exchange rate overvaluation and scored well on the financial deepening index. The misclassified low-growth countries, Jamaica and Venezuela, however, do reasonably well on these productivity indicators, except for Jamaica's external debt measure, so the answer to their high investment and low-growth pattern must be sought elsewhere.

5   Conclusions and lessons for country studies

Long-run growth is clearly a complicated process. While it is relatively easy to ascertain causes of short-run growth fluctuations, long-run growth depends on a host of underlying factors covering all aspects of the organization and behaviour of human societies. In this chapter –

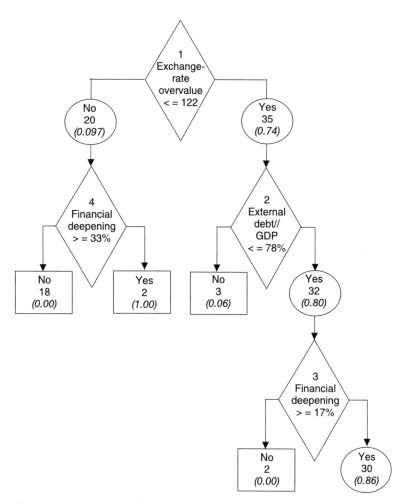

Figure 1.4   Productivity of investment: benchmark case
Note: Values in parenthesis refer to probability of high productivity of investment, conditional on being at the current node.

and in this book – we hope to show that while cross-country studies and regional analysis can shed considerable light on where to look, more in-depth country-level study is necessary to determine the many interrelationships, including political, societal and cultural factors, affecting growth patterns. Clearly, general policy shifts such as more investment in education or opening up to foreign trade by themselves are likely to have limited effects. An obvious fact is that some invest-

Table 1.3   Characteristics of misclassified countries

Country	Key variables in growth			Key variables in productivity of investment		
	Growth in labour force	Investment	Inflation	Exchange rate over-valuation	External debt	Financial deepening
Peru	0.5	22	425	132	56	17
Guinea-Bissau	–0.4	27	51		179	14
Venezuela	0.6	25	24	91	44	26
Jamaica	0.7	26	20	118	99	37
Gabon	–0.3	35	7	146	58	17
Israel	0.1	25	56	118	n/a	54

ment – whether in machines, infrastructure or education – is much more effective than other investment. The critical question is why does this continue to be such a strong result in the long-run?

Since the Second World War, the study of economic development has gone full circle. It began with a strong emphasis on fairly general growth models, then moved to analysis of different aggregate elements needed for the growth process. In both cases the analysis most often relied on cross-country data or observations. In the 1970s there was a strong movement to country-level studies, more and more focusing on one or a small number of sectors or policy areas. It even seems that for some time the bigger picture of growth had been largely lost.[12] In the mid-1980s new growth theory arrived, bringing with it lots of elements of old growth theory. This new paradigm helped to put development specialists back into focus. Like its predecessor, the new growth theory began by looking at aggregates and cross-country comparisons. Similarly, it first focused on the direct 'ingredients' of growth, but quickly moved on to the variables affecting the quantity and quality of these ingredients. However, the point has now been reached where the returns to this type of work are limited as the processes are too complex and go far beyond traditional economics.

The time has come for country analysis again, however this time without losing sight of the bigger picture and the interdependencies inherent in a successful growth process.

Notes

1 This project grew out of a project on growth in Sub-Saharan Africa, organized by the African Economic Research Consortium.

2   Regions include East Asia, South Asia, Latin America and Caribbean, Eastern Europe and Former Soviet Union, Middle East and North Africa, and Sub-Saharan Africa.

3   Among the resource persons are Angus Deaton of Princeton University, Robert Solow of MIT, and Joseph Stiglitz, former chief economist of the World Bank, now at Columbia University.

4   For a different view see Easterly and Levine (1999).

5   Least-squares growth rate, r, is estimated by fitting a linear-regression trend line to the logarithmic annual value of the per capita GDP in the relevant period. Least-squares growth rates are used whenever there is sufficiently long time series to permit a reliable calculation. The regression equation takes the form $\ln X_t = a + bt$, which is equivalent to the logarithmic transformation of the compound growth equation, $X_t = X_0 (1 + r)^t$. The average annual growth rate, r, is obtained as $[\exp(b^\star) - 1] * 100$, where $b^\star$ is an estimate of b. The calculated growth rate is an average rate that is representative of the available observations over the entire period. See World Bank, World Development Report (2000).

6   Except for institutional variables, all others are measured as averages over the sample period 1968–98. Institutional variables are measured as averages over the period 1982–95 due to limited availability of data.

7   In their work, Ghosh and Wolf (1998) also find the investment threshold to be 22 per cent.

8   Terms-of-trade shocks and the black-market exchange-rate premium are also found to be relevant, but each only helps categorize one additional country.

9   When institutional variables are introduced, risk of repudiation of contract by government emerges as the most important discriminant.

10 When institutional variables are included, the results are very similar with exchange-rate overvaluation, financial deepening, and the external debt ratio being the most important determinants of the productivity of investment.

11 Note that if the original classification analysis of growth is done with the investment variable omitted, the same variables emerge as when the classification is done on the productivity of investment. This could be interpreted to mean that the most important thing after the quantity of investment is the quality of investment.

12 One of the authors of this chapter taught undergraduate development economics throughout the 1980s. Most textbooks were organized by sectors, and typically one or two lectures were devoted to long-run growth.

References

Aghion, P. and P. Howitt (1998) *Endogenous Growth Theory* (Cambridge, Mass.: MIT Press).

Azariadis, C. and A. Drazen (1990) 'Threshold Externalities in Economic Development', *Quarterly Journal of Economics,* vol. 105, pp. 501–26.

Barro, R. (1997) *Determinants of Economic Growth: A Cross-Country Empirical Study* (Cambridge, Mass.: MIT Press).

Barro, R. and J. Lee (1994) '*Sources of Economic Growth*', Carnegie-Rochester Conference Series on Public Policy, no. 40, pp. 1–46.

Breiman, L., J. H. Friedman, R. A. Olshen and C. J. Stone (1984) 'Classification and Regression Trees', The Wadsworth Statistics/Probability Series.

Easterly, W. (1994) 'Economic Stagnations, Fixed Factors, and Policy Thresholds', *Journal of Monetary Economics*, vol. 33, pp. 525–57.

Easterly, W. and R. Levine (1999) 'It's Not Factor Accumulation: Stylized Facts and Growth Models', mimeo, Policy Research Group, The World Bank, Washington, DC.

Ghosh, A. and H. Wolf (1998) 'Threshold and Context Dependence in Growth', Working Paper no. 6480, National Bureau of Economic Research, Cambridge, Mass.

Guha-Khasnobis, B. and F. Bari (2000) 'Sources of Growth in South Asian Countries', paper prepared for GDN Global Research Project, mimeo, Indian Council for Research on International Economic Relations, New Delhi, India and Lahore University, Lahore, Pakistan.

Hahn, Chin Hee and Kim, Jong-il (2000) *Sources of East Asian Growth: Some Evidence from Cross-Country Studies* paper prepared for GDN Global Research Project, mimeo, Korea Development Institute and Dongguk University.

Knack, S. and P. Keefer (1996) 'Institutions and Economic Performance: Cross-country Test Using Alternative Institutional Measures', *Economics and Politics*, vol. 7(3) pp. 207–27.

Lucas, R. (1988) 'On the Mechanics of Economic Development', *Journal of Monetary Economics*, vol. 22, pp. 3–42.

O'Connell, S. and B. Ndulu (2000) 'Africa's Growth Experience: A Focus on Sources of Growth', paper prepared for GDN Global Research Project, mimeo, Swarthmore College, Swarthmore, Pennsylvania.

Sachs, F. and A. Warner (1995) 'Economic Reform and the Process of Global Integration', *Brookings Papers on Econimic Activity*, vol. 1, pp.1–18.

Sala-í-Martin, X. (1997) 'I Just Ran Two Million Regressions', *American Economic Review*, vol. 87(2), pp. 178–83.

World Bank (2000) *World Development Report*, Washington, DC.

2
Sources of Aggregate Growth in Developing Regions: Still More Questions than Answers?

Charles C. Soludo and Jongil Kim

1 Introduction

In the last 40 years of the twentieth century, economic growth was a puzzle and a surprise, defying orthodox predictions and prescriptions.[1] Growth has varied tremendously across and within developing regions, and over time. A selected group of Asian developing countries was the only region to have experienced persistent and high growth over the period. In others, especially Africa and Latin America, growth has been very disappointing and highly volatile, despite huge inflows of development finance and significant economic reforms since the 1980s. The transition economies have experienced larger initial drops in their GDP than anticipated by economists, and the Arab countries have witnessed marked volatility in their performance. In all of this period, and despite massive development assistance and a plethora of special global initiatives directed at eliminating underdevelopment traps, only Botswana and Mauritius have graduated from the list of least-developed countries. Rather, more countries continue to join the league, and currently there are 49 such countries with 34 of them in Sub-Saharan Africa. The economic recovery since the mid-1990s in most developing regions has been minuscule relative to the requirements for poverty reduction, and for Africa even the best performers are projected to remain very poor in 2020 if present trends continue (Berthelemy and Soderling, 2001).

What is the reason for all these disappointing results and what can economists tell us about their causes? From Adam Smith's seminal *Inquiry into the Nature and Causes of the Wealth of Nations* (1776), through the neoclassical growth models, development economics,

and the recent extensions in the endogenous growth models, understanding economic growth has always been the fulcrum of economic
science. Despite the eternal interest and the burgeoning literature on
the subject, it would be fair to say that if the disappointing growth
performance is a measure of economists' ignorance, then there is
plenty of it. Our ideas about why nations prosper and others
stagnate remain largely fickle and contentious. Even in our state of
ignorance, however, there are certain fundamental insights that our
current state of knowledge and methodology permit us to draw. The
goal of this chapter is to illuminate the state of play by summarizing
what we know, what we don't know, and what we should know
about the sources of growth in developing regions in the last
40 years. We draw primarily from six regional papers on growth
written for the GDN growth project to highlight both the areas of
consensus and agenda for further research. The six regions covered
include Sub-Saharan Africa (SSA), the Middle East and North African
(MENA) region, Latin America, Transition Economies, South Asia,
and the Southeast Asian region. Our key finding is that the literature
has come a long way to underscore some of the growth fundamentals consistent with our educated guesses. However, we admit that
the largely unresolved issues tend to raise more questions than
answers.

The chapter is organized into four sections. Section 2 summarizes the
broadly agreed growth-accounting framework and the evidence from
the regional studies and empirical literature. In section 3, we evaluate
the various cross-national 'regression-based' approaches to decomposing the sources of growth and summarize the findings. Section 4 summarizes the major themes that emerge as 'unresolved issues' or as an
agenda for further research and concludes the paper.

2   Aggregate growth-accounting framework

Growth results from two major sources – the accumulation of factor
inputs (physical capital and labour), and the efficiency of factor use
(total factor productivity, TFP). Why does the source of growth matter
for policy? The answer lies in the nature of factor accumulation and
the concern for long-run sustainability of growth. According to the
neoclassical growth model, which is supported by empirical evidence,
factor accumulation exhibits diminishing returns. Thus, for sustainable
long-run growth, a country cannot rely solely on accumulation of
factor inputs, but must have growth in TFP.

Empirical growth-accounting exercises use the aggregate neoclassical production function to decompose the growth rate of aggregate output into contributions of growth of measured inputs and improvement in TFP. The results of the exercise depend critically on the specification of the production function. In the literature, the Cobb–Douglas production function, with the share of capital set to a 'benchmark' value of one-third for all countries, is typically used (see Young, 1993, 1995; Krugman, 1994; and the extensions by Collins and Bosworth, 1996; and Sarel and Robinson, 1997). If we start from a simple case with two inputs, capital and labour, we can specify an aggregate production function as follows:

$$Y = A\, f(K, L) \tag{1}$$

where Y, K and L are output, capital and labour, respectively, and A denotes the level of productive efficiency, so called total factor productivity.[2] If we take the natural logarithms of both sides of the above production function and differentiate them with respect to time, we get the growth rate of output decomposed into the sources of growth: improvement in productive efficiency $(\frac{\dot{A}}{A})$ and the increase in produc tive capacity $(\frac{\dot{K}}{K}$ and $\frac{\dot{L}}{L})$,

$$\frac{\dot{Y}}{Y} = \frac{\dot{A}}{A} + \frac{Af_K K}{Y}\frac{\dot{K}}{K} + \frac{Af_L L}{Y}\frac{\dot{L}}{L} \tag{2}$$

Here, Af_K and Af_L are the marginal products of capital and labour, respectively, which are equal to the rental and wage rates if factor markets are competitive and firms maximize their profits. Then, $\frac{Af_K K}{Y}$ and $\frac{Af_L L}{Y}$ are the shares of the compensation to capital (α_K) and labour (α_L) in total output, respectively. Since the share of capital income is one minus the share of labour income under the assumption of constant returns to scale, the growth rate of output is decomposed into TFP growth and the weighted sum of the growth of capital and labour as follows,

$$\frac{\dot{Y}}{Y} = \frac{\dot{A}}{A} + (1 - \alpha_L)\frac{\dot{K}}{K} + \alpha_L \frac{\dot{L}}{L} \tag{3}$$

Having data on the growth rates of output and input along with factor income shares, we can measure TFP growth from the above equation as residual output growth, after subtracting the contribution of measured input growth from output growth.

For the purpose of accounting for long-run macroeconomic performance, output is usually measured as GDP. Capital input is measured as gross fixed capital stock – the accumulation of past gross fixed capital investment – under the assumption that the flow of services from capital stock is proportional to the stock. Among the variables, the accuracy of the capital stock is the most controversial since we need the depreciation rate and benchmark capital stock for the initial period, which are not readily available from official statistics.[3] Labour input is measured as the number of hours worked if the data on working hours are available. However, since the data on working hours are not so reliable for less-developed countries, labour input is sometimes measured as the number of workers. In addition, due to the emerging importance of human capital that may affect worker quality, labour input is adjusted by a quality change, generally measured by the increase in schooling years. Finally, the labour income share can be measured as the share of compensation to labour in GDP from national accounts. For developed countries for which data are reliable, the labour income share is believed to be about two-thirds of total income. However, in less-developed countries, a large portion of labour comprises family firms and self-employment, the data for which are not so reliable. While some studies apply two-thirds as the labour income share in the growth accounting of less-developed countries, others directly estimate the factor elasticities from the production function (for example, Senhadji, 1999).

There have been numerous attempts to account for the growth of many countries since Abramovitz (1956) and Solow (1957) initially applied the methodology to the US economy. Both Abramovitz and Solow reported the surprising result that the output growth of the US economy in the first half of the twentieth century could be mostly attributed to TFP growth. It stimulated many growth-accounting exercises that tried to explain the huge contribution of TFP growth, since TFP growth is a measure of ignorance to some extent. Many studies such as Denison (1967) and Jorgenson, Gollop and Fraumeni (1987) extended the methodology to account for other factors such as education, economies of scale, resource allocation, the advance of knowledge, input quality change, and so on. For cross-country comparison, Christensen, Cummings and Jorgenson (1980) exercised growth accounting for the economic growth of the OECD countries for the period 1947–73, and again found that TFP growth contributes heavily to the economic growth of developed countries in the post-Second World War period. Even with numerous efforts, the studies show that TFP growth has been an important source of growth in the postwar growth of developed countries, although TFP growth slowed down after the mid-1970s.

Recently, Young (1992, 1993 and 1995) made a major effort in accounting for the economic growth of four rapidly growing East Asian newly-industrialized economies (NIEs). He suggested the controversial result that these East Asian countries grew mostly due to factor growth rather than TFP growth, in contrast to the experience of developed countries. This implies that East Asian growth cannot be sustained in the long run since the economic growth rate in the long run is determined by TFP growth according to the neoclassical growth model. Young's studies have stimulated analyses by Sarel and Robinson (1997) and Collins and Bosworth (1996). Although the estimates are somewhat different among the studies, they all confirm an important role of factor growth in East Asian economic growth.

As shown in the above two controversial cases initiated by the use of growth accounting, the key issue of growth accounting is the role of TFP growth in economic growth. Since TFP growth is residual output growth, the estimate of TFP growth first of all depends on the basic assumptions of the growth-accounting framework such as Hicks-neutral technical progress, optimization under competitive factor market, and constant returns to scale. These assumptions may be too restrictive to reflect the true characteristics of production in developing countries. Second, the magnitude of each source of growth critically depends on how we define input and estimate labour income share. In much of the empirical literature (including the studies under the GDN network), the remuneration of physical capital is typically set to one-third for all countries, implying identical production technologies across countries. If the data fail to support the assumption of identical technologies, and there are many reasons to believe that technologies differ across countries and regions, then the comparison of the sources of growth across countries and regions may be flawed (Senhadji, 1999). Furthermore, it is not easy to compare the results from growth accounting of different countries if the data are measured differently across countries. Third, although TFP growth is usually considered as an index of technological progress, it is quite sensitive to the short-run noises of the business cycle and external shocks. Therefore, growth accounting for a period long enough to smother these effects is required to detect the true efficiency improvement. In addition, TFP growth includes all the factors that may affect output growth except for input growth. The possible candidates are the effects of resource allocation from structural transformation, political and macroeconomic instability, climate change, and institutional factors that may influence the overall efficiency of economic operation.

Evidence

To have a fair comparison of sources of growth across countries, it is important to apply a consistent framework and data to the compared countries. Two recent extensive growth-accounting exercises (see Collins and Bosworth, 1996; Senhadji, 1999) have been relied upon by the regional studies in evaluating the comparative sources of growth among the regions. The O'Connell and Ndulu (2000) study for Africa draws on Collins and Bosworth (1996), while the De Gregorio and Lee (2000) study for Latin America benefits from both, and Makdisi *et al.* (2000) employs the methodology used by Senhadji. Both studies (Collins and Bosworth and Senhadji) include education as an input, which enhances the quality of labour (*H*). Thus, the growth rates of output are represented as total factor productivity growth and the weighted sum of the growth of capital and labour and improvement in labour quality due to education as follows:

$$\frac{\dot{Y}}{Y} = \frac{\dot{A}}{A} + (1 - \alpha_L)\frac{\dot{K}}{K} + \alpha_L(\frac{\dot{L}}{L} + \frac{\dot{H}}{H}) \tag{4}$$

While Collins and Bosworth impose the share of capital income $(1-\alpha_L)$ to be 0.35, identical across countries, Senhadji tries to estimate the factor elasticities based on the specification of a Cobb–Douglas production function by using either individual country time series or regional panel data. Thus, Senhadji allows different shares of capital income across regions, and also estimates this capital income share with two different estimation methods – in level as well as first difference forms. Table 2.1 reports the growth accounting from the two studies showing the regional means for the contributions of each source of growth.

What can we learn from these results? Senhadji (1999) summarizes some of the major lessons from the growth-accounting exercises, and the results of the regional studies largely confirm them, as follows. The contribution of TFP to output growth depends crucially on the share of physical capital in real output (alpha). The higher is alpha, the lower is the contribution of TFP, because decreasing alpha lowers the contribu-

Table 2.1   Sources of economic growth by region, 1960–94

		Collins and Bosworth Contribution by component			Growth of
	Capital income share	TFP	K/L	H	Y/L
Africa	0.35	−0.6	0.8	0.2	0.3
Latin America	0.35	0.2	0.9	0.4	1.5
South Asia	0.35	0.8	1.1	0.3	2.3
East Asia	0.35	1.1	2.5	0.6	4.2
Middle East	0.35	−0.3	1.5	0.5	1.6
Developed	0.35	1.1	1.5	0.4	2.9

		Senhadji Contribution of the growth of				Growth of
	Capital income share	TFP	K	L	H	Y
Level equation estimation						
Africa	0.43	−0.56	1.79	1.39	0.22	2.83
Latin America	0.52	−0.39	2.31	1.22	0.28	3.42
South Asia	0.56	0.55	2.87	0.99	0.25	4.66
East Asia	0.48	0.28	4.50	1.27	0.44	6.49
Middle East	0.63	−0.03	3.99	0.84	0.25	5.05
Developed	0.64	0.06	2.87	0.27	0.19	3.39
First difference equation estimation						
Africa	0.50	−0.66	2.08	1.22	0.19	2.83
Latin America	0.30	−0.52	2.75	0.97	0.22	3.42
South Asia	0.42	0.94	2.08	1.31	0.33	4.66
East Asia	0.30	1.34	2.86	1.71	0.59	6.49
Middle East	0.54	0.28	3.42	1.04	0.31	5.05
Developed	0.58	0.25	2.6	0.31	0.22	3.39

Sources: Collins and Bosworth(1996), Senhadji(1999).

tion of physical capital, and increases the contribution of labour. Add this to the fact that physical capital generally grows faster than labour, and the result leads to the negative correlation between the contribution of TFP and the level of alpha.

Reasonable variations in alpha preserve the TFP ranking of the sample countries (88 of them) even if the (log) level of TFP is sensitive to the value of alpha. This relative insensitivity of the TFP ranking across countries to changes in the value of alpha stands out more clearly when short-term fluctuations in TFP are smoothed out by taking averages over time. A detailed analysis shows that while the cross-country ranking is generally well-preserved, even under large variations in alpha, the individual country time series of TFP are more sensitive to variations in alpha. In essence, the level of TFP depends heavily on the specification of the production function – that is, the share of physical capital (alpha) in the simple Cobb–Douglas production function. For example, if one believes Senhadji's results that the average estimate of alpha for the whole sample is between 0.52 and 0.55, the contribution of TFP in real output growth has likely been negative for the whole sample period 1960–94. For alpha = 0.6, for example, physical capital would explain 3.05 per cent of the 3.80 per cent output growth for the whole sample. The implication, of course, would be that most of the growth during 1960–94 came from physical capital accumulation. Particularly for the regions with high capital accumulation such as East Asia, the change in income share makes a huge difference in the contribution to growth of capital accumulation. Thus, it may not be appropriate to conduct growth accounting by simply assuming identical income shares across countries as in Collins and Bosworth (1996). For country studies, it is necessary to estimate the income share based on national accounts and other complementary data as done by Young for the East Asian newly industrialized economies (NIEs), and for the MENA and Latin American growth studies. However, as it is quite difficult to get reliable estimates of income shares for most developing countries, in such cases it may be a necessary evil to impose the conventionally-guessed labour income share.

In all growth decomposition exercises, Africa remains the worst performer (see Table 2.1). The sources of the lower African growth (2.83 per cent for Africa relative to 3.80 per cent for the entire sample during 1960–94) are lower physical and human capital accumulation and lower TFP growth. From Collins and Bosworth, the MENA region had the next worst TFP performance, followed by Latin America. On the contrary, Senhadji's results reverse the ranking for the second and third worst performers. Asia remains the star performer in both studies.

Does the method of estimation matter much? Probably. Senhadji shows that estimating the production function in levels or first differences can lead to important differences in the results of growth decomposition. However, the differences in the estimates of alpha can be smoothed out when taking regional averages. Taking such averages shows that except for East Asia, estimates of alpha from a production function in levels and first differences are relatively close. For the East Asian countries, the level equations yield an average estimate of alpha of 0.48, while the first difference equations yield an average estimate of 0.30. Of course, these two estimates yield different results in the growth accounting. In the literature, first-difference estimation is becoming fashionable, but theoretically the level equations may be more appropriate.

Between factor accumulation and TFP growth. From the empirical results, it can be seen that factor accumulation is an important factor differentiating income growth across regions. Comparing rapidly growing East Asia with other regions, East Asia's high performance comes from the rapid growth in all three factors – that is, physical and human capital and labour (see also Young 1994, and Krugman 1994). Among the factors, physical capital accumulation turns out to be the most important factor differentiating growth performance. In contrast, human capital accumulation makes a relatively modest difference, although it may be due to the measure relying on schooling years that intrinsically change slowly over time. Although it depends somewhat on how we estimate the labour income share, TFP growth appears to be as important as capital accumulation in explaining differences in output growth. If we compare fast-growing East Asia with slow-growing Africa and Latin America, TFP growth differentials resulted in as much as 1.7 and 0.9 percentage point differences in output per labour, respectively, and capital growth differentials contributed 1.7 and 1.6 percentage points, according to Collins and Bosworth (1996). On the other hand, physical capital accumulation accounted for most of the growth performance in the industrial countries, while labour accounted for much less.

Furthermore, it is observed that TFP growth is closely associated with capital accumulation across regions – the regions that achieved high capital accumulation tend to have high TFP growth. Even at the country level presented in the sources of growth papers, there also seems to be a close correlation between TFP growth and capital accumulation. Over the 1960–94 period, Africa was a clear outlier in the sense of having very low capital accumulation and the atypically low TFP explains over half of the growth shortfall relative to other regions (O'Connell and Ndulu, 2000), while the transition economies experienced huge output collapse due to the sharp declines in TFP (Campos and Coricelli, 2000). O'Connell and Ndulu (see pp. 8–9) provide a good summary of the literature on the causes of the low TFP in Africa as follows. A large literature, for example, stresses the impact of tax and tax-like policies in generating an inefficient *composition* of aggregate investment in Africa. Such distortions produce a negative residual by gradually undermining the quality of the capital stock. A general bias against private-sector accumulation, emphasized by Mkandawire and

Soludo (1999), would produce the same effect unless justified by an unusually high marginal productivity of public capital. In a Chenery framework, slow movement of factors of production out of agriculture would also produce a low or negative TFP, given the presumption of a difference in sectoral marginal productivities.

Also, Sachs and Warner (1997) and Bloom and Sachs (1998) have recently emphasized geography as an additional factor in African growth, either in undermining the health status of workers or in imposing high transaction costs that discourage market integration. Some of these effects operate on the *level* of A rather than on its growth rate. For example, a chronic health deficit that reduced labour quality by 15 per cent would be equivalent to a reduction in A by $(0.15)^{.3}$, with no ongoing effect on the residual. *Changes* in average health status, in contrast – like the emergence of HIV/AIDS – can have major effects on the productivity residual. Moreover, structural features that impede the flow of information and trade, even if unchanged over time, can lower the TFP by limiting the scope for agglomeration economies and the diffusion of existing technological knowledge (Barro and Sala-í-Martin, 1995).

In addition to the influences cited above, the literature suggests a variety of other potential sources of a low TFP in Africa. These include falling capacity utilization, sometimes emphasized in systems of exchange control as in Tanzania between 1979 and 1985; high rates of depreciation of physical capital, associated for example with poor maintenance of public infrastructure, itself sometimes attributed to a bias of aid donors against recurrent spending; climate shocks that undermine total factor productivity in agriculture; and civil strife. At shorter frequencies, the residual may also reflect fluctuations in aggregate demand, which would affect output via capacity utilization and the degree of underemployment (both of which are implicitly assumed fixed in the calculation).

When the sample period is divided into sub-periods, interesting results are obtained depending on the choice of the sub-periods. However, a consistent pattern that emerges is that except for Asian countries, growth declined steadily in other regions from the first decade through to the 1990s. Loss of productivity and weakening of investments could be at the root of the growth slowdown. Table 2.2 presents the sources of growth by region and by period from Collins and Bosworth (1996). We find that growth rates are highly unstable over time except for East Asia, and the growth of all other regions including the developed countries slowed down after 1973. In particular, the growth rates in Africa and the Middle East plummeted after 1973, even reaching negative figures. Using time-series econometrics, Ben-David and Papell (1997) report that there exist significant structural breaks in postwar growth rates in a majority of countries, with most breaks found in the mid-1970s. Using a somewhat different method, Pritchett (2000) also classifies the different patterns of growth across countries. Most East Asian countries belong to the group of 'steep hills' and many developed countries show a pattern of 'hills'. Most Latin American and Middle Eastern countries experienced a meltdown in growth showing a pattern of 'plateaus and mountains'. Many African countries belong to the group of 'mountains and plains'. In this respect, the persistence as well as the rate of growth appears to be a key to the differential performances across regions.

Unlike output growth, the rates of factor accumulation in Table 2.2 appear to be very persistent over time. Education per worker has risen persistently regardless of periods and regions. Even capital accumulation shows a persistency. Easterly, Kremer, Prichett and Summers (1993) computed the cross-decade correlation of each component of output growth between the periods 1960–70s and 1970–80s. The correlation coefficient of the investment rate was around 0.85 and that of labour-force growth was around 0.6. However, the coefficient of TFP growth was very low at 0.15. Thus, the slowdown after the mid-1970s in most developing countries may be due to low TFP growth. Furthermore, capital accumulation sharply deteriorated for the period 1984–94. In this respect, TFP growth seems to be equally a critical factor determining the overall growth of countries.

The transition economies experienced a drastic fall in both output and TFP initially and there is evidence of a 'Baltic puzzle' (see Campos and Coricelli (2000), pp. 15–17). An interesting addition to the cross-country growth regression comes from the transition economies. The well-known cross-country studies for transition economies using a growth-accounting framework are De Broeck and Koen (2000), which focuses on the former Soviet Union countries, and Estrin and Urga (2000), which focuses on Central and Eastern Europe. Both studies cover the period 1970–97, and use data for labour and capital which were not corrected for hours worked or capacity utilization (so the reported TFP results after 1990 entirely reflect the impact of the transition). In both studies, the shares of labour and capital are assumed to be 0.7 and 0.3 respectively. One major result, which is also consistent

Table 2.2 Sources of growth by region and period

Region		Contribution by component			Growth of
		TFP	K/L	H	Y/L
Africa	1960–73	0.3	1.3	0.2	1.9
	1973–94	–1.3	0.4	0.2	–0.6
	1973–84	–2.0	1.2	0.2	–0.6
	1984–94	–0.4	–0.4	0.3	–0.6
Latin America	1960–73	1.8	1.3	0.3	3.4
	1973–94	–0.8	0.6	0.4	0.3
	1973–84	–1.1	1.1	0.4	0.4
	1984–94	–0.4	0.1	0.4	0.1
South Asia	1960–73	0.1	1.4	0.3	1.8
	1973–94	1.3	0.9	0.3	2.6
	1973–84	1.2	0.9	0.4	2.5
	1984–94	1.5	1.0	0.3	2.7
East Asia	1960–73	1.3	2.3	0.5	4.2
	1973–94	1.0	2.5	0.6	4.2
	1973–84	0.5	2.8	0.6	4.0
	1984–94	1.6	2.2	0.6	4.4
Middle East	1960–73	2.3	2.0	0.4	4.7
	1973–94	–1.9	1.1	0.5	–0.3
	1973–84	–2.2	2.2	0.6	0.5
	1984–94	–1.5	0.0	0.5	–1.1
Developed	1960–73	2.2	2.3	0.4	4.8
	1973–94	0.4	1.0	0.4	1.7
	1973–84	0.2	1.1	0.6	1.8
	1984–94	0.7	0.8	0.2	1.7

Source: Collins and Bosworth (1996).

with the other regional results, is the exhaustion of the growth capacities of these economies over the last three decades. While the general pattern of growth slowdown is evident, the radical structural break is not easily observed. Declines in TFP appear to be rather large *vis-à-vis* the decline in factor accumulation rates, indicating the rapid deterioration of the growth potential of the Soviet-type economy. This happened despite the variety of ways in which changes in the numbers of the employed occur, ranging from increases in non-participation (for example early retirement schemes) to open unemployment (Blanchard, 1997), as well as despite investment falling below replacement levels especially in the early transition years.

Another very important result is that the output fall during the onset of the transition is accounted for mainly by declines in TFP rates. Yet, the year-to-year results referred to above show a 'V-shaped' pattern in TFP growth during transition (large initial falls followed by rapid recovery), which lead De Broeck and Koen (2000) to note the coexistence of temporary and permanent elements. Among the former, they mention price and trade liberalization, while among the latter, disorganization. To investigate this issue, the authors apply the cross-sectoral decomposition of TFP. The decomposition involves separating out the contribution of productivity changes within sectors from that of changes in the sectoral composition to aggregate TFP growth. The second component is particularly interesting as it is expected to be positive if factors are reallocated from lower to higher productivity sectors. The results show that this component was negative until the late 1980s, turning positive in the early transition. Yet, the authors conclude that the change in the share effect was small, indicating that sectoral input reallocation did not have a major impact on productivity.

Furthermore, growth decomposition in the transition economies finds evidence of a 'Baltic puzzle'. Estonia, Latvia and Lithuania all had output contractions comparable to other former Soviet Union countries, but their recovery has been much faster and more pronounced. Even more puzzling is the fact that the Baltic experience seems to turn the received wisdom in the literature on its head. For example, in the Baltics, investment rates declined dramatically in the early 1990s (*vis-à-vis* other transition countries), and this was also the only group for which the share of government consumption in GDP was rising throughout the transition period. Thus, rapid growth recovery occurred in spite of the drastic investment decline and huge government consumption.

Summing up, it is evident that growth accounting is a mechanical decomposition of output growth into TFP growth and factor accumulation that may be the result of economic development *per se* rather than its true source. In the regional studies and the literature, both factor accumulation and TFP growth have been confirmed to be very important (albeit to varying degrees) in the regional experiences. The specific weight of each depends on the weights of physical capital and labour in the growth accounting. Regional differences and 'puzzles' remain with respect to their growth performances. In the next section, we turn to the regional studies and empirical growth literature for insights into the determinants of the cross-national growth differences.

3 Comparative analysis of sources of growth across regions: cross-country growth regression

Given that both factor accumulation and TFP matter for growth, the key question then is, why are these higher in some countries or regions than in others? This section explores the literature on the major determinants of per capita income growth rates for the last four decades, based on the general framework of cross-country regressions, which puts the experience of individual countries in a global context. The basic framework is based on an extended version of the neoclassical growth model, which is predicated on the assumption of conditional convergence (see Barro, 1991, 1997; Barro and Lee, 1994; Sachs and Warner, 1995). According to the neoclassical growth model, economies converge to the steady state where the growth rates of the economies are determined only by TFP growth. Provided economies converge to the same steady state, poorer economies should grow faster, which is called absolute convergence. Baumol (1986) provided evidence that there may have been absolute convergence among developed countries. However, absolute convergence does not hold for a broad range of countries including many developing countries, whose steady states may be far away from those of developed countries. Instead of absolute convergence, Barro (1991) suggested conditional convergence, which states that the farther away an economy is from its steady state, the faster it should grow.

Thus, the typical equation for a cross-country growth regression can be represented by:

$$\log(\frac{Y_{Ti}}{Y_{0i}}) / T = \beta_0 + \beta_1 \log(Y_{0i}) + \beta_3 x_i + \varepsilon_i \tag{5}$$

The dependent variable is the growth rate of per capita income for the period T for country i, and the explanatory variables are y_{0i}, the initial level of per capital income, and X_i, a set of variables that may determine country i's steady-state level of per capita income. ε_i is the country-specific disturbance term.

The empirical literature on the determinants of cross-national differences in growth performance using the above equation has faced several fundamental difficulties. These problems include the lack of clear guidance from theory on the vector of variables to constitute the 'x'; specification uncertainty and robustness of the estimated parameters (Levine and Renelt, 1992; Sala-í-Martin, 1997; Ley and Steel, 1999; Senhadji, 1999); and estimation technique (Hoeffler, 1999; O'Connell and Ndulu, 2000).

Economic theory does not provide a precise guide about the determinants of factor accumulation or productivity growth. Numerous variables have been proposed as the determinants of the steady state level, but since income growth is a result of a complicated process of economic development, it is almost impossible to specify an explicit causal mechanism from determinants to growth. Furthermore, there is probably a feedback effect from growth to its determinants, and thus the direction of causality is not clear.

The methodological problems pertain to the correct definition, measurement and specification of the dependent and explanatory variables, as well as the choice of estimation technique. In the first instance, it is not certain how the dependent variable should be defined or measured. In most of the empirical literature, the growth rate of real output is the left-hand-side variable. De Gregorio and Lee (2000) provide a justification for this: 'differences in productivity growth by itself cannot explain differences in growth rates across countries, and hence differences should stem from the distance between each country's output and its steady state'. Senhadji (1999, p. 15) disagrees: 'recent theoretical as well as empirical arguments ... point to the level of TFP as the more relevant variable to explain'[4]. Most empirical literature has not focused on cross-country differences in TFP, and, with the exception of Hall and Jones (1998), those that did focused on the cross-country differences in *growth rates of TFP*. Thus, there is both an issue with the choice of output versus TFP and level versus growth rates. Berg *et al.* (1999) argue strongly in favour of using output levels rather than growth rates on the basis of statistical tests. However, Campos and Coricelli (2000) confirm that the qualitative results of the growth-rate-based regression are consistent with the level-based results. Beside the debate on the levels versus growth rates and TFP versus GDP, there is the issue of the 'benchmark' variable against which to contrast TFP or income. For example, Senhadji measures the dependent variable as the level of TFP for each country relative to the level of TFP in the United States. Many empirical papers attempt to explain the 'gap' between the individual countries and 'best-practice' country or region (for example the East Asian countries). These seemingly subtle differences should matter or at least should be borne in mind while interpreting the results of empirical estimation.

Another fundamental problem pertains to the estimation technique. Hoeffler (1999) and O'Connell and Ndulu (2000) argue that the orthogonality of the right-hand-side (RHS) variables to each other and to the residual is a major requirement for the regression-based decomposition of the contributions of individual explanatory variables to produce unbiased and consistent 'parameters of interest'. O'Connell and Ndulu show that in practice, the orthogonality assumption fails to hold, thus producing two problems for regression-based decompositions. The first one is an estimation problem – how to obtain consistent estimates of the parameters. In some cases, there is an endogeneity problem, and estimation methods that ignore it will produce biased and inconsistent estimates. The instrumental variable technique can be used to deal with the endogeneity problem. Also, unobserved country effects might have similar effects if they are correlated with the explanatory variables. Although fixed effects estimation can obtain consistent estimates, it comes at a cost – we give up a lot of the sample variation in the process. Furthermore, the dynamic panel literature has shown that consistency holds only if the time dimension of the panel increases along with the number of countries. The second pertains to both multicollinearity and an attribution problem. While multicollinearity produces difficulties in small samples, with unstable point estimates and a tendency towards weak and non-robust significance tests for individual variables, it also produces an attribution problem between the regressors and the residual that persists in large samples.

These problems, summarized by O'Connell and Ndulu, in part lead to the weak robustness of the estimated parameters in cross-country regressions as shown by Levine and Renelt (1992). Several authors have tried to deal with the problem in different ways. In a review of the regional growth papers of the GDN network, Easterly (2000) particularly challenged O'Connell and Ndulu's insistence on orthogonality as a condition to obtain precise estimates. According to Easterly,

> In theory, regression analysis should be able to sort out the effects of independent variables, even if they are correlated. The authors' insistence on orthogonality as a prerequisite to decomposition seems odd, unless they believe that some RHS variables are themselves functions of other RHS variables – but why not estimate such a system explicitly?

Indeed, O'Connell and Ndulu do present decompositions based on Hoeffler's (1999) system-GMM estimates (Table 2.3) of the augmented Solow model for 85 countries. The system-GMM approach is believed to impose sufficient orthogonality conditions to ensure consistent estimates of these parameters even if investment is endogenous and/or unobserved time-invariant country effects are correlated with the observed variables.

Table 2.3   Components of fitted growth by region, Hoeffler (1999)

Region	Initial income (1)	Investment (2)	Education (3)	Replacement investment (4)	Fixed period effects (5)
Contributions to fitted growth deviation					
SSA	3.08	–2.99	–0.17	–0.86	–0.03
LAC	–0.2	0.02	0.03	–0.37	0.01
SAS	2.74	–3.13	–0.19	–0.44	0.01
EAP	0.71	1.2	0.03	–0.32	0.01
MENA	–0.38	1.1	–0.02	–0.28	–0.01
INDU	–3.92	3.01	0.2	1.71	0.01
All countries	0.00	0.00	0.00	0.00	0.00
Beta coefficients					
All countries	–1.01	1.14	0.06	–0.44	–

Notes: The beta coefficient for variable x_i is calculated as $b_i*[sd(x_i)/sd(\text{growth})]$, where b_i is the estimated coefficient and *sd* denotes a standard deviation. The standard deviation of annualized growth in real GDP per capita in the sample is 3.00. SSA = Sub-Saharan Africa; LAC = Latin America and the Caribbean; SAS = South Asia; EAP = East Asia and Pacific; MENA = Middle East and North Africa; INDU = Industrialized Countries.
Source: O'Connell and Ndulu (2000) table 4.2b, calculated from Hoeffler (1999) SYS-GMM results for the Augmented Solow model.

This system-GMM still leaves the problem of attribution since the explanatory variables are largely correlated and potentially endogenous. In the attempt to evaluate the contributions of policy to growth, O'Connell and Ndulu use equation (5) above to estimate a 'baseline' regression in which the conditioning variables are plausibly determined (see Tables 2.4 and 2.5), and then incorporate the policy variables one by one – thus examining the partial correlation between policy variables and growth conditional on the predetermined variables. Finally, they develop a full specification that includes the predetermined variables along with a set of variables capturing different aspects of the institutional and policy environment, and use it to estimate the relative contributions of the RHS variables (see Tables 2.6 and 2.7). Such a 'full' specification does not orthogonalize among the explanatory variables in calculating the decomposition. The estimated residuals suggest the presence of unusual period and/or country-specific factors in the growth process. Also, the contributions of individual variables or groups of variables identify growth syndromes for which there are theoretical justifications but which may involve two-way causality. Of course, the possibility of two-way causation in the cross-country regressions is a constant reminder that these regressions indicate correlations but not necessarily causation.

Other authors have tried to deal with the problem of parameter robustness and relative contributions of the RHS variables in other ways. The pioneering work of Levine and Renelt (1992, 1999) uses a variant of the Extreme-Bounds Analysis (EBA) introduced in Leamer (1983, 1985), and concludes that very few regressors pass the extreme-bounds tests. Sala-í-Martin (1997) uses a less severe test to evaluate the relative importance of explanatory variables. His method considers the distance of the point estimates from zero, averaged over a set of regression models. In effect, if the averaged 90 per cent interval of a regression coefficient does not include zero, he would classify the corresponding regressor as a variable that is strongly correlated with growth. On the basis of this method, Sala-í-Martin identifies a large number of variables as important for growth regressions. Ley and Steel (1999) try to deal with both model and parameter uncertainty using the Bayesian framework (Bayesian Model Averaging, BMA). Their finding, based on the same data-set as those of Sala-í-Martin, broadly support the view that many more variables (than admitted by Levine and Renelt) are important RHS variables for explaining cross-country growth performance. However, the list of which variables are important differs substantially from Sala-í-Martin's results. In effect, the list of which variables are judged to be 'robust' growth determinants in cross-national regressions depends crucially on the methodology employed.

Among the regional growth papers, there is significant methodological pluralism (OLS in the East Asian paper; seemingly unrelated regression (SUR) for Latin America, principal component technique for transition economies, and so on). Despite this methodological pluralism and differing lists of important variables in the literature, it is remarkable how a group of 'standard' variables show up in most regression analysis, consistent with our educated guesses.[5] These variables fall under four main groups: initial conditions, exogenous shocks, policy and institutions, and human resources. Each of the groups, however, has a fairly large number of potential candidate variables, and sometimes the location of particular variables within each category differs among researchers as is evident in the regional growth studies.

The regional studies for East Asia, South Asia, Latin America, and the Middle East and North Africa (MENA) regions adopt approaches that are fairly 'standard' in much of the literature and produce largely 'standard' results.[6] Two papers, O'Connell and Ndulu (2000) (for Sub-

Table 2.4 Baseline pooled regressions

	Dependent variable growth in real GDP per capita. Full sample				Developing countries only				
	(1) Coef.	*Beta*	*(2) Coef.*	*Beta*	*(3) Coef.*	*(4) Coef.*	*(5) Coef.*	*(6) Coef.*	*Beta*
Initial conditions									
ln(initial income)	-1.356	-0.46	-1.479	-0.50	-1.064	-1.574	-0.949	-1.580	-0.39
	-5.326		*-6.022*		*-3.438*	*-5.340*	*-2.842*	*-5.082*	
Initial life expectancy	0.103	0.42	0.093	0.37	0.102	0.102	0.108	0.104	0.34
	4.392		*3.777*		*4.132*	*4.008*	*4.201*	*3.808*	
Demographics									
Age dependency	-0.057	-0.34	-0.046	-0.27	-0.058	-0.045	-0.060	-0.048	-0.22
	-5.470		*-4.773*		*-5.127*	*-4.337*	*-4.961*	*-4.335*	
gr(LF) – gr (pop)	0.704	0.12	0.500	0.09	0.604	0.495	0.598	0.468	0.08
	2.976		*2.210*		*2.197*	*1.898*	*2.067*	*1.707*	
External shocks									
Terms-of-trade shock	0.055	0.07	0.053	0.07	0.056	0.046	0.052	0.045	0.06
	1.900		*1.822*		*1.840*	*1.494*	*1.694*	*1.439*	
Trading partner growth	0.574	0.22	0.406	0.15	0.591	0.390	0.604	0.390	0.15
	3.187		*2.417*		*2.995*	*2.140*	*3.039*	*2.075*	
Geography									
Landlocked	-0.821	-0.10	-0.380	-0.05	-0.636	-0.206	-0.593	-0.209	-0.02
	-2.744		*-1.342*		*-1.673*	*-0.581*	*-1.577*	*-0.588*	
Investment and aid									
Investment/GDP	–	–	0.157	0.39	–	0.172	–	0.171	0.42
	–		*6.539*		–	*6.411*	–	*6.040*	

Table 2.4 Baseline pooled regressions   *continued*

	Dependent variable growth in real GDP per capita. Full sample				Developing countries only				
	(1) Coef.	*Beta*	*(2) Coef.*	*Beta*	*(3) Coef.*	*(4) Coef.*	*(5) Coef.*	*(6) Coef.*	*Beta*
Aid ex TC Grants/GDP	–	–	–	–	–	–	0.046	0.003	0.01
							1.881	*0.126*	
Constant	10.453		8.577		8.550	8.731	7.547	9.008	
	4.519		*3.990*		*3.296*	*3.580*	*2.767*	*3.427*	
# of observations	615		592		490	478	468	457	
R^2	0.317		0.423		0.302	0.428	0.293	0.416	
Root MSE	2.488		2.293		2.697	2.452	2.726	2.490	

Note: All regressions include half-decade dummy variables. *t*-statistics are in italics. A decomposition of predicted growth deviations by region, using the regression in column I, appears in Table 2.5.

Source: O'Connell and Ndulu (2000), table 5.1.1.

Table 2.5   Decomposition from the baseline regression, by region

Region	Observed growth rate	Deviation from sample mean		Residual	Implied country effect
		Observed	Predicted		
SSA	0.69	−1.23	−1.16	−0.06	−0.06
LAC	1.39	−0.53	−0.12	−0.41	−0.41
SAS	2.33	0.42	0.43	−0.01	−0.01
EAP	4.49	2.58	1.52	1.06	1.06
MENA	2.93	1.02	0.35	0.67	0.67
INDU	2.74	0.82	1.06	−0.23	−0.23
All countries	1.91	0	0	0	0

Implied contributions of:

	Initial conditions	Demography	External shocks	Geography	Time effects
SSA	−0.07	−0.85	−0.05	−0.15	−0.04
LAC	0.18	−0.21	−0.17	0.07	0.03
SAS	0.58	−0.22	0.10	0.04	−0.07
EAP	0.27	0.60	0.56	0.12	−0.04
MENA	0.15	0.24	−0.09	0.12	−0.07
INDU	−0.42	1.26	0.07	0.03	0.11
All countries	0	0	0	0	0

Source: O'Connell and Ndulu (2000), table 5.1.2. Calculated from the regression coefficients in column 1 of Table 2.4. The decomposition applies to the regression sample only.

Saharan Africa, SSA) and Campos and Coricelli (2000) (for economies in transition), are more adventurous both in terms of innovative choice and definition of variables as well as estimation procedure.[7] The SSA paper contains extensive results for all regions except the transition economies (see Tables 2.4–2.7). We use the results in the SSA paper to focus the discussion of the key conclusions of these papers, drawing attention to the differences with other regional papers where applicable. The transition economies' paper is an important contribution to the growth literature – to the extent that the experience of these economies confirms some of the accumulated empirical evidence and also poses its own puzzles.[8] The major conclusions are as follows:

Initial conditions matter

Cross-country growth regressions have consistently shown that initial conditions matter. A 'standard' variable used in most studies and consistent with the conditional convergence hypothesis is the initial GDP

Table 2.6 Growth, policy and institutions: pooled sample

Dependent variable: growth in real GDP per capita	Specification 1		Specification 2		Specification 3		Specification 4	
	(1)	Beta coeff. (2)	(3)	Beta coeff. (4)	(5)	Beta coeff. (6)	(7)	Beta coeff. (8)
ln(initial income)	-1.765 / -6.104	-0.631	-1.698 / -4.951	-0.580	-1.833 / -5.778	-0.657	-2.065 / -6.087	-0.772
Life expectancy	0.089 / 2.872	0.375	0.076 / 2.136	0.300	0.085 / 2.424	0.353	0.079 / 2.613	0.327
Age dependency ratio	-0.052 / -4.222	-0.338	-0.043 / -3.125	-0.269	-0.047 / -3.492	-0.308	-0.051 / -2.988	-0.348
Growth of potential LF participation	0.728 / 2.711	0.126	0.786 / 2.622	0.131	0.661 / 2.359	0.114	0.785 / 2.504	0.138
Terms of trade shock	0.004 / 0.146	0.006	0.016 / 0.530	0.023	0.016 / 0.546	0.023	-0.016 / -0.546	-0.025
Trading partner growth	0.540 / 2.759	0.231	0.607 / 2.962	0.249	0.516 / 2.463	0.220	0.488 / 1.876	0.191
Landlocked	-0.912 / -2.725	-0.113	-1.185 / -2.949	-0.143	-0.874 / -2.246	-0.106	-0.694 / -1.559	-0.086
Political instability	-0.975 / -4.220	-0.137	-1.062 / -4.382	-0.154	-0.740 / -3.040	-0.109	-0.780 / -2.565	-0.122
Financial depth (M2/GDP)	– / –	–	0.021 / 2.842	0.164	– / –	–	–	–
Inflation	-0.004 / -1.830	-0.051	– / –	–	-0.003 / -1.170	-0.032	-0.002 / -0.766	-0.030

Table 2.6 Growth, policy and institutions: pooled sample   *continued*

Dependent variable: growth in real GDP per capita	Specification 1		Specification 2		Specification 3		Specification 4	
	(1)	*Beta coeff. (2)*	*(3)*	*Beta coeff. (4)*	*(5)*	*Beta coeff. (6)*	*(7)*	*Beta coeff. (8)*
Black market premium	-0.007	-0.134	-0.008	-0.153	-0.008	-0.153	-0.009	-0.176
	-2.403		*-2.687*		*-2.399*		*-2.293*	
Gov nonprod. cons./GDP (Barro/Lee (1993))	-0.113	-0.254	-0.105	-0.225	-0.113	-0.252	-0.100	-0.239
	-4.555		*-3.931*		*-4.210*		*-3.681*	
Ratio of manufacturing trade to GDP	–	–	–	–	0.026	0.137	0.029	0.175
					2.721		*3.032*	
Fiscal deficit after grants/GDP	–	–	–	–	–	–	-0.103	-0.181
							-2.928	
Constant	15.347	–	12.782	–	13.934	–	16.883	–
	5.365		*4.449*		*4.903*		*5.053*	
# of observations	422		364		363		258	
F	15.58		13.58		13.68		12.53	
Prob > F	0		0		0		0	
R-squared	0.407		0.402		0.417		0.467	
Root MSE	2.186		2.278		2.179		2.005	

Notes: All regressions include half-decade dummy variables; *t*-statistics are in *italics*.

Table 2.7a Decompositions based on full pooled regression

Region	Deviation of actual growth from sample mean	Contribution of:			
		Baseline variables	Political instability	Policy	Residual
	(1)	(2)	(3)	(4)	(5)
Column 1 of Table 2.6					
SSA	−1.24	−0.53	0.12	−0.73	−0.12
LAC	−0.61	−0.31	−0.14	0.00	−0.19
SAS	0.12	1.06	−0.22	−0.76	0.06
EAP	2.13	1.38	0.08	0.33	0.38
MENA	1.00	0.21	−0.01	0.19	0.69
INDU	0.57	0.06	0.05	0.61	−0.16
Column 2 of Table 2.6					
SSA	−1.4	−0.42	0.15	−1.01	−0.17
LAC	−0.62	−0.14	−0.17	−0.24	−0.09
SAS	0.53	1.26	−0.27	−0.76	0.34
EAP	2.42	1.53	0.11	0.25	0.56
MENA	1.02	0.13	0	0.49	0.45
INDU	0.57	−0.31	0.07	1.1	−0.27
Column 3 of Table 2.6					
SSA	−1.26	−0.32	0.10	−0.89	−0.19
LAC	−0.61	−0.25	−0.10	−0.14	−0.15
SAS	0.42	1.31	−0.20	−0.91	0.28
EAP	2.32	1.41	0.07	0.50	0.37
MENA	0.91	0.14	−0.01	0.28	0.56
INDU	0.38	−0.26	0.03	0.78	−0.16
Column 4 of Table 2.6					
SSA	−1.14	−0.12	0.11	−1.05	−0.15
LAC	−0.93	−0.2	−0.1	−0.18	−0.46
SAS	0.68	1.59	−0.21	−1.17	0.57
EAP	2.35	1.48	0.07	0.65	0.14
MENA	0.71	0.18	−0.03	0.04	0.56
INDU	0.18	−0.65	0.04	0.8	0.01

Source: O'Connell and Ndulu (2000), table 5.3.2, Calculated using regression coefficients from Table 2.6. The decomposition applies to the regression samples only.

per capita (the beginning period average, usually half-decade). In the regional studies and the growth literature, this variable turns out with a negative coefficient and is statistically significant, providing strong evidence for conditional convergence. For example, De Gregorio and

Table 2.7b   Relative contributions to growth differentials between East Asia and other regions, 1960–90 (percentages)

	Developed	Latin America	Middle East	South Asia	Sub-Saharan Africa
Initial income	–187	–45	–47	49	57
Human resources					
Schooling	18	–4	–16	–22	–43
Institution and policy	*61*	*–43*	*–49*	*–134*	*–87*
Government consumption	3	–4	2	–25	–20
Openness	–1	–11	–13	–29	–23
Institution	58	–28	–38	–80	–44
Exogenous factors	*8*	*–8*	*12*	*8*	*–26*
Resource endowment	8	–7	–2	13	–25
Terms of trade	1	–1	13	–5	–1

Source: Hahn and Kim (2000).

Lee (2000) estimate a coefficient of (–0.021) and a standard error = 0.003 for initial income, implying that a poor country at half the income level of another country grows by 1.45 percentage points faster than the richer country. O'Connell and Ndulu also include life-expectancy at birth as one of the 'initial conditions' and it turns out with a strongly positive and large coefficient.

An important addition to the growth literature is the reinforcement of the importance of initial conditions by the experiences of the economies in transition. Based essentially on the economies in transition, Campos and Coricelli (2000) distinguish their work by using the principal components technique to isolate a limited number of vectors of significant initial conditions (see also EBRD, 1999, for a similar approach). Specifically, the authors consider (i) measures of initial distortions, associated with both the structure of the economy (namely the degree of over-industrialization) and policy-induced distortions, such as the premium of the black-market exchange rate over the official exchange rate; (ii) 'natural' characteristics, such as the physical distance from Western European markets, and the endowment of natural resources; (iii) weight of the inheritance from the previous regime, measured by the time spent under central-planning; and (iv) the degree of development of market mechanisms. The results obtained are quite illuminating (see Campos and Coricelli, 2000, pp. 22–7). The first two principal components explain about 80 per cent of the variance. The first component shows a large negative weight for initial liberalization and a large positive weight for initial distortions, such as repressed inflation, dependence on CMEA trade, black-market premium, distance from Brussels and years spent under communist regime. A positive coefficient on this variable implies the predominance of the effects of initial distortions, while a negative coefficient implies the predominant role of initial market liberalization. The second component shows large weights to initial income per capita and the degree of urbanization. The results of the first principal components are consistent with expectations and the growth literature; namely, initial distortions and distance from market economies, both in physical and economic terms, exert a strong negative effect on growth. The result of the second principal component, which implies that a higher level of initial income per capita is associated with faster growth after reforms, is however more difficult to interpret, especially in the context of the conditional convergence hypothesis. Experience in many countries (especially in Africa) is that 'economies in transition' especially following a prolonged civil strife and operating from a very low base tend to grow much faster after reforms. One possible explanation for the outcome in the former communist countries might be related to the existence, in higher-income countries, of the minimum threshold of capital stock required for initiating higher growth after reforms. If higher income levels are associated with higher savings–investment rates, a new momentum for cumulative growth could be unleashed following reforms that eliminate most distortions.

Growth 'fundamentals' and non-policy variables also matter

In most growth regressions several variables, which have both direct and indirect effects on growth, are included together in the regression. Clearly, many of the variables have their impact on growth through their effects on factor accumulation and efficiency. O'Connell and Ndulu (2000) carefully isolate three clusters of variables – 'fundamentals', non-policy plus initial conditions, and a full (pooled) sample incorporating the three groups. This presents very interesting results that are both informative and boldly underscore the problem of model uncertainty, as the decomposition weights for each of the groups of variables depend crucially on the specification chosen (see Table 2.7).

Growth 'fundamentals' here refer to the variables usually included in the vector 'x' of the augmented Solow model: (i) the national saving rate, proxied by the ratio of investment to GDP; (ii) a variable measuring replacement investment requirements and dominated in practice by population growth; and (iii) a measure of saving for human capital accumulation. The decomposition of Hoeffler's (1999) system-GMM result is presented in Table 2.3. Hoeffler uses educational attainment as the more relevant measure of human capital, in preference over enrolment rates (here defined as the average years of schooling achieved by the population aged 15 or older). One of the important findings of the Hoeffler system-GMM regression is, according to O'Connell and Ndulu, that

> there is little evidence in these data, once the GMM estimates are used, of a set of slow-moving or time-invariant growth determinants that are specific to SSA. The 'Africa dummy variable', so often large and statistically significant in the growth literature, is both small in magnitude and statistically insignificant.[9]

Second, the result of the decomposition (see Table 2.3) confirms the usual suspects – initial income and investment ratio are highly significantly correlated with growth. Other regional papers and the growth literature support this finding. Education (here a proxy for human capital) is surprisingly unimportant in the Hoeffler results (although consistent with the sources of growth decomposition reported in Collins and Bosworth, 1996). The SSA paper argues that 'not only is its average effect small, but its beta, at 0.03, indicates that almost none of the cross-country variation in growth around its mean is attributed to cross-country dispersion in educational attainment'. This is consistent with the results in some empirical studies, especially Africa-specific studies (see for example, Sacerdoti *et al.*, 1998; Pritchett, 2000). However, the cross-national regression in the Latin American study (see De Gregorio and Lee, 2000) argues on the contrary that

> the educational attainment variable, which is measured by the average year of secondary and tertiary schooling, has a positive and significant effect on the growth rate: the estimated coefficient on the schooling variable is 0.005 (s.e. = 0.002) ... Therefore, the coefficient indicates that one standard-deviation increase in the secondary and tertiary schooling raises the growth rate of per capita income by about 0.7 percentage points per year. (p. 16)[10]

Campos and Coricelli (2000) also find a much higher coefficient on secondary education in the regression for transition economies.

The 'baseline' regression in the SSA paper (see Tables 2.4 and 2.5) considers initial conditions, demographic factors, geography, aid excluding technical cooperation grants, and external factors. The regional differences in terms of these variables are revealing. Africa is the obvious outlier in terms of demography and more so with regard to geography. In terms of external shocks and demography, the East Asia and Pacific region is a positive outlier, implying that effective demographic transition and favourable external shocks may have played decisive roles in the growth differences between the East Asian countries and others. What is surprising in the results, however, is the apparent unimportance of the external shocks – proxied by terms-of-trade effects – even for the SSA region and the MENA region. Makdisi *et al.* (2000, p. 7) confirm that 'some of the variables portraying the impact of external shocks and volatility were found to be insignificant for the whole sample'. Contrary to the SSA paper, however, the authors find that 'these same variables turned out to be very significant for the MENA group'. In contrast to these two papers, the Latin American study finds a 'significant relationship between changes in the terms of trade and per capita GDP growth' for the whole sample. Specifically, the study finds that

the estimated coefficient on the growth rate of the terms of trade is 0.136 (s.d. = 0.029), indicating that countries with favorable terms of trade shock by one-standard deviation of 0.035 in the 1985–95 period grew by 0.5 percentage points per year greater than other countries.

The reason for the differing results could be located in the differences in measurement. The popular approach in the empirical literature is to use the average year-to-year percentage changes in the barter terms of trade. However, Easterly (2000) contends that a preferable measure on theoretical grounds is the income effect of the terms of trade, which multiplies the relative price change by the share of the trade in GDP. A separate issue, however, is whether to use the average year-to-year change or a measure of cumulative income effects, and O'Connell and Ndulu opt for the later, while acknowledging that both measures are substantially different. This is an issue that needs further empirical investigation since it seems that the result one obtains depends on how the terms-of-trade variable enters the regression equation.

The evidence indicates that the SSA region is atypically constrained by its geography (measured in terms of landlockedness). There is also evidence of resource-curse as the measure of resource endowment consistently turns out to be negatively correlated with growth. There is therefore support for the hypothesis that natural resource-abundant countries tend to grow slowly due to the Dutch-disease syndrome and unproductive rent-seeking activities. Political instability, which negatively affects factor accumulation and efficiency of resource use, consistently hurts growth.

Policy and institutions are decisive for growth

Most empirical growth studies have shown that policy and institutional variables matter. The lingering controversy pertains to the channels of effects, the measurement of the variables, the choice of variables, and the weights that these policy variables carry relative to the non-policy variables and growth fundamentals (summarized by O'Connell and Ndulu, 2000, in their 'baseline' regression). Sometimes, the debate about the appropriate weight to be attached to policy/institutions versus others has swung to extremes. In the extreme, those who see the world of economic performance only through the policy prism argue that the non-policy variables – geography, demography and external shocks – only hurt growth in the context of poor policy. While disputing the destiny argument implied by these non-policy variables, the 'policy-only' school believes that sound policies can obviate or eliminate the potential negative effects of the non-policy variables (see Bloom and Sachs, 1998, and the critique by Collier, 1998). While the debate on the relative weights to be attached to the various groups of determinants is unlikely to go away soon, many analysts also question the sense of determinism sometimes unconsciously implied in the conclusions of the non-policy advocates. Ultimately, whether or not non-policy variables dominate growth, it would require discretionary actions such as policies to get the particular countries out of the constraints imposed by the non-policy variables. Here lies the significance of the debate. A clear identification of the particular non-policy variables that constrain growth, for example, has specific implication in terms of which 'policy' choices are required to eliminate them. If geography (landlockedness) is a major constraint, then policies that favour investment in infrastructure and regional integration might be required to reduce the impact of adverse geography. Geography and the policy variable that indirectly affects growth through its effect on infrastructure might be highly correlated if included jointly, thus affecting the precision with which the coefficients can be estimated.

This in itself raises another fundamental problem with the cross-national growth regressions, namely, the tight covariation of 'policy' with non-policy variables (especially the initial conditions). Which policy variables turn out to be significant depend crucially on the conditioning variables (especially the initial conditions) as well as other policy variables included in the regression. Evidence, however, shows that while individual policy variables rarely perform consistently across alternative specifications, it is rare for a set of policy variables to be jointly insignificant in a growth regression (Levine and Renelt, 1992). The 'experimental design' by O'Connell and Ndulu (2000) of sequentially introducing the policy and institutional variables one-by-one and examining the partial correlations and beta coefficients as well as the 'pooled' full specification of baseline and policy, institutional, and political instability variables confirm this point by Levine and Renelt (see Tables 2.6 and 2.7).

In the literature there is a remarkable convergence of views around sets of policy variables that matter for growth – adequate macroeconomic policy, adequate openness and private-sector orientation, adequate governance and institutional quality, size and composition of government expenditure (see all the regional growth papers; Pritchett, 2000 Easterly, 1996, and so on). Each of these sets can be proxied by several variables, and individual studies often differ markedly in their choice of 'representative' variables. To varying degrees, all the regional growth papers confirm the importance of these sets of variables irrespective of the definition of variables (see particularly Table 2.7 for the joint effect of policy and institutional variables relative to other growth determinants). The decomposition of the 'contributions' of various groups of determinants to the growth deviations results in varying weights to policy and non-policy variables, depending on the particular specifications.

What is particularly striking in the results reported in Table 2.6 is that aid does not enter these regressions significantly once policy variables are included, nor does better policy enhance the predicted effect of aid (consistent with Burnside and Dollar, 1997). In contrast to Burnside and Dollar, O'Connell and Ndulu find that the net marginal contribution of aid is positive even when policy is poor. A strong interaction term (of policy and aid) emerges only if the authors remove Zambia in the late 1980s – an outlying country/period observation with very modest growth and very weak policy indicators – from the regression sample. While this result is interesting in the sense of a new perspective on the policy–aid interaction, it also highlights the fundamental flaw of the 'add and drop' methodology of cross-national growth regressions.[11]

Another striking feature of the regional studies is the evidence from the transition economies, which largely corroborates the results for other developing countries. Campos and Coricelli (2000, p. 20) note that 'the similarity with results obtained for developing countries is somehow reassuring on the fact that after liberalization growth in transition economies is affected by factors that are similar to those conditioning growth in developing countries'. The authors find that macroeconomic stability, proxied by the rate of inflation; economic distortions such as the premium in the black market for foreign exchange; quality of infrastructure fundamental for the functioning of a market economy, proxied by telephone lines; human capital endowment (secondary-school enrolment); and the initial level of per capita income all play important roles in affecting the rates of growth in transition economies. Campos and Coricelli correctly observe, however, that this standard set of variables is too narrow to account for the fundamental differences between the experience of transition economies, characterized by a process of radical structural and institutional change, and developing countries, characterized by highly imperfect but nevertheless well-established market economies.

In addition to the 'standard' explanation of growth differences, Campos and Coricelli introduce variables and explanations they believe could tell the 'story' of the transition economies. For example, in the set of initial conditions, they include measures of initial distortions, macroeconomic imbalances, degree of market liberalization, natural endowment, income per capita and output growth before liberalization. As the starting point for each country, they use the year in which full-fledged reforms began. Three key results of the transition-economies study are worth highlighting since they are of direct importance to the policy and growth debate.

The first important result is the ambiguity of the impact of reforms on growth (at least in terms of the liberalization indicators constructed by the EBRD). Domestic price liberalization tends to reduce growth, while opening up to external trade is good for growth.[12] An important finding, however, is the interaction between reform indicators and initial conditions. Such an interaction term suggests that the effects of domestic price liberalization are a powerful stimulus for growth in countries characterized by unfavourable initial conditions, while the opposite obtains for external liberalization. The key message, according to the authors, is that the effects of liberalization measures crucially depend on the initial conditions of the countries.

The second important finding is the puzzling role of the presence of IMF programmes for growth. Macroeconomic instability (typically the central concern of IMF programmes), proxied by inflation and budget deficits, have significant adverse effect on growth. However, the presence of IMF programmes also adversely affect growth. The authors caution that the negative correlation of the programmes with growth should be interpreted with caution since the presence of such programmes signals underlying macroeconomic difficulties. Nevertheless, according to the authors, 'the fact that IMF programmes are accompanied in most cases by output decline, or an acceleration of it, should be taken as an indication of the *possibility* that such programmes contributed to the fall in output, and thus were partly ill designed'.

The third major result pertains to the composition of government expenditures. Following Barro's (1991) influential work, several empirical studies on growth have typically found government consumption to GDP ratio to be a powerful constraint on growth. In the same tradition, Fischer *et al.* (1998) foresee better growth performance for the transition economies if government consumption is permanently reduced to 10 per cent of GDP. The result could, however, be different if one focuses on government expenditure rather than consumption (the difference being mainly transfers). Campos and Coricelli (2000) disaggregate government expenditure into three key components that are likely to have different effects on growth rates and levels – social expenditure, capital spending, and consumption spending. They find that social expenditure is strongly positively correlated with growth in the transition economies. This is consistent with the results for selected market economies in which Easterly and Rebelo (1993) found that social expenditure and public investment tend to be positively correlated with growth, while other expenditures – mainly government consumption – have an adverse effect on growth. Campos and Coricelli find that the effect of social expenditure is stronger and statistically more significant in the transition economies. However, contrary to the evidence in popular literature, the authors find that capital expenditure is not significant, and this may indicate the inefficient nature of this type of expenditure in the initial stages of transition. Despite all the well-known caveats regarding the inclusion of fiscal variables in growth regressions, especially the possibility of reverse causation, Campos and Coricelli conclude that the strong effect of social expenditure on growth lends support to the view that far-reaching reforms and structural change require an accompanying social safety net. Without this safety net the system cannot sustain a massive realloca- tion of labour across sectors. Workers would lack the incentives to abandon inefficient enterprises and face a period of unemployment, which would result in a lack of political support for reforms. The key message is simple: 'the development of a growing market economy requires building of institutions and the presence of adequate social safety nets. "Wild" capitalism, Russian style, is not an unfortunate byproduct of a fast growing market economy, but may represent a major obstacle to the development of markets and growth' (Campos and Coricelli, 2000, p. 26).

Finally, all the regional studies reaffirm what most growth regres- sions have found, namely, that institutional quality matters, and that openness to trade is necessary for growth. For institutions, O'Connell and Ndulu (2000) use the ICRG indices of government corruption, quality of bureaucracy, and rule of law. Taken together, the authors find that their net effect is big – an increase from the African average to the average for the high-performing Asian economies that also includes Malaysia, Thailand and Indonesia – three countries whose governance scores are low by the standards of the group – would increase long-run growth by nearly a third of a percentage point per year. For the transition economies, Campos and Coricelli (2000) use a similar data-set from ICRG,[13] and point out the uniqueness of their study, which is that previous studies did not control for the complete set of initial conditions, macroeconomic reform and reform variables that they included. Still they conclude from their results that market reforms are effective if they are able to create the necessary institutions for the functioning of a market economy. All the regional studies (except the transition economies) use the Sachs–Warner (SW) openness index, and reach the usual conclusion that openness is strongly corre- lated with growth.

Rodrik (2000b) does not explicitly disagree with the conclusion that quality institutions and openness matter for growth. However, he is disappointed with the measures of these variables used in the regional growth papers as well as in the popular growth literature, namely the Sachs–Warner openness index and the Knack–Keefer (KK) index of institutional quality.[14] He notes that these indices do the heavy lifting in three of the regional papers (East Asia, Latin America, and South Asia) in the sense that the differential performance in each of the regions in question is attributed in large part to differences in openness and institutions, as measured by these two indices. Given that these two indices are problematic, Rodrik (2000b, p. 2) argues that the conclusions from these studies obfuscate rather than clarify:

> The SW index is not a measure of openness. It is an index that essentially distinguishes countries that are either in Africa or have had high black market premia from countries that fit neither of these criteria. This index tells us nothing about the effects of trade openness proper (in the sense that we usually think of openness, namely low tariff and non-tariff trade barriers) ... The point rather is that the SW index is a misleading and biased indicator of what it purports to measure. It should not be used as an indicator of trade openness, period.[15]

On the KK index of institutions, Rodrik raises two concerns. One is that this is a highly subjective measure, based on survey responses. For example, let us take the case of two countries with identical institutions, but with large differences in growth rates. The natural bias in survey responses will be to rate the institutions of the high-growth country as being superior to those in the low-growth country. The second problem is that the ratings pertain to the 1980s, but are typically used in growth regressions spanning a time period that antedates the 1980s. The possibility of reverse causation is very real, as it is possible for high-growth countries to eventually acquire better institutions. In this case, an instrumental variable technique could be used to deal with the problem. Rodrik concludes by suggesting that authors of cross-national growth studies use more direct measures of trade policy, and an instrumental variable approach to institutions as a way of bringing their work 'closer to the frontier of the cross-national growth literature'. In effect, Rodrik raises the red flag on the measurement of these variables that many empirical growth studies advertise to drive much of the observed cross-national growth differences. What can we conclude from the foregoing?

4   Conclusions: comparative lessons learnt and matters arising

When we combine the insights of the growth accounting in section 2 with the regression-based estimation results in section 3, we have a basis to evaluate the lessons learnt and summarize the remaining agenda. It is evident that there is an emerging 'consensus' on the broad list of factors that could explain cross-regional differences in accumulation and efficiency, but there is also a raging controversy pertaining to the appropriate methodology – both measurement and estimation procedures. On balance, it would be fair to conclude that we know as much as we don't in terms of what determines the differences in cross-national growth performances. This is especially true given that it is still not easy to pinpoint from these results which factor is the most dominant and how they affect economic growth since all the factors considered are intertwined and changing along with the development process.

Basically the literature and the regional studies confirm much of our educated guesses, especially with guidance from neoclassical theory and empirical evidence rooted in it. From a policy perspective, the cross-country evidence largely confirms the major aspects of the *extended Washington consensus* – that is, with the quality of institutions included. All the variables that form the core of that consensus turn out to be important, at least given various permutations and combinations of the variables. In some regressions, variables that proxy 'exogenous shocks' turn out to be unimportant – still a reconfirmation of the basic logic of the Washington consensus even though terms-of-trade shocks have been highlighted to be important in many country-specific studies.

How useful are these results to the policy-maker, especially in developing regions? Quite frankly, we believe that the answer is not much. To be sure, the results are a reassuring confirmation of the key elements of the Washington consensus. Hence, policy-makers are at least reassured with empirical evidence that they are not making a mistake by improving institutions that guarantee the rule of law and ensure macro stability. On the other hand, the state of play in these models simply gives the policy-maker a long list of important things to do, without any sense of their order of importance.[16] The sense of 'everything is important' one gets from the various regression results adds little value to the policy-makers' knowledge tool kit. Sometimes, one cannot help asking whether the efforts put into these cross-country growth regressions and the controversies generated by them are justified by the results. Indeed, the sometimes conflicting evidence on the importance of some of the key variables, such as education and trade, can be confusing to the policy-maker. This raises the importance of the other complementary studies under the GDN network that focus on markets, political economy and microeconomic issues. In other words, for policy-makers looking for answers to specific questions, the results of the cross-country regressions should be read in tandem with these other studies as well as the case studies in order to have a more complete picture.

The methodological issues raised by Levine and Renelt (1992), Sala-i-Martin (1997), Ley and Steel (1999), Hoeffler, (1999), O'Connell and Ndulu (2000), Senhadji (1999) and others raise more questions than answers and underscore the caution that should be exercised in interpreting the estimated results, especially in using them for policy. Questions about model 'specification' and the 'robustness' of the parameters of interest will remain for some time, while the measurement problems will continue to persist. The 'add and drop' methodology mentioned earlier might continue to make the results sensitive to the sample selection. Recall that by simply dropping one country – Zambia – from their sample, O'Connell and Ndulu (2000) obtain results that change the qualitative impact of the aid–policy interaction term. Although there are procedures for directly testing for these biases, they are rarely done in much of the reported studies. Employing a different estimation procedure – the system-GMM – Hoeffler (1999) eliminates the Africa dummy without including any of the usual variables that have been used to do the magic, and thus in a fundamental sense alters some of the well-known 'insights' about Africa's slow growth. Furthermore, for even the basic growth-accounting exercise, what you get in terms of the contributions of TFP depends largely on the 'choice' of the size of alpha (share of physical capital in the production function). Several growth-accounting exercises simply 'impose' the alpha across all developing countries due mainly to data problems. Attempts by Senhadji (1999) to directly estimate the alpha from national data is a bold beginning, but given the questions surrounding the 'con structed' capital stock data, such an effort must be interpreted as only a pointer in the direction to go while awaiting future improvements in data quality to produce more reliable estimates. Senhadji has also shown that estimating production in levels or first-difference forms can lead to important differences in the results. Equally daunting is the problem of variable definition and measurement and getting relevant proxies for policy and institutional variables. Easterly (2000) has raised a red flag on how we measure institutions and openness, and work needs to begin to respond to these concerns. A lot of work still needs to be done in 'constructing' more relevant indices or proxies. The summary is that a huge research agenda on the methodology of cross-national growth regressions is yet to begin.

Furthermore, there is a huge agenda of unresolved issues regarding growth and its characteristics. A point to be emphasized here is that very specific contexts matter greatly beyond what is illuminated in the country fixed-effects parameters. Detailed country case studies need as much attention as has been devoted to the cross-country regression analysis. This is the other *emerging* consensus. Both at the national and regional levels, there are very specific growth puzzles that remain to be illuminated. For example, the regional growth papers show that growth has been highly variable (or volatile) in Latin America, the Arab region and Africa, with clear evidence of a lack of growth persistence (except in a few cases such as Botswana and Mauritius in SSA). Southeast Asia is the only region in the world to have experienced faster TFP growth following the oil-price shock of the 1970s. Some have attributed the outcome to institutions and policy, which helped them to respond appropriately to the shocks of the 1970s as well as attenuate the negative snowball effects of the shocks. However, it still needs to be understood why countries in that region were unique in developing such institutions or better policy and not others, and why not all countries within the region were equally successful. Many Latin American countries have undertaken significant reforms since the 1980s and yet have still grown very slowly. The output collapses in most transition economies were certainly not anticipated in the magnitude that they occurred, but even beyond that recovery among the countries has been highly uneven. These issues need in-depth case studies.

Beside aggregate regional puzzles, national features and drivers of growth need urgent attention, and here our ideas are still essentially fickle. We provide three illustrations. First, in his Prebisch Lecture, Stiglitz (1998) stressed this point by drawing attention to the chasm between north and south Italy. According to Stiglitz:

> no trade barriers separated the north from the south; the overall macroeconomic framework in both regions was the same; and the south even benefited from economic policies specifically designed to encourage it. Yet while the north boomed, the south stagnated. This by itself should have suggested that there was more to development than acknowledged by the technical approaches.

Understanding the growth experiences of societies such as southern Italy would require a broader understanding of development as a transformation process within which context the explanations of growth makes sense. Evidently, understanding the effects of such 'society-related' variables on development goes far beyond the confines of an economistic approach – something which many of the studies that have introduced destiny-related explanations – geography, ethnic fractionalization, contagion effects of growth, religion, and so forth – have tried to do. Even within the confines of an economistic approach, there is simply so much that remains to be understood. Take the obvious example of what the cross-country growth regressions sell to be self-evident, namely, that an 'excessive' fiscal deficit is bad for growth. The issue really is not whether 'high' or 'excessive' deficits are bad or good, but *how* 'high' deficits could be deleterious in specific circumstances.[17] Case studies are needed to illuminate such specific contexts. Another example to illustrate the point is the Baltic puzzle reported in the paper on transition economies (Campos and Coricelli, 2000). As stated earlier, this group of countries had output contractions comparable to other former Soviet Union countries but experienced a much faster recovery. The puzzle, however, is that they did some of the 'wrong' things: investment rates declined sharply relative to other transition countries, and the share of government consumption to GDP was rising throughout the period. From the results of the cross-country growth regressions this is, indeed, a great puzzle. Again, this is another example to illustrate the importance of the other complementary studies on markets, political economy, institutions and microeconomic issues.

Among the many unresolved issues on the sources of growth, we highlight two for illustrative purposes. The first is the central issue of growth variability and volatility, and the second pertains to the conflicting results on the role of openness to trade.

Growth variability and structural vulnerability are two interrelated issues which cross-national growth studies have rarely focused upon. Easterly (2000) points out that observed growth varies much more strongly over time than any of the explanatory variables, and researchers should worry about this. From a national economic point of view, the average growth rate over time 'reveals relatively little about the economy. The pattern of growth rates over time generates substantially more information about the nature of the economy and, to a certain extent, about the economy's relation to the international markets' (Weeks, 2001, p. 3). For example, in 40 years, Burkina Faso and Rwanda had average growth rates of 3.4 and 3.3 per cent per annum respectively. But the standard deviation of the growth rate for Burkina Faso was 3.4 and for Rwanda 12.2. Within shorter sample periods, growth variability is even more acute.[18] Growth variability or volatility has been a key feature of the SSA, Arab and, to a lesser extent,

Latin American economies. For Africa it is difficult to discuss growth without this fundamental feature. Understanding the nature and causes of this evident lack of growth persistence is a major challenge to researchers. To a large extent, growth variability is linked to structural vulnerability (which means the risk of being negatively affected by unforeseen events beyond the control of the country). In turn, structural vulnerability could be a consequence of the state of underdevelopment. These factors and linkages are very important to a proper understanding of growth and feasible policy responses because, according to the *World Development Report*, 1996, 'countries' characteristics – their unique advantages and disadvantages – influence what policies can be chosen and what leaders can accomplish'. If structural vulnerability – which has an historical and social basis – is found to be central to the phenomenon of growth volatility in these countries or regions, it would have far-reaching implications for the design of policies. This is because, according to Weeks (p. 2), 'short-term macroeconomic policy may have limited impact on growth variability, though they may affect the average in the short term'.

Another key issue that should be hot on the agenda for research is the role of openness or external-account liberalization in the growth process. Basic theory still posits openness, especially for small countries, as an essential factor for growth. However, the empirical evidence is shrouded in controversy about measurement and robustness of evidence. Given that such a variable does the heavy lifting in many cross-country growth regressions, it is important to rise to the challenges raised by Rodrik (2000b), stated earlier, namely to throw away the Sachs–Warner 'openness index' and measure trade policy more directly. He also disputes the claim that countless other studies have found openness to lead to growth. This is consistent with Rodrik's consistent attempts to show that there is no robust empirical evidence linking openness to economic performance. Commenting on an advance copy of Dollar and Kraay (2001) on 'Trade, Growth, and Poverty', Rodrik (2000a) summarizes his bottom line as follows:

> The analysis in this paper of the post-1980 'globalizers' is extremely misleading. When the analysis focuses on indicators of trade policy, we find no evidence that rapid/deep trade liberalizers did better than other countries (and some evidence to the contrary). Direct indicators of trade policy (tariff averages and NTB coverage ratios) do a reasonably good job of ranking countries *vis-à-vis* each other with respect to trade policy openness. Trade volumes (as share of GDP) are

correlated with incomes but this is devoid of policy content unless one is able to trace out links from policy via trade to growth. The cross-country evidence is consistent with the hypothesis that the quality of institutions (appropriately instrumented) is the driving force behind both trade and incomes. The authors' claims regarding the beneficial effects of trade liberalization on poverty have to be seen as statement based on faith rather than evidence.

The literature on the growing dissent based on empirical evidence cannot be summarized here. Suffice it to note also that the results of detailed country studies (see Ganzua, Taylor and Vos, 2000) are sobering. At their best – and the best cases were infrequent – liberalization packages generated modest improvements in economic growth and distributional equity; at their worst they have been associated with increasing income inequality and slower growth, even in the presence of rising capital inflows. The point to be stressed here is not that anyone can successfully defend autarky as the better policy, but that the importance of trade policy needs to be measured and evaluated in such a manner that can provide information on the specific elements of trade policy that matters most and how to achieve them. Simply regressing the trade to GDP ratio and running with the strong conclusion that openness is good for growth does not further the frontier of growth research. Research needs to be deepened both on the conceptual issues and data.

From the foregoing, it is evident that the cross-country empirical studies to date on the sources of growth have come a long way. However, given the myriad of methodological, conceptual and empirical issues that remain, we can conclude that there are still more questions than answers. Rigorous empirical research is required to fill the huge gaps that still exist in the literature.

Notes

1 The authors drew heavily upon the regional papers on the sources of growth by Campos and Coricelli (2000), De Gregorio and Lee (2000), Guha-Khasnobis and Bari (2000), Hahn and Kim (2000), Makdisi *et al.* (2000) and O'Connell and Ndulu (2000).
2 Here, we assume productive efficiency is independent of the input accumulation, so-called Hicks-neutral technical progress or output-augmenting. This assumption is needed for our purpose of breaking down the output growth into the contribution of input accumulation and technical progress.
3 If we have long enough data on past investment before the concerned period, we do not have to worry about the benchmark but we cannot do without a depreciation rate.

4   Senhadji provide three reasons why levels matter more than growth rates. First, growth rates are more important only to the extent that they are a determining factor of levels. Second, recent contributions to the growth literature focus on levels instead of growth rates. For example, Easterly *et al.*, (1993) show that growth rates are only weakly correlated, suggesting that cross-country differences in growth rates may essentially be transitory. Moreover, several recent models of technology-transfer across countries imply convergence in growth rates as technology transfer prevents countries from drifting away from each other indefinitely. In these models, long-run differences in levels are the pertinent subject of analysis. And, third, the cointegration literature has clearly demonstrated the superiority of level equation versus first-difference equations when series are nonstationary. Formal unit root tests show indeed that these variables cannot reject the unit-root hypothesis.

5   The 'robustness' of these variables to different estimation techniques could stem from their actual empirical regularity or consistency with theory. Alternatively, it could be a result of measurement or definitional errors in these variables which are then repeated in most regressions. For example, Easterly vigorously challenges most of the variable measurements as contained in the regional growth papers, especially the Sachs–Warner 'openness' measure and the index of institutions. For the Sachs–Warner 'openness' index, Easterly argues that it does not make 'sense to derive the estimates of trade openness on growth from an indicator that is designed to yield the maximum measured impact', and goes ahead to suggest that 'it should not be used as an indicator of trade openness, period'.

6   With little variation, the choice and definition of variables as well as estimation techniques are largely common in the literature. The results also confirm much of what is fairly known in the literature about the determinants of cross-national growth differences.

7   See also Easterly's comments on the regional papers for a similar conclusion.

8   Our summary also draws liberally from Campos and Coricelli (2000).

9   This is an important methodological issue. A distinguishing feature of earlier empirical work on African growth was that after accounting for most of the 'traditional' determinants plus policy variables, a significant unexplained variation remained (the 'Africa dummy'). However, several extensions of the growth model that include measures of institutional environment, risk and uncertainty, openness to trade, geography and ethnic diversity, and experimentation with dynamic panel estimation, have resulted in the elimination of the 'Africa dummy'. In the Hoeffler result, the system-GMM ensures that the 'Africa dummy' is eliminated even without including the myriad of variables enumerated above.

10 We return to this issue in the next section of the chapter. Is the issue related to measurement or to method of estimation?

11 Results obtained are highly sensitive to country sample selection, periodization, and grouping of variables in the same regression. In the case under reference, adding or dropping a variable or country could significantly change the qualitative results as the dropping of Zambia from the sample has shown. It simply cautions that the results be interpreted with much caution.

12 Liberalization indicators are a measure of cumulative liberalization achieved. Thus this variable indicates that liberalization has long-lasting effects on growth, as changes in previous years are embodied in such a cumulative indicator. It is worth noting that the heterogenous signs of each liberalization indicator implies that the impact of a summary measure of liberalization, generally used in previous work, is the net result of conflicting forces. Nevertheless, given the possible collinearity among different liberalization indices, the results show that on balance liberalization has a positive effect on growth. However, this result is far from being robust, and the sharp differences in sign and significance of the various components calls for caution in interpreting the result (Campos and Coricelli, p. 23).

13 The data from ICRG are meant to capture (i) the strength of the legal environment and the lack of uncertainty on contract enforcement and respect of laws, and (ii) the quality of bureaucracy, a proxy for effectiveness in the functioning of the state, and consequently an easier environment for business activities.

14 See Knack and Keefer (1996). We state Rodrik's criticisms of these indicators below.

15 In various studies, Dani Rodrik has tried to show that a properly measured openness variable in terms of tariffs and non-tariff trade barriers does not exert significant impacts on growth. Indeed, Rodrik has demonstrated that the SW openness index is driven essentially by the exchange-rate distortion. Once the exchange-rate distortion is eliminated, the SW index becomes insignificant.

16 The attempt in various studies to decompose the 'contributions' of the various groups of variables should be interpreted with caution especially since the authors acknowledge that the 'parameters of interest' were imprecisely estimated given the plethora of methodological difficulties.

17 Fischer (1994, p. ix) amplifies this point. According to him, 'adjectives such as "prudent" and "excessive" are inadequate guides to action. It is generally agreed that budget deficits which, since 1986, have exceeded 8 per cent of gross national product (GNP) bear much of the blame for the economic disaster in the former Soviet Union. But Pakistan's fiscal deficits have exceeded 8 per cent of GNP each year since 1985. If a deficit of 8 per cent a year is excessive, why did Pakistan experience steady growth along with single-digit inflation in the 1980s? Or are some countries able to sustain large deficits for some time without ill consequences? If so, what determines the size and duration of sustainable deficits?'.

18 Although the long-run growth outcomes might be identical, the nature and path of the growth process is equally important. Typically, cross-country growth regressions use half-decade or decade averages, and within such short sample periods there is significant growth variability. Thus, measures of 'long-run growth' depend on where and how we define the cut-off points – half-decade, one decade, or two–four decades' averages?

References

Abramovitz, M. (1956) 'Resource and Output Trends in the United States since 1870', *American Economic Review*, vol. 46, pp. 5–23.

Barro, R.J. (1991) 'Economic Growth in a Cross Section of Countries', *Quarterly Journal of Economics*, vol. 106, pp. 407–43.

Barro, R. (1997) *Determinants of Economic Growth: A Cross-Country Empirical Study* (Cambridge, MA: MIT Press).

Barro, R. and J.W. Lee (1993) 'International Comparisons of Educational Attainment', *Journal of Monetary Economics*, vol. 32(3), pp. 363–94.

Barro, R. and J. Lee (1994) 'Sources of Economic Growth', Carnegie-Rochester Conference Series on Public Policy, no. 40, pp. 1–46.

Barro, R. and X. Sala-i-Martin (1995) *Economic Growth* (New York: McGraw-Hill).

Baumol, W. (1986) 'Productivity Growth, Convergence, and Welfare', *American Economic Review*, vol. 76, pp. 1072–85.

Ben-David, D. and D. H. Papell (1997) 'Slowdown and Meltdowns: Postwar Growth Evidence from 74 Countries', NBER Working Paper, no. 6266.

Berg, A. E. Borenzstein, R. Sahay, and J. Zettelmeyer (1999) 'The Evolution of Output in Transition Economies: Explaining the Differences', Washington DC: IMF Working Paper no. 9973.

Berthelemy, J.-C. and L. Soderling (2001) 'Will there be New Emerging Countries in Africa by the Year 2020?', Paper presented at the Conference on Development Policy in Africa, Oxford University, CSAE, 29–31 March.

Blanchard, O. (1997) *The Economics of Post-Communist Transition* (Oxford: Clarendon Press).

Bloom, D. and J. Sachs (1998) 'Geography, Demography, and Economic Growth in Africa', *Brookings Papers on Economic Activity,* vol. 2, pp. 207–73.

Burnside, C. and D. Dollar (1997) 'Aid, Policies and Growth', *World Bank Policy Research Working Paper,* no. 1777, June.

Campos, N. F. and F. Coricelli (2000) 'Growth in Transition: What We Know, What We Don't, and What We Should', paper prepared for the Global Research Project on 'Explaining Growth'.

Christensen, L. R., D. Cummings and D. W. Jorgenson (1980) 'Economic Growth, 1947–73: An International Comparison', in J. W. Kendrick and B. Vaccara (eds), *New Developments in Productivity Measurement and Analysis,* NBER Conference Report, Chicago, University of Chicago Press.

Collier, P. (1998) 'Comment on Bloom and Sachs: Geography, Demography, and Economic Growth in Africa', *Brookings Papers on Economic Activity,* vol. 2, pp. 274–89.

Collins, S. and B. P. Bosworth (1996) 'Economic Growth in East Asia: Accumulation versus Assimilation', *Brookings Papers on Economic Activity,* no. 2, pp. 135–203.

De Broeck, M. and V. Koen 'The Great Contradictions in Russia, the Baltics and Other Countries of the Former Soviet Union' IMF Working Paper WP00/32.

De Gregorio, J. and J.-W. Lee (2000) 'Economic Growth in Latin America: Sources and Prospects', paper prepared for the Global Research Project 'Explaining Growth'.

Denison, E. F. (1967) *Why Growth Rates Differ* (Washington, DC: The Brookings Institution).

Dollar, D. and A. Kraay (2001) 'Trade, Growth and Poverty' *Finance and Development*, vol. 38 (3), pp. 16–19.

Easterly, W. (1996) 'Why is Africa Marginal in the World Economy?', in G. Maasdrop (ed.), *Can South and Southern Africa Become Globally Competitive*

Economies? (New York: St Martin's Press; London: Macmillan–Palgrave), pp. 19–30.

Easterly, W., M, Kremer, L. Pritchett and L. H. Summers (1993) 'Good Policy or Good Luck? Country Growth Performance and Temporary Shocks', *Journal of Monetary Economics,* vol. 32, pp. 459–83.

Easterly, W. and S. Rebelo (1993) 'Fiscal Policy and Economic Growth; An Empirical Investigation', *Journal of Monetary Economics,* vol. 32, pp. 471–58.

Easterly, W. (2000) 'Review Comments on Six Regional Growth Studies', mimeo, Global Development Network, Washington, DC.

Estrin, S. and G. Urga (2000) 'Accounting for Growth in Transition Economies, 1970–1995', London Business School and City University Business School, mimeo.

European Bank for Reconstruction and Development (various issues), *Transition Report* (London: EBRD).

Fischer, S. (1994) 'Foreword', in W. Easterly *et al.* (eds), *Public Sector Deficits and Macroeconomic Performance* (Oxford: Oxford University Press).

Fischer, S., R. Sahay and C. Vegh (1996) 'Stabilization and Growth in Transition Economies', IMF Working Paper no. WP/96/31.

Ganzua, E.,L. Taylor and R. Vos (eds) (2000) *External Liberalization and Economic Performance in Latin America and the Caribbean* (New York: United Nations Development Programme).

Guha-Khasnobis, B. and F. Bari (2000) 'Sources of Growth in South Asian Countries', paper prepared for the Global Research Project 'Explaining Growth'.

Hahn, C.-H. and J.-il Kim (2000) 'Sources of East Asian Growth: Some Evidence from Cross-country Studies', paper prepared for the Global Research Project 'Explaining Growth'.

Hall, R. and C. Jones (1998) 'Why do Some Countries Produce So Much More Output per Worker than Others?', mimeo, Stanford University.

Hoeffler, A. (1999) 'The Augmented Solow Model and the African Growth Debate', CSAE, University of Oxford, March: Background Paper (revised April 2000).

Jorgenson, D. W., F. M. Gollop and B. M. Fraumeni (1987) *Productivity and US Economic Growth* (Cambridge, MA: Harvard University Press).

Knack, S. and P. Keefer (1996) 'Institutions and Economic Performance: Cross-country Tests using Alternative Institutional Measure', *Economics and Politics,* vol. 7, pp. 207–28.

Krugman, P. (1994) 'The Myth of Asia's Miracle', *Foreign Affairs,* vol. 73(6), pp. 62–78.

Leamer, E. E. (1983) 'Let's take the Con out of Econometrics', *American Economic Review,* vol.73, pp. 31–43.

Leamer, E. E. (1985) 'Sensitivity Analysis Would Help', *American Economic Review,* vol. 75, pp. 308–13.

Levine, R. and D. Renelt (1992) 'A Sensitivity Analysis of Cross-Country Growth Regressions', *American Economic Review,* vol. 82, pp. 942–63.

Levine, R. and D. Renelt (1999) 'Where Did All the Growth Go? External Shocks, Social Conflict, and Growth Collapses', *Journal of Economic Growth,* vol. 4, pp. 385–412.

Ley, E. and M. F. J. Steel (1999) 'We Just Averaged over Two Trillion Cross-Country Growth Regressions', *IMF Working Paper,* WP/99/101.

Makdisi S., Z. Fattah and I. Limam (2000) 'Determinants of Growth in the Arab Countries', paper prepared for the Global Research Project 'Explaining Growth'.

Mkandawire, T. and C. Soludo (1999) *Our Continent, Our Future: African Perspectives on Structural Adjustment* (Trenton, NJ: Africa World Press).

O'Connell, S. A. and B. J. Ndulu (2000) 'Africa's Growth Experience: A Focus on Sources of Growth, 2000', paper prepared for the Global Research Project 'Explaining Growth'.

Pritchett, L. (2000) 'Understanding Patterns of Economic Growth: Searching for Hills among Plateaus, Mountains, and Plains', *World Bank Economic Review*, vol. 14, no. 2, pp. 221–50.

Rodrik, D. (2000a) 'Comments on "Trade, Growth and Poverty by D. Dollar and A. Kraay"', October, Harvard University mimeo.

Rodrik, D. (2000b), 'Review Comments on Six Regional Growth Studies', mimeo, Global Development Network, Washington, DC.

Sacerdoti, E., S. Brunschwig and J. Tang (1998) 'The Impact of Human Capital on Growth: Evidence from West Africa', IMF Working Paper, WP/98/162.

Sachs, J. and A. Warner (1997) 'Sources of Slow Growth in African Economies', *Journal of African Economies,* vol. 6(3), pp. 335–76.

Sachs, J. and A. Warner (1995) 'Economic Reform and the Process of Global Integration', *Brooking Papers on Economic Activity,* vol. 1, pp. 1–95.

Sala-i.-Martin, X. (1997) 'I Just Ran Two Million Regressions', *American Economic Review*, vol. 87, pp. 178–83.

Sarel, M. and D. J. Robinson (1997) 'Growth and Productivity in ASEAN Countries', IMF Working Paper, no. 97/87.

Senhadji, A. (1999) 'Sources of Economic Growth: An Extensive Growth Accounting Exercise', IMF Working Paper no. 99/77.

Solow, R. M. (1957) 'Technical Change and the Aggregate Production Function', *Review of Economics and Statistics*, vol. 39, pp. 312–20.

Stiglitz, J. E. (1998) 'Towards a New Paradigm for Development: Strategies, Policies, and Processes', paper presented at the 1998 Prebisch Lecture at UNCTAD, Geneva, October.

Weeks, J. (2001) 'Growth Variability Among and Within African Countries: The Key to Sustained Development', paper presented at the UN Expert Growth meeting on African Economic Growth, February.

Young, A. (1992) 'A Tale of Two Cities: Factor Accumulation and Technical Change in Hong Kong and Singapore', *NBER Macroeconomic Annual*, pp. 13–54.

Young, A. (1993) 'Lessons from the East Asian NICS: A Contrarian View', NBER Working Paper, no. 4482.

Young, A. (1995) 'The Tyranny of Numbers: Confronting the Statistical Realities of the East Asian Growth Experience', *Quarterly Journal of Economics*, vol. 110(3), pp. 641–80.

3
Microeconomic Determinants of Growth Around the World

Sergei Guriev and Djavad Salehi-Isfahani

1 Introduction

This chapter aims at summarizing the findings of the Global Research Project (GRP) on the microeconomic determinants of growth in non-OECD countries in 1950–2000.[1] We study the behaviour of the main microeconomic agents, namely firms and households, the decisions they make, and the constraints they face with a particular emphasis on the implications for growth. The paper is mainly (but not exclusively) a survey of regional papers on microeconomics of growth, and therefore complements the effort made within the GRP to explain huge variations in growth rates around the world. Unlike other studies, this project does not exclusively rely upon cross-country regressions that include institutional variables; the idea is rather to understand what is behind the institutional and structural variables, what determines the productivity growth and factor accumulation at the microeconomic level. Regressions generally explain the variation in growth rates across countries by the large variations in the accumulation of physical and human capital, they do not explain how these variations arise in the first place. The GRP attempts to go beyond just the variation in inputs.

Many important decisions that affect growth, such as to save, invest, innovate and accumulate human capital, are the results of decisions taken by microeconomic agents. Therefore, any understanding of the mechanics of growth must begin with the behaviour of micro agents. We assume that firms and households across the globe are rational but make different decisions because they operate under different constraints. The regions under the GRP study have vastly different growth experiences in the twentieth century. To what extent has this been the result of differences in firm and household behaviour? We believe that comparative analysis of microeconomic determinants of growth in different regions (for example East Asia vs Africa) may shed light on this question. The purpose of the regional papers was to study how these constraints in each region gave rise to differences in firm and household behaviour, which may have contributed to differences in aggregate growth. In this review, we take stock of the knowledge generated by these studies in an attempt to learn some general lessons. These lessons should be used as guidelines for further studies of economic growth at the country level. In this sense, this paper should be considered a bridge between regional papers and country studies. Our goal is to identify the most important issues emerging from the regional papers and provide a unified framework for the authors of the country studies so that all the country studies will be produced on the same grounds.

Other overview papers dealing with the macro view (Soludo and Kim, Chapter 2, this volume), markets (Jurajda and Mitchell, Chapter 4, this volume), and political economy (Castanheira and Esfahani, Chapter 5, this volume) similarly attempt to summarize the findings of the regional papers in their respective areas and act as a bridge to country studies. This chapter is perfectly complementary to the chapter by Jurajda and Mitchell on the role of markets on growth. They describe the environment in which micro agents operate and we study how microeconomic agents respond to that environment. We take the incentive structure defined by the markets and institutions as given while they explain where the incentives come from. Part of the environment and the institutional structure that we take as given is a product of the policy choices studied in the political economy chapter. At the same time, since the behaviour of the microeconomic agents feeds back on policy choices and helps shape the environment, our paper provides input to the papers on markets and growth and political economy. For example, while political economy explains which policies are chosen, understanding how they are *implemented* and what the *outcomes* are requires understanding the behaviour of microeconomic agents. For example, the outcome of a policy to promote gender equity depends very much on how families make intra-household allocation decisions. Similarly, the effects of an educational subsidy intended to even the playing field for the disadvantaged depend on household behaviour, which determines the extent to which child education depends on parental education. An important distinction with the macro chapter, and to some extent with the other overview chapters, is that the microeconomic determinants of growth exhibit huge variations not only across regions but within countries. Thus, speaking of African and Latin American scenarios can be rather misleading: many differences arise at the microeconomic level. This is not to deny that regional similarities exist that may allow one to compare the 'typical' African case with the typical 'East Asian' case, only that one should keep in mind the limitations of such abstract concepts.

The structure of the paper is as follows. In section 2 we provide a general structure for a microeconomic analysis of determinants of growth; we describe the main microeconomic agents and discuss in what ways their behaviour can influence growth. Then, in the main part of the paper (sections 3 and 4) we provide a more specific account of what has actually happened in different regions and countries of the world, what factors have been more important and why. In section 3 we concentrate on households, and in section 4 we focus on firms. Section 5 contains concluding remarks and discusses possible avenues for future research.

2   An overview of microeconomic determinants of growth in non-OECD economies

The main microeconomic agents are firms and households. For economic growth to take off, households should supply factors of production (labour, physical capital and human capital) and firms should put these factors to the best use (adopt better technologies). A closer look at these decisions reveals a great number of factors that can promote or hinder growth at the microeconomic level. In this section we briefly consider households and firms in turn.

Households

The most important household decisions that affect economic growth are to procreate, to save, and to transfer knowledge and assets to the next generation. These decisions are interdependent and are affected by the environment in which families find themselves. For example, parents who wish to provide for their old age will consider the options to purchase a financial or physical asset, have many children to increase the probability that they will be taken care of, or invest in the human capital of a few children hoping that they would have the means to help. Which options they take will depend on the expected benefits and costs. These benefits and costs are largely determined by the endowments, institutions, and the level of development of the country, while at the same time they influence economic growth. Households make other important decisions that primarily affect the static allocation of resources, but that have implications for growth. For example, how to cope with risk and how much labour to supply are decisions that affect production, but their impact on growth is indirect through factor accumulation and improvement in the overall efficiency of the economy.

A firmly established finding of the development literature is that economic growth fundamentally transforms household decisions. In the course of economic development strategies based on high fertility and low investment in children give way to those based on low fertility and high investment in human capital (Becker, Murphy and Tamura, 1990). This change is often accompanied by a reversal in the direction of intergenerational transfers, a point which Caldwell (1976) has highlighted as a key feature of the development process. He describes developed countries as those in which net intergenerational transfers are from parents to their children, in the form of human capital and other assets, and developing countries as those in which transfers are from children to parents, in the form of farm labour and provision of old-age security. The process through which this transformation takes place – the demographic transition – is well-known, but how and why countries and regions enter this phase is less clear. The key to a better understanding of this transition is to analyse the factors that motivate the individual units – households – to shift from a regime of high fertility and low investments in children to its converse. We return to this point later in section 3.

Savings and investment decisions are also closely intertwined with fertility and human-capital decisions. One important link between the two sets of decisions arises because of intertemporal consumption smoothing. It is widely believed that high fertility serves in part the purpose of providing for old age. Where credit markets are developed, they enable households to postpone consumption by lending when young and consuming when old. In these circumstances households would be less inclined to have large families and thereby switch to greater bequest in the form of human capital. The need for intergenerational transfers provides another link between household investment decisions on human and financial capital. Personal savings intended for bequest can serve as a substitute for human-capital investments in children. In other words, altruistic parents may choose to leave their bequest in the form of human capital or other assets depending on the productivity of each investment.

Firms

The other microeconomic agents, crucial for growth, are firms that use the factors supplied by the households through the factor markets and make production and investment decisions. We distinguish between two types of firms: small businesses and large firms.[2] The challenges these two types of agents face may be quite different. For a small business the main challenge is to survive and grow, whilst the large firm has already achieved (or overgrown) the optimal scale so that the main task is to restructure in response to changing external conditions and to increase productivity.

In most non-OECD countries small businesses are much more important than in the developed economies (precisely due to barriers to growth that we discuss below). For example, in the Middle East and North Africa (MENA) large firms (greater than 100 employees) account for only 2 per cent of employment. Table 3.1 presents the distribution of employment across plant sizes brought together from different sources by Tybout (2000). This table is very instructive since it presents the dichotomy between two development scenarios: in some countries (such as Ghana, Zambia, Indonesia, Sierra Leone) small business is the dominant form of industrial organization, while in many other countries, where small firms still occupy a disproportionately large share of the economy (relative to the United States), there is a substantial share of employment in large firms as well. What is striking about the latter scenario is that there are almost no medium-sized firms. Tybout (2000) refers to the latter situation as the 'missing middle'.[3]

In most of the non-OECD countries, small businesses operate in a rather hostile environment facing numerous barriers to entry and growth, including credit and insurance-market imperfections, rent-seeking by private rackets, predatory regulation and taxation by government officials. Hence many potentially efficient small businesses are not established, some do not survive, and some do not grow to their optimal scale and/or scope. Also, some firms prefer to stay in the informal rather than the formal sector. We will try to understand which constraints are binding in different countries and what the implications for growth are. As for the large firms, the incentives to restructure and invest in new technologies also depend on the external environment. We will discuss the role of financial imperfections, domestic and foreign competition, privatization, and institutions of contract and property-rights enforcement.

Treating the distinction between small and large firms as static may be misleading. As mentioned above, the essence of the development

Table 3.1 Distribution of employment shares across plant sizes.

	Numbers of workers					
	1–4	*5–9*	*10–19*	*20–49*	*50–99*	*>99*
United States, 1992[a]	1.3	2.6	4.6	10.4	11.6	69.4
Mexico, 1993[b]	13.8	4.5	5.0	8.6	9.0	59.1
Indonesia, 1986[c]	44.2	17.3		38.5		
Korea, 1973[d]	7.9		22.0		70.1	
Korea, 1988[e]		12		27		61
Taiwan, 1971[c]		29.1			70.8	
Taiwan, 1986[f]		20		29		51
India, 1971[g]		42		20		38
Tanzania, 1967[g]		56		7		37
Ghana, 1970[g]		84		1		15
Kenya, 1969[g]		49		10		41
Sierra Leone, 1974[g]		90		5		5
Indonesia, 1977[g]		77		7		16
Zambia, 1985[g]		83		1		16
Honduras, 1979[g]		68		8		24
Thailand, 1978[g]		58		11		31
Philippines, 1974[g]		66		5		29
Nigeria, 1972[g]		59		26		15
Jamaica, 1978[g]		35		16		49
Colombia, 1973[g]		52		13		35
Korea, 1975[g]		40		7		53

Source: Tybout (2000).. [a] 1992 US Census of Manufacturing, unpublished Census Bureau calculations. [b] INEGI (1995). [c] Steel (1993). [d] Little, Mazumdar and Page (1987, table 6.5). [e] 1988 Census of Manufacturing, Republic of Korea, calculations of Bee-Yan Aw. [f] Chen (1997, table 2.2). [g] Liedholm and Mead (1987).

process is the transformation of small (and informal) firms into large (and formal) ones.[4] However, due to the barriers that small businesses face, many of them are stuck in the informal sector and cannot grow. Therefore, many economies find themselves in a (low-level) equilibrium where the size of the informal sector remains very high.

The main findings of the regional papers

Households

To the extent that behaviour at the micro level determines the rates of physical and human capital accumulation, a careful study of firm and household behaviour in different parts of the world should reveal deeper sources of variation in growth than we have been able to uncover so far using cross-country regressions. The role of the six regional studies on the theme of the microeconomics of growth has been to define the key issues for each region and help coordinate the country studies that would follow. Although on the whole the micro thematic papers have succeeded in raising the key issues, the main part of the task of identifying the micro sources of variation in growth remains for country studies.

The thematic papers were asked to follow the model set by Collier and Gunning (1999), the microeconomics paper on Africa. Collier and Gunning chose two types of micro agents, manufacturing firms and rural households, which play the critical roles in African growth, and then proceeded to analyse the actions of these agents in light of the environment in which they operated. Several other regional papers similarly chose to limit their focus. Except for Africa and South Asia, the regional papers chose to focus on urban households as key micro-economic agents that contribute to growth. This is not surprising as urban households predominate in the populations of all regions except Sub-Saharan Africa and South Asia.

The main question for all micro studies was to assess the contribution, or lack thereof, of these micro agents to growth given the environment they faced. The aim was to assess the degree to which the variation in growth experience of different regions of the world could be explained by the behaviour of rational agents facing different constraints as defined by the external environment. For this purpose, the environment would be defined in such a way as to be exogenous to household decisions. Success in explaining good and bad outcomes of household decisions depends very much on the extent to which one can assume exogeneity of the constraints.

For Sub-Saharan Africa, Collier and Gunning (1999) identify risks arising from soil and climate conditions and disease as the environment that has shaped the behaviour of micro agents in general and rural households in particular. They argue that in the absence of appropriate insurance markets, these risks force micro agents into inefficient diversification that inhibits growth. Micro agents in the traditional economy were able to develop organizations and institutions that helped them cope with risk, but these solutions were costly in terms of growth, because they required investments in lineage and foregone specialization.

In MENA, Salehi-Isfahani (2000) identifies the strong role of state and social norms regarding gender as the important characteristics of the environment that distort household choices. Preponderance of public employment and regulation of the private labour markets in

MENA have led to reduced individual effort as well as unproductive investment in human capital. Gender norms have limited women's choices, in particular discouraging them from working outside the home, thereby reducing returns to female education, slowing down fertility decline and human-capital accumulation. For Latin America and the Caribbean (LAC), Behrman *et al.* (2000) focus on the unstable macroeconomic environment as the major constraint that has limited the contribution of households to economic growth. They show that periods of downturn have coincided with lower educational achievement of the cohorts who were school age at the time. In the case of Central and Eastern Europe and Former Soviet Union (CEE-FSU), Guriev and Ickes (2000) have to deal with two different environments, one facing households during the planned socialist period and the other during transition. The socialist environment reduced income risk to households, caused rapid human-capital accumulation and very high labour supply levels for women. The transition environment, which is presumably not permanent, increased income risks, reduced household savings and the labour supply of women.

These characterizations of the environment are first and foremost hypotheses to be tested by country studies that will follow the regional papers. As such they are subject to challenge on two grounds at least, significance for growth and exogeneity. To be sure, characteristics of the environment that are in a significant way shaped by household decisions should not be used to explain the behaviour itself. For example, the social norms regarding women's role in society defined in Salehi-Isfahani (2000) are in some sense the product of household behaviour. It may be argued that individual agents have the incentive to enforce only those norms that in one way or another correspond to their preferences. However, as Salehi-Isfahani argues, norms inherited from the past can influence decisions for a long time after they have ceased to serve any purpose. The question then becomes why in MENA such social norms arose in stronger form and lingered while in other regions they either did not arise or disappeared quickly.

Similarly, one could question the role of risk. Is the African environment riskier than environments elsewhere? Or have the institutions and markets to help them cope with the risks been slower to develop? Collier and Gunning (1999) argue the first, and cite a substantial literature on African geography and development to back it up. This literature notwithstanding, there is room for doubt. For risk to be a convincing explanation for African underdevelopment one must show that the risk present in the African environment is greater or harder to cope with than that faced by farmers in other regions, such as farmers in South Asia or the European settlers of Africa and the Americas two hundred years ago. The pitfall with this reasoning is that the very success in coping with risk may hide its initial importance. For example, take two types of risk mentioned in Collier and Gunning, that of low and irregular rainfall and morbidity. Risk of the former kind can and has been mitigated by investments in irrigation, as note Ranade and Siddiqui (2000) for South Asia and Salehi-Isfahani (2000) for MENA, and the risks of disease in newly-settled regions by investment in health. Thus both types of risk can be regarded as in part endogenous, in the sense that they reflect household decisions not to invest. The question to ask, then, is why in some regions returns to risk management are lower than in others, or why markets and institutions to help alleviate the risks did not develop in Africa? In this sense, factors that inhibit investment in risk management are the real culprits in inhibiting growth rather than the risk itself. One well-known line of reasoning, due to Boserup (1965), argues that reducing such risks, for example with irrigation, is only economical when population density reaches a certain level, a condition which was not fulfilled for a long time in many parts of Africa.

Papers on East and South Asia do not identify any specific regional characteristics that explain household behaviour in their regions. In East Asia, Kuncoro (2000) sees the effective role of households in physical and human capital accumulation as the product of several factors: a good policy environment that emphasized the supply of primary education, the development of labour intensive industries that raised the return to such education, and a relatively equal income distribution. For South Asia, where the focus is on rural households, the authors mention risk and inequality as factors that inhibit household accumulation of savings and human capital.

Firms

Our knowledge of the behaviour of firms in developing countries is still far behind our understanding of firms in OECD economies, and there are at least three important reasons why this is the case. First, given that human capital both in the private and in the public sector is still very low, there is no wonder that the quality of official statistical data is far from satisfactory. Second, most of the statistical data cover only large firms, while the majority of employment is by small businesses and farms. Third, the official statistics cover virtually none of the informal sector which constitutes a much larger share of GDP than in OECD economies.[5]

Therefore it is no wonder that our knowledge of firms' behaviour is rather patchy. All six regional papers on microeconomics recognize the importance of modern firms for growth, but only three papers (Collier and Gunning, 2000, on Sub-Saharan Africa (SSA); Guriev and Ickes, 2000, on CEE and FSU; and Abdel-Fadil, 2000, on MENA) discuss incentives at the firm level. One paper (Behrman *et al.*, 2000, on LAC) does not discuss firms at all, two papers (Kuncoro, 2000, on East Asia, and Ranade and Siddiqui, 2000, on South Asia) discuss production mainly at the sectoral level.

The major theme that is discussed in all the papers, but especially in Collier and Gunning (1999) and Abdel-Fadil (2000), is the hostile environment faced by small businesses. It turns out, however, that although the set of challenges and constraints is common (predatory regulation, lack of financial depth, risk and volatility, poor infrastructure), regional authors identify different *binding* constraints: what is the key barrier to growth in one region may be rather unimportant in others. Both Abdel-Fadil (2000) and Collier and Gunning (2000) suggest that in the MENA and SSA regions the main constraint for growth of a firm is risk and volatility due to weather and instability of world prices for raw materials. This problem is of course aggravated by poor and monopolized infrastructure, predatory regulation, poor contract enforcement, lack of agglomeration and financial underdevelopment, but both papers emphasize risk as being the main problem.

In the papers on East Asia and South Asia, the emphasis shifts to the large firms. Ranade and Siddiqui (2000) argue that the contribution of small firms to growth in South Asia is minor and concentrate on large industrial enterprises. Most South Asian countries have pursued central-planning and protectionist policies for almost all the period under study. Since liberalization, opening up and deregulation have started only recently it is too early to analyse their impact. This is why the authors mainly discuss the reform packages rather than their effect on productivity and growth.[6] However, they do provide limited evidence that the reform has increased efficiency but also resulted in job losses.

Kuncoro (2000) discusses the factors that have contributed to the successful economic development in East Asian economies. He argues that the main factors behind the East Asian miracle are rapid accumulation of human capital, high saving rates, competition and openness. The author then looks at the role of financial markets. Most East Asian countries have pursued financial repression policies until very recently, so it is interesting to compare the impact of financial repression and subsequent financial liberalization on efficiency. The paper argues that financial repression has resulted in misallocation of investment and even overinvestment in large firms.[7] Loans were directed towards large firms while small businesses were liquidity constrained. Financial liberalization has helped to reallocate domestic credit to small firms but the small firms still borrow at significantly higher rates. There is insufficient microeconomic data to carry out firm-level analysis, but the evidence from industry-level analysis confirms that openness, FDI and access to external finance result in higher factor productivity. Guriev and Ickes (2000) study both small and large firms in the CEE-FSU region. The paper identifies two growth scenarios – 'typical CEE' and 'typical FSU' ones. In the typical CEE scenario, small businesses grow to their optimal scale while in the FSU case they stay small (and to a large extent informal) because of the predatory regulation by government. Large firms that restructure rather successfully in the CEE countries fail to do so in the FSU. The authors explain the growth in CEE by competition and openness (determined both by policies and Soviet-time legacies) and elimination of direct and implicit subsidies. The paper also emphasizes the role of EU accession for the CEE countries that serves as an anchor to coordinate expectations (which is essential for getting out of the lack-of-restructuring trap). It is interesting that some countries (for example Romania) fall into the CEE category in terms of small business development, while following an FSU scenario in terms of large-firm restructuring.

3 How households contribute to growth

Recent theories of economic growth recognize a greater role for households than before. The shift in emphasis in growth theory from physical to human capital, beginning with Lucas (1988), places the household at the centre of the accumulation process: parents take the key decisions regarding fertility and investment in education that affect human-capital accumulation and thereby growth. In older vintage growth models, households were also present but played a less central role in the dynamics, as savers and suppliers of labour (population growth). In this section we consider, in turn, household choices to save, supply labour, procreate and invest in human capital. For each choice we ask: does the decision have a large impact on growth? In what regions has this impact been observed? And, finally, where the impact has been smaller than expected, are there identifiable constraints that can explain the low impact?

Savings

For the answer to the first question, the importance of household savings for growth, we first turn to theory. We consider both aggregate growth models that define the role of savings in growth and micro models that account for individual behaviour. Neoclassical theory, for example Solow (1956), emphasizes the role of private savings with no clear distinction between household and corporate savings. While in the steady state, savings determine the level of per capita income but not the rate of growth, during transition higher savings lead to higher growth rates. The classical development literature, as in Lewis (1954), equates savings with retained earnings of firms, thus minimizing the role of households in capital accumulation. Furthermore, the classical approach reverses the causation implicit in the neoclassical models of growth, taking the saving rate as endogenous. According to Lewis, growth takes place as a result of structural transformation in which resources shift from the low-saving sectors into high-saving sectors, causing the overall savings rate to increase. In models designed to explain individual behaviour we can find causation running in both directions. The Keynesian savings function assumes that incomes drive savings, but the reverse is generally true of the intertemporal models of saving behaviour. For example, in the life-cycle model of saving causation runs from growth to savings; in times of rising incomes households engage in larger intertemporal transfers of resources, which results in more savings (Modigliani, 1970). Masson, Bayoumi and Samiei (1998) report a positive effect of growth on private savings.

While a positive association appears to exist, empirically it is not possible to support or reject either view of the causation (Gersovitz, 1988). Indirect evidence of the impact of savings on growth has come from the examination of the impact of changing demographics on savings. The rising proportion of savers to the dependent population that followed the fertility transitions in East Asia is shown to have stimulated growth by increasing national savings (Bloom and Williamson, 1998; Higgins, 1998). National savings are composed of public, private corporate, and household savings, which makes it difficult to gauge the contribution of households.

To determine the significance of household savings for growth we also need to know how important household savings are as a proportion of private and national savings. The literature reports surprisingly little quantitative information on household savings in developing countries. Micro data on household income and expenditures from which we can expect to obtain household savings are notoriously lacking or inaccurate in developing countries. For the poorest regions, Sub-Saharan Africa and South Asia, low family incomes imply low savings, so there we would not expect household savings to initiate economic growth. But even in those cases where high savings and rapid growth have gone hand in hand, such as East Asia, it is difficult to attribute a significant role to household – as distinct from corporate – savings. Kuncoro's (2000) paper on East Asia acknowledges the importance of private savings in the East Asian growth success, but notes that within the private sector the dynamic role was played by corporate rather than household savings, even though quantitatively the two had roughly equal shares. In Japan and Taiwan, household and corporate sectors have equal shares in total private savings, while in Thailand, one of the few developing countries for which the break-down between personal and corporate savings is available, household savings are only one-fourth of total private savings. The experience of the transition economies and MENA also suggest a limited role for household savings, at least in the initial phases of growth. In both cases the overall supply of savings seems not to have been a major con-straint on growth. In CEE-FSU, Guriev and Ickes (2000) argue that, given the large amount of capital that has fled certain countries of the region, the supply of savings has not been a constraint on growth. In some oil-rich MENA countries the large supply of public savings has discouraged private savings (Salehi-Isfahani, 2000).

Although theory is not strong on a role for household savings, there is general agreement that improved financial institutions can increase the impact of household savings on growth (McKinnon, 1973; Shaw, 1973). Where financial markets are underdeveloped, household savings (whatever its share) does not always find its way into productive investments. This is particularly important where long-term smoothing – life-cycle purposes or bequest – is the reason why households save. Good financial institutions can help increase the productivity of these savings by shifting them from, say, real estate to manufacturing. Even in the case of short-term smoothing, financial deepening can help turn rural savings into long-term investments. In the South Asia paper, Ranade and Siddiqui (2000) argue that households in rural South Asia save primarily for short-term consumption smoothing. In many African countries, lack of credit markets prevents poorer rural house-holds from smoothing their consumption even on a short-term basis. Unlike in South Asia where private money-lenders operate, in Sub-Saharan Africa even informal credit markets are hampered by lack of private property in land which can serve as collateral (Collier and

Gunning, 1999). Perhaps this is one reason why other credit institutions, such as rotating credit associations, are more prevalent in Africa than elsewhere.

Savings are also sensitive to instability in the macroeconomic environment. As the chapters in this volume by Soludo and Kim on sources of growth (Chapter 2) and Jurajda and Mitchell on markets and growth (Chapter 4) note, there is consensus that macroeconomic stability is good for savings, but the consensus is much weaker on the role of financial liberalization. Stability increases confidence in the financial system and encourages households to place their savings in instruments that channel resources to firms. But higher real interest rates that better reflect the scarcity of funds, a main objective of financial liberalization, may not increase savings. There is evidence that a rise in real interest rates increases capital formation (Fry, 1979), but it is not clear that it actually promotes household savings. Kuncoro (2000) credits macroeconomic stability for the savings boom in the East Asian economies, even though it was in part achieved with financial repression that reduced both inflation and lending rates at banks. Household savings appear to have benefited from the stability offered by low-inflation without suffering much from the low interest rates. Economic theory is not clear on the role of interest rates on personal savings; in the life-cycle model, for example, the impact of low or negative interest rates on personal savings may go either way.

Labour supply

The supply of labour, the most important factor of production, in the short and the long run results from household choices between work and leisure, work at home or in the market, and fertility. The significance of labour-force increase for economic growth is best documented by the growth experience of the fast growing East Asian countries. Young (1995) attributes much of the economic growth in East Asia to factor accumulation in general, and growth of the labour force in particular. In South Korea, for example, simple growth accounting shows that more than half of the growth rate – nearly 4 per cent – was due to the growth of the labour force alone, compared to only 0.7 per cent for human capital (Topel, 1999). Bloom and Williamson (1998) emphasize the role of fertility decline in the rapid increase in the growth of labour force relative to population, a phenomenon which in their words is a 'demographic gift' to these countries.

Participation of women in market work is perhaps the most important source of labour-force growth in the early phase of industrialization, a process which is most clearly seen in the experience of the former Soviet Union and East Asian countries. Across the developing world the labour supply of men is much more uniform than that of women (Figure 3.1), suggesting that the variation in growth rates is more likely to be related to the variation in the labour supply of women than men. Both theory and micro evidence suggest that the participation of women in market work, mainly in the urban areas, has an important indirect effect on growth through a decline in fertility and an increase in investment in child education. Women's ability to earn income from market work raises the opportunity cost of their time at home which can lead to lower fertility and increased investment in human capital. East Asia, where fertility decline and increased participation of women have gone hand in hand, provides the strongest evidence of a link between labour force allocation decisions and growth. East Asia now has the highest rates of participation for women, followed by transition economies of FSU-CEE (Figure 3.1). In Sub-Saharan Africa women also report a high incidence of market work but it is mostly in household production in rural areas, which is not as significant for growth as wage work because it does not raise the cost of children and therefore does not affect the fertility choice.

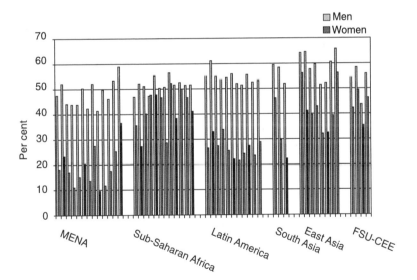

Figure 3.1 Activity rates of men and women aged 15–65 in developing regions
Source: *World Development Indicators*, World Bank (2001).

At the other extreme is the MENA region, where female labour-force participation is the lowest in the world, especially in view of the relatively high level of female education in several countries of the region. For example, in Iran less than 15 per cent of women report market work compared to about 60 per cent in Malaysia with similar levels of female education and fertility. Salehi-Isfahani (2000) identifies restrictive social norms in MENA, mainly disapproval on the part of husbands and parents, which limit women's access to market work as a constraint on household choices that has inhibited the contribution of households to economic growth. Because women's labour-force participation is closely linked with fertility and child investment decisions, the low level of female participation in MENA may have negatively affected growth through delayed fertility decline and slower accumulation of human capital. Karshenas (2001) has argued that these restrictions may have inhibited the ability of MENA countries to successfully implement structural-adjustment reforms necessary for economic growth. Social norms against market work for women prevent male wages from responding to competitive wage pressures because the norms reduce the possibility of supplementing the declining male wages with female labour income.

Household choices of jobs and sectors of production also influence overall productivity and hence growth. The most well-known, if not well-documented, labour reallocation which enhances growth is that from low to high-productivity sectors, sometimes equated with rural–urban migration. The classical models of growth, from Ricardo to Lewis, consider the gains from reallocation of labour from rural and informal production to urban manufacturing as an important source of growth during the initial phase of development (R. E. B. Lucas, 1997). Migration across borders in response to better earning opportunities can also help the exporting country, but if and only if remittances more than compensate for the loss of productivity of the migrants (Razin and Sadka, 1997).

This grand reallocation of labour from low to high productivity sectors *à la* Lewis has received more attention in the development literature, but job allocation at a smaller scale, within industries or even firms, also affects labour productivity and growth (Topel, 1999). Labour supply decisions that affect the level of worker effort and the quality of the match between workers and jobs matter for growth. As discussed in Jurajda and Mitchell in Chapter 4 of this volume, a well-functioning labour market provides the incentives for individuals to apply effort, to search for jobs that match their skills, and accumulate the type of human capital that is most productive. Where labour markets have been inflexible, such as in MENA and CEE-FSU before transition, the low quality of job matches have lowered labour productivity and reduced incentives for learning specific skills (Salehi-Isfahani, 2000).

Labour-market rigidities associated with implicit and explicit promises of tenure in employment discourage labour turnover and thereby reduce worker incentives to supply effort and to acquire human capital, as well as reduce the likelihood of optimal job matches. Although we know that labour-market institutions differ across countries, we know little about how different institutions affect economic growth. In general the study of the role of labour markets and growth has not gone beyond the recognition that human capital matters for growth (Topel, 1999). Country studies commissioned under the GRP should be able to throw light on this important link.

Fertility and human capital

The increasing importance of human capital in growth theory has focused attention on the central role of fertility and child investment decisions of household in economic development (Lucas, 1998). The new human-capital-based models of growth assume that, first, household choices regarding the level of investment in their children determine the rate of accumulation of human capital in the economy, and, second, fertility and child investment decisions are made jointly. These assumptions are well-grounded in empirical research. Econometric studies based on micro data from many countries, even where public provision of education is strong, report that family characteristics play a large role in the determination of child education (Strauss and Thomas, 1995; Behrman, 1997). Studies on early childhood education support the notion that not only parental decisions influence the human capital of their children, but much of that human capital is actually produced at home (World Bank, 1996; Shonkoff and Phillips, 2000). Other studies provide evidence in favour of the quality–quantity tradeoff (for example Hanushek, 1992; Rosenzweig, 1995).

The development economics literature has always considered fertility decline as a precondition for growth. The new literature sees fertility decline as part of a larger change in household behaviour, from high fertility and low investment in child education to low fertility and high investment, that promotes economic growth. Becker, Murphy and Tamura (1990) (hereafter BMT), was one of the first papers to integrate the micro decisions regarding quality and quantity of children with macro outcomes and show the possibility of multiple equilibria.

According to their model, households with the same preferences and facing the same technology can, in equilibrium, behave in very different ways: In the 'low-level equilibrium' characterized by high fertility and low human capital, household behaviour reproduces the low human-capital equilibrium because households have no incentives to change their behaviour. Because the cost of children and returns to education are low at low levels of human capital, households opt for high fertility and low investment in children. Conversely, in the 'high-level' equilibrium, characterized by low fertility and high levels of human capital, returns to human capital are high, inducing parents to choose low fertility and high investment in children. There are two important implications of this model. First, that growth and development are not linear processes; if a country is stuck in the lower equilibrium there will be no steady growth, but once a certain threshold is broken, steady growth is difficult to stop. The model therefore offers a precise definition for the Rostow notion of 'take-off'. Secondly, that household decisions are the key determinants of whether a country is or is not taking off. While the model does an excellent job of showing how the micro behaviour and macro outcomes are connected, it does not say much about how a country moves from one equilibrium to another.[8]

Is there empirical support for this view? Using cross-section data, Ahituv (2001) has found that models with endogenous fertility perform better than the traditional growth models. We can illustrate the relevance of the BMT here with a few simply graphs: the data plotted in Figures 3.2–3.6 depict the total fertility rate (TFR) against the average schooling of the adult population, the two key household-choice variables.[9] Taking the multiple equilibria story of BMT seriously, we pick, for demonstration purposes, the critical values of TFR and average schooling that represent the threshold levels of these variables that separate the low- from high-level equilibria. The straight lines marking the TFR of 3 and average schooling of 5 years (completed primary education) delineate four quadrants. The upper-left and lower-right quadrants correspond to the low- and high-level equilibria, and the other two represent unstable equilibria in which either fertility or education are inconsistent with a long-run stable choice. A regression line shown in all graphs represents the mean levels of TFR for given values of schooling (computed from the entire sample) and helps us compare the outcome for a particular country with the 'average choice'. We notice, as expected, that the poorer countries fall mainly in the upper-left quadrant (low-level equilibrium), and the richer and

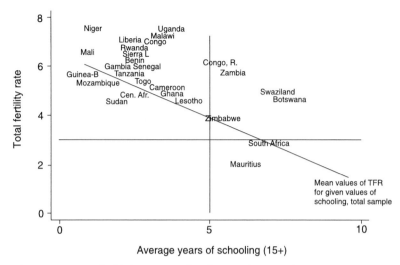

Figure 3.2 Household choices in Sub-Saharan Africa, 1998.
Source: World Bank, *World Development Indicators*, 2001.

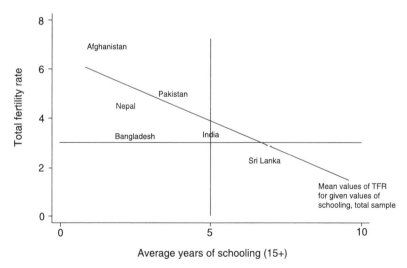

Figure 3.3 Household choices in South Asia, 1998.
Source: World Bank, *World Development Indicators*, 2001.

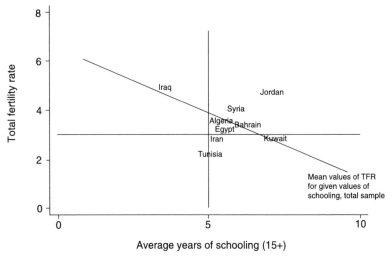

Figure 3.4   Household choices in Middle East and North Africa, 1998

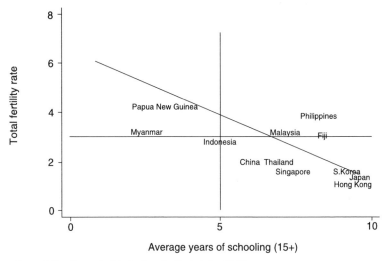

Figure 3.5   Household choices in East Asia, 1998
Source: World Bank, *World Development Indicators*, 2001.

faster growing countries in the lower-right quadrant (high-level equilibrium). The average growth rate for countries in the upper-left quadrant is much lower than those in the lower-right quadrant.

Two observations based on these data are consistent with the BMT model: first, there is a fair degree of coherence of the regional group-

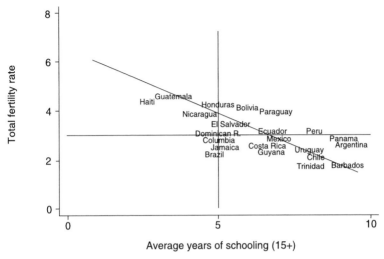

Figure 3.6 Household choices in Latin America and the Caribbean, 1998
Source: World Bank, *World Development Indicators*, 2001.

ings and, second, a strong association exists between growth performance and the quadrant in which the country appears. The behaviour of Sub-Saharan Africa and East Asia represent the two polar cases.
Almost all African and South Asian countries fall in the upper-left
quadrant (the low-level equilibrium), with high fertility and low education. In contrast, most East Asian countries are located in the lower-
right quadrant, with low fertility and high education, implying a sense
of take-off into long-run growth. Latin American countries also
predominate in the same quadrant, implying their relative proximity
to the high-level equilibrium. MENA countries fall mostly in the upper-
right quadrant, where education is relatively high, but fertility is also
high. In keeping with the logic of the model and with historical experience, we can claim that countries in this quadrant are in an unstable
situation. They will either reduce their fertility and move down to the
high-level equilibrium, or will find it too hard to maintain their educational level and fall back to the low-level equilibrium.

In 1960 most of these countries were located in the upper-left quadrant, but 40 years later only the East Asian countries as a group can be
said to have cleared the thresholds for take-off. Countries of Sub-
Saharan Africa and South Asia are still in the same general location;
MENA countries still have some distance to go; and Latin American
countries are to be found on both sides of the threshold. The question is

what has prevented so many countries for so long from moving to the lower-right quadrant? There are several possible explanations, mostly based on an exogenous shift in technology of one sort or another that affects household decisions. The best-known technological argument, most popular in the demographic literature, considers the technology of fertility control as the exogenous factor that has limited household choices. With the availability of birth-control technology, households are in a position to choose the low-fertility high-education bundle if that is indeed the desirable option. This argument is less popular in the economics literature, where it is believed that while differential access to birth control cannot be ruled out as an explanation of high fertility in some countries, after decades of worldwide dissemination it is difficult to explain much of the international variation in fertility in this way (Schultz, 1994). A technological hypothesis of a different kind by Galor and Weil (1994) can also explain how fertility decline is initiated. Technological change increases the return to mental labour thereby raising the wages of women relative to men and thereby increasing the cost of children and lowering fertility. The model does not include human capital as an explicit variable.

Perhaps the most important argument has to do with exogenous increases in the returns to education, and two factors can be considered as causing an exogenous shift in returns to human capital. First, a decline in mortality, specifically youth mortality, increases the likelihood that infants will survive to become productive adults and therefore increases the returns to investing in them. Second, technological change can increase returns to skills (Schultz, 1975; Huffman, 2001) and initiate a decline in fertility. Arguments pertaining to low returns to education are reported in the regional studies but they do not all arise for the same reasons. For Africa, where fertility transition has been particularly slow, Collier and Gunning (1999) offer low returns to education as an explanation for high fertility. In rural areas, private returns are the constraint because social returns are considered to be high. Nor is the higher private rate of return in the urban labour markets sufficient to induce rural households to invest in child education because the probability of employment there is low.

Gender bias may also lower returns to education for the whole economy. In South Asia, where the gender gap in education is particularly wide, Ranade and Siddiqui (2000) note that poverty and lack of access to credit forces parents to limit investment in female children. Because of the central role played by female education in human-capital accumulation, this lowers education in the long run. Low female education lowers the cost of child quantity relative to quality, thereby favouring high fertility over education in family decision-making. At the same time, low female education raises the cost of child quality, because mothers provide important input into child education. A positive association between mother and child education (usually stronger than father–child education) has been widely observed in developed and developing countries (Strauss and Thomas, 1995). In MENA countries, social norms that restrict women's choice of market work similarly lower returns to female education (Salehi-Isfahani, 2000). This is a plausible explanation for why MENA countries, after Sub-Saharan Africa, have had the slowest fertility transition. For Latin America and the Caribbean, Behrman *et al.* (2000) discuss the quantity–quality choice by noting that macroeconomic instability and the low quality of public schooling have limited the accumulation of human capital.

As Pritchett notes in Chapter 6, the conclusion to this volume, empirical studies of growth find very low impact of education on growth. Most growth regressions show that the initial level of a country's human capital is important for growth, whereas increase in human capital is not (Topel, 1999). The low observed social returns are in sharp contrast with the high rates of private return estimated from micro data, which, presumably, guide private actions. One possibility for resolving this apparent puzzle is that institutional variation in the markets for labour and human capital, where private returns are determined, lead to variation in the social returns. In other words, high private returns can be consistent with low social returns if the labour market provides incentives for the accumulation of the wrong type of human capital. This is the argument advanced by Salehi-Isfahani (2000) in his thematic paper on MENA, where the anomaly between increasing education and stagnant growth is particularly glaring (Pissarides, 2000; Pritchett, 1999). A large public sector, with interventionist labour market policies which set employment rules for itself as well as for the private sector, has guided households to accumulate too much formal schooling that does not enhance individual productivity (Salehi-Isfahani, 2000). These policies reduce turnover, which causes the signal of productivity conveyed by an individual's level of formal schooling to dominate those for less observable types of human capital, such as creativity, teamwork, and attitudes towards work. In an inflexible labour market in which it is costly to lay off unproductive workers or reward productivity with higher wages independently of the level of schooling, individuals overinvest in formal schooling, causing social returns to schooling to decline. Thus the inflexible labour markets of the region promote investment in degrees and credentials first, in knowledge second, and in other types of human capital, such as creativity and teamwork, a distant third.

This argument may appear at odds with the experience of East Asia, where formal schooling has also become the focus of human-capital accumulation, but remains a favourite explanation for the East Asian miracle (Kuncoro, 2000). There are two significant differences between MENA and East Asia in the type and quality of formal accumulated. In term of years of schooling, in 1960 East Asia was not that far ahead of the average developing country and was actually behind Latin America. What appears to have been the East Asian advantage is the high enrolment rate at the primary level. MENA countries have surpassed East Asia in tertiary enrolments throughout the period 1960–90, but have been far behind in primary enrolment. Recent evidence shows that quality of schooling, in addition to its quantity, can explain variations in growth (Hanushek and Kimko, 2000). Expenditure data on education, particularly at the primary level, shows a wider difference between East Asia and other developing countries.

A related question is whether the educational system can also be considered a constraint, as distinct from the labour market, that shapes household choices in human-capital accumulation. Do labour-market signals shape the educational system or can schools produce their own type of human capital independent of what the market wants? To what extent are the more flexible labour markets in East Asia responsible for the better quality of education, especially the emphasis at the primary level?

Flexible labour markets send clearer signals about the value of various types of human capital – writing versus mathematics – and the premium for secondary and tertiary education over primary education. Presumably, the human capital produced at home reflects parental preferences, which are in turn influenced by what is rewarded in the labour market. Do schools respond to market signals in the same way? It is reasonable to assume that private schools behave in a more responsive way and provide the type of human capital preferred by parents. But this assumption may be too strong for public schools. In democratic countries in which elected local authorities run public schools, labour-market signals will influence curriculum choice through parental oversight. But this is not the case in many developing countries. Government interventions in the labour market may go hand in hand with control of educational priorities. In this case, as in MENA, the incentives produced in the labour market are echoed through the educational system, creating a formidable barrier to more efficient household decision-making (Salehi-Isfahani, 2000). Research at the country level may produce insights into these issues.

4   Firms

In this section we discuss the main themes on the contribution of firms to growth as analyzed in the regional papers. We start with a short survey of the ideas of each paper, then we go through all factors that promote or constrain growth in small and large firms, discussing whether these factors are relevant in different regions and why. Finally we summarize the findings from the regional papers in the form of 'growth scenarios' trying to classify the growth experience of regions and sub-regions into three broad categories.

Small-business development

Here we discuss incentives and constraints relevant for the establishment and growth of the small business, and the choice of formal and informal sectors of the economy. Even given the data limitations, it is common knowledge that in many non-OECD countries it is hard to establish a small business and, once established, small firms rarely manage to reach the minimum efficiency scale (De Soto, 1989, 2000; Tybout, 2000). On the other hand, the economic growth in developing countries presumes that small firms take off and become modern industrial corporations (in the success story of East Asia, almost all of the 30 leading corporations have grown out of small family businesses). This is why in this section we will try to understand which factors constrain the growth of small business in non-OECD regions.

The most widely discussed constraint for small-business establishment and growth is the lack of access to credit. Indeed, even if credit markets exist in a developing economy (which is rather rare), they usually cater to large firms; there are increasing returns to scale in transaction costs of processing a loan, and the risk of default is higher for smaller firms. However, the recent empirical evidence seems to suggest that the finance constraint is usually *not* binding (see Abdel-Fadil, 2000; Johnson *et al.*, 2002; EBRD, 1999). Among the regional papers, only Kuncoro (2000) points to financial constraints as a major problem for small-business development, whilst Collier and Gunning (1999), Abdel-Fadil (2000), Guriev and Ickes (2000) suggest that while finance is a problem, it is not the most important barrier for the growth of small businesses.

Apparently, loans are obtained through the informal credit markets and the institutions of micro credit (see Morduch, 1998; Besley, Coate and Loury, 1993, Woolcock, 1996). This is rather intuitive. First, the economies of scale in lending are often correlated with the increasing returns in savings. The banks do not offer high rates on small deposits, therefore there is a substantial supply of savings (that banks are not interested in) which are used to finance the establishment of small businesses either through the informal credit market or intra-family transfer. The family networks in the developing countries are relatively extensive and often include family members working abroad and sending their wages back as remittances.[10] The firms are so small that financing through family networks or informal credit markets may be sufficient. Moreover, the other barriers to growth result in limited competition and large unattended market niches so that the firms that do survive can finance their needs by reinvesting current profits.

A more important problem is the limited access to insurance. In non-OECD countries, entrepreneurs face risks which are related to weather, world prices for raw materials, macroeconomic instability and so forth.[11] Those risks cannot be insured by the informal insurance markets since the latter are usually locally-based and therefore cannot diversify against region-wide risks. The problem is aggravated by the lack of agglomeration and poor transportation infrastructure that keeps small businesses very specialized and therefore highly vulnerable to risk.

The businesses that cater to metropolitan areas or foreign markets are more protected from volatility since customers' income is sufficiently diversified. This suggests the importance of economic geography: large cities and densely populated areas are privileged, while landlocked and isolated areas are disadvantaged (see Sachs *et al.*, 1999, for cross-country evidence, and the regional papers by Abdel-Fadil, 2000; Collier and Gunning, 1999; Guriev and Ickes, 2000). The situation can and should be improved by investing in infrastructure. On the other hand, investment is necessary but not sufficient: in many countries physical infrastructure is available but is monopolized and run inefficiently.

At the same time, these same regional papers on MENA, SSA and CEE-FSU document the importance of predatory regulation as a barrier to entry and growth.[12] Why is this the case? Governments have incentives for predation both at the high level (policy choice) and the low level (policy implementation). Given that the small businesses are dispersed and politically weak, public policy is more supportive of large firms that get more subsidies and protection from foreign competition.[13] At the level of policy implementation, the corrupt bureaucrats (and even judges) use their discretion to extend red tape and introduce new regulations in order to extort bribes that would complement their meagre wages. It is very important to distinguish these two phenomena: in many countries, the central government adopts policies conducive to business growth, but in virtually all non-OECD countries (except East Asia, see Kuncoro, 2000) low-level corruption undermines implementation of these policies.[14]

Corruption and the overregulation that it breeds is not only burdensome for small businesses, it also causes businesses to slide into the informal sector. Table 3.2 shows that informal employment is a rule rather than an exception in developing economies. Entrepreneurs cannot comply with all the regulations and simply bribe the officials that allow them to operate in the shadow economy.

The large spread of the informal economy has important implications for growth. First, it strips the government of tax revenues so that the government has to increase the tax burden on those who remain in the formal sector, or decrease spending on law and order. In both cases the incentives to stay in the shadow sector increase further, making the informal economy self-perpetuating. Second, small businesses have an additional disincentive to grow; larger firms are more visible, and growth results in entry to the official economy, which is costly. Table 3.2 shows the informal labour force as a percentage of total employment for various countries.

Table 3.2 Informal labour force in urban areas

Country	*Year*	*Percentage of total employment*
Bolivia	1996	57
Chile	1997	30
Colombia	1996	53
Côte d'Ivoire	1996	53
Ecuador	1997	40
Ethiopia	1996	33
Gambia	1993	72
Madagascar	1994	43
Mexico	1996	35
Peru	1996	51
Philippines	1995	17
South Africa	1995	17
Tanzania	1995	67
Uganda	1993	84

Source: ILO (1999).

In addition to predatory regulation, governments contribute to the hostility of the small-business environment by the failure to protect property rights and enforce contract law. The private sector responds to this government failure by creating its own enforcement institutions, often criminalized and violent (mafia-like networks), but still more effective than corrupt and slow courts. Once small businesses resort to using these informal institutions, they fall into the vicious circle of the informal economy. Entrepreneurs become vulnerable to rackets and bribe-extortion by organized crime and corrupt bureaucrats.

To illustrate how important is government predation for the growth of small businesses, let us consider the example from the CEE-FSU regional paper. Some Central European governments have managed to provide small businesses with a friendly environment, while FSU countries are similar to the typical non-OECD case (see Table 3.3). This helped small business growth to take off in CEE so that the number of small businesses per capita is *ten* (!) times higher in Poland (and other CEE countries) than in Russia (Guriev and Ickes, 2000). Not surprisingly, the growth performance of Poland is much better than that of Russia.[15]

Predatory regulation creates high entry barriers that result in limited competition. It is worth noting, though, that the surviving businesses do not enjoy their monopoly power since rents are taxed away in bribes or through payments to private rackets. Rent-seeking also distorts the incentives for adoption of new technologies. If there is little or no rent-seeking (as in the case of Poland) entry is high, so the main problem of small business is competition – as indeed shown by surveys, see Frye (1999). Hence, firms have incentives to adopt technologies that reduce

Table 3.3   Government vs private contract enforcement for small businesses

Country	Romania (4 cities)	Poland (Warsaw)	Russia (Moscow)
Used courts in last two years	0.20	0.14	0.19
Needed to use courts but did not	0.15	0.10	0.45
Can use courts against government	0.51	0.41	0.50
Can use courts against business partner	0.67	0.45	0.65
Contacted by racket in the last 6 months	0.00	0.08	0.39
Does one need a 'roof' ('umbrella') to operate?	0.01	0.06	0.76

Note: 'Roof' and 'umbrella' are euphemisms for mafia protection in Russia and Poland respectively.
Source: Pop-Eleches (1998), Frye and Shleifer (1997).

marginal costs. In the case of uncontrolled rent-seeking, the additional revenue created by such technologies is taken away. The rent-seekers cannot commit to allow firms to retain substantial benefits from innovation; hence firms have low incentives to invest.

Large industrial firms

Industrial firms play a major role in economic development. Contrary to widespread opinion inherited from the early views of developing countries, the share of industry in GDP in non-OECD countries is comparable to that in OECD economies[16] (see Figure 3.7).

The existing large manufacturing firms in most developing countries were created in non-market conditions or under heavy protection from domestic and/or foreign competition;[17] therefore improvements in economic performance depend on enterprise restructuring. Our purpose in this section is to understand what determines the incentives to restructure, what the relevant constraints are, and what explains the characteristic differences in restructuring experiences around the world.[18]

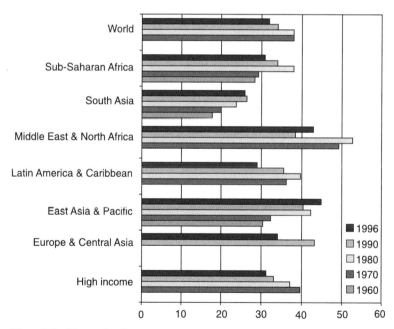

Figure 3.7   Share of industry in GDP, value added (percentages)
Source: *World Development Indicators*, World Bank.

The pressure on managers to undertake restructuring may come from a few sources. The first and the most important one is ownership: privatization and enforcement of property rights of outside owners. The second is competition (we will distinguish between domestic and foreign competition). The third is hard budget constraints and elimination of subsidies. In theory it is clear that each of these factors reduces the room for 'managerial slack' and provides incentives for restructuring. The question is which of these factors has a larger effect on managerial incentives, and whether these factors are substitutes or complements in affecting the performance of individual firms.

We will also discuss how the factors that influence *incentives* to restructure interact with imperfections of financial markets that constrain *ability* to restructure. As Jurajda and Mitchell (2000) argue, the development of financial markets is very low in most non-OECD countries; only East Asian (see Kuncoro, 2000) and Central and East European firms (Guriev and Ickes, 2000) have access to finance at interest rates comparable to their OECD counterparts.

Although there exists a growing literature on productivity in manufacturing firms in developing countries, solid microeconomic evidence is still limited (Tybout, 2000). There is an array of research on transition economies (see Frydman *et al.*, 1999; Djankov and Murrell, 2002) and selected countries in Latin America (Tybout, 2000), East Asia (Kuncoro, 2000), Africa (Clerides *et al.*, 1998; Tybout, 2000) and India (Banerjee and Duflo, 2000). Even these studies often suffer from poor quality of the data. The most obvious problem is selection bias: it is not clear whether private firms are doing better because private ownership is superior, or because better firms were privatized in the first place. Analysis of the effect of competition may be subject to the endogeneity problem – the market structure is *not* independent of efficiency (Nickell, 1996).[19] Certainly, panel-data analysis would help, but large balanced panels are usually not available, so most research resorts to cross-sectional analysis.[20]

Theoretically, efficiency-enhancing restructuring would be undertaken once a firm is privatized. The evidence, however, implies that privatization does not always bring restructuring and productivity gains (Guriev and Ickes, 2000) and there are several reasons for this. First, in many countries corporate governance is still underdeveloped so that outside owners have little control over management (see the paper by Jurajda and Mitchell in Chapter 4 of this volume). Moreover, development of corporate governance institutions may be very difficult politically. Some authors insist that fully-fledged investor protection is not feasible at this stage in non-OECD countries, so one should concentrate on protection of majority shareholders and large creditors (Berglof and von Thadden, 1999).

Another issue is elimination of subsidies and soft-budget constraints. As Shleifer and Vishny (1994) show, a manager-owner of a private firm may prefer not to restructure to preserve excess employment, and subsidies are the main tool to make side payments from politicians to reward a manager's compliance with the political agenda. The modern theory of soft-budget constraints (Berglof and Roland, 1998) suggests that the soft-budget constraints emerge due to the lack of commitment on the creditors' side, which is of course very common in developing economies. The evidence from transition (Djankov-Murrell, 2002) and developing (Kuncoro, 2000) countries suggest that subsidies (and cheap credit) do distort incentives to restructure, and may even result in a vicious circle of survival-without-restructuring; managers keep delaying restructuring in hopes of a bailout from the government. Therefore, the elimination of soft-budget constraints is complementary to privatization to promote growth-oriented restructuring.[21]

The existing literature suggests that the strongest incentives for restructuring are provided by competition. To various extents, the effect is observed in all countries (Brown and Earle, 2000; Guriev and Ickes, 2000; Ranade and Siddiqui, 2000; Kuncoro, 2000; Djankov and Murrell, 2002; Tybout, 2000). The literature addresses a number of issues. First, what kind of competition has the strongest effect: domestic versus foreign, product market competition versus competition in the factor markets and so on. The other question is whether the effect is linear. The third question is whether the effect of competition is stronger in more mature institutional environments and in privatized industries.

There are still no clear and unambiguous answers to these questions. Apparently, in CEE and Latin American countries, the major effect comes from competition from imports. In East Asian economies exporting firms that are subject to competition in the global economy also benefit from foreign competition. In the CIS countries, domestic demonopolization plays the key role while the role of import penetration is less clear. Djankov and Murrell (2002) suggest that the effect of import competition in the FSU is often insignificant, but this may be driven by the quality of data. In the only panel-data analysis available (Brown and Earle, 2000), the effect is positive and significant.

There are very few studies that look into the effect of the factor market structure. This is not because it is unimportant (see the chapter by Jurajda and Mitchell in this volume), but rather because measuring the labour and capital-market structure is hard. Kuncoro (2000) argues that capital-market liberalization has significantly improved incentives and relaxed financial constraints for East Asian firms, but the evidence is rather qualitative (before and after reform). One notable exception is Brown and Earle (2000) who look at the effect of local labour-market competition in Russia. Given the low geographical mobility of Russian workers and lack of unionization, local labour-market concentration gives employers a monopsony power (Friebel and Guriev, 2000). Brown and Earle (2000) show that local labour-market concentration negatively affects firm-level productivity.

The other question is whether there can or cannot be 'too much' competition. Theoretically, the higher competition is, the better. However, once financial-market imperfections are taken into account, it turns out that the effect is ambiguous: while incentives to restructure do indeed increase with competition, the sources of finance dry up. If the credit market is imperfect, then firms have to finance restructuring out of their profits. Thus, if competition is too harsh, firms just cannot afford productivity-enhancing restructuring. This is precisely the finding of EBRD (1999), which shows that while monopolies restructure less than firms having one to three competitors, any further increase of competition (more than three competitors) makes the firms less likely to undertake restructuring. This suggests that directed credit policies in East Asia (Kuncoro, 2000), although distortionary, may have mitigated this problem, giving East Asian firms a chance to finance their growth under harsh competition in the global economy.

The effect of openness on restructuring and growth is not limited to increases in competition, it may also facilitate diffusion of modern technologies. There are a number of papers (Clerides *et al.*, 1998; Yudaeva *et al.* 2001) that show that outward orientation does help to move towards better practice in developing and transition countries. At the macro level, the positive effect of openness on growth is not as clear; cross-country analysis has not yet established either a positive or negative effect of openness on growth (Rodríguez and Rodrik, 2000). As Rodríguez and Rodrik (2000) argue, opening up immature economies can result in specialization in traditional production which may slow down rather than accelerate learning by doing. On the other hand, the firm-level evidence in many countries does suggest that openness provides incentives to restructure (Kuncoro, 2000; Guriev and Ickes, 2000; Ranade and Siddiqui, 2000).

It is interesting that productivity may go up not only after an actual increase in foreign competition, but also after a credible promise of opening up. In many CEE countries, the announcement of EU accession has made a substantial difference, providing an important benchmark: the only way to survive in five years is to start restructuring now.

Growth scenarios

Summing up the analysis of findings of the regional papers along the dimensions above, one can come up with three broad 'growth scenarios':

1 *Successful development* (East Asia, CEE, LAC in recent years). Openness and foreign competition provide large firms with incentives to restructure and invest (including through foreign direct investments). Government does not prey upon small businesses, so they grow until they face financial constraints.
2 *Muddling through* (FSU, South Asia, LAC before recent reforms). Government predation is the major constraint for small-business development. Financial markets are not developed but financing is not the binding constraint for small businesses. Lack of openness and competition results in limited incentives for large firms to restructure. Rather, they are involved in politics, lobbying for protectionism and subsidies.
3 *Lagging behind* (MENA, SSA). Poor infrastructure and lack of agglomeration make risk and volatility the binding constraint for business development. Government predation and financial imperfections are also present, but are relatively less important (especially financing) for small-business growth. Large firms are virtually absent, and there is almost no chance for a small business to grow beyond the family size and to survive the founder.

5   Concluding remarks

This chapter has summarized the findings from the GRP regional papers on the microeconomic determinants of growth around the world. We have discussed the decisions by households to supply factors of production and by firms to put the factors to the best use. Although the microeconomics of growth varies greatly across regions and countries, it turns out to be possible to distinguish several growth scenarios and set an agenda for further research in the country studies.

No set of common factors explains the lack of effective contributions by households to growth, and there are two lessons that have emerged so far. First, although it is difficult to get an agreement on the role of household savings in growth, it is possible to say that a stable macro environment and effective financial intermediation enhance this role. Secondly, the role of households in human-capital accumulation is probably the most important role they play in modern economic growth. The household is the principal unit through which the transfer of human capital from one generation to the next takes place. Family decisions regarding family size probably have the greatest impact on the effectiveness of this intergenerational transfer. Returns to education not only influence fertility decisions, but also the decisions regarding how much human capital and of what type to accumulate.

The other microeconomic impediments to growth emerge at the firm level. Although small businesses around the globe face similar constraints, in different regions different constraints are binding. Lack of access to finance is an important barrier to growth only in the advanced regions, while in others it is government predation and volatility.

On the other hand, the determinants of restructuring and productivity growth in large firms are similar in all the regions. It turns out that the major forces that provide incentives to restructure are competition and openness. Competition contributes to restructuring and growth both directly and through reinforcing the effects of privatization and helping to eliminate soft budget constraints. Openness is not only a source of external competition, but also facilitates the foreign direct investment which helps to overcome financial underdevelopment.

The microeconomic determinants of growth identified by the regional studies have to be further explored by the country studies. While we have been able to define regional 'growth scenarios', at the country level the growth experience may not purely fall into one of the scenarios. However, our discussion of the regional paper findings may be used as a framework for the analysis at the country level.

Notes

1 The authors drew heavily upon the regional papers on microeconomics and growth by Abdel-Fadil (2000), Behrman, Duryea, and Székely (2000), Collier and Gunning (1999), Guriev and Ickes (2000), Kuncoro (2000), Ranade and Siddiqui (2000), and Salehi-Isfahani (2000).

2 Certainly, the distinction between 'small' and 'large' firms is vague. In some countries, a firm employing 50 people would qualify as 'small', while in others it would be necessarily a 'large' one (Abdel-Fadil, 2000; Guriev and Ickes, 2000).

3   In Section 4 we argue that the missing middle is consistent with the set of growth scenarios described in the regional papers.

4   The fact that small size of average business is negatively correlated with growth in developing countries has been established both through cross-country analysis (Liedholm and Mead, 1987; Banerji, 1978), and through analysis across time within countries (Little, Mazumdar and Page, 1987; Steel, 1993).

5   This issue is very important in some transition countries as well. On the other hand, the first and the second problems seem to be relatively less important.

6   There is no wonder that authors of both South Asia and CEE-FSU regional papers are reluctant to bore the audience with a detailed discussion of the central-planning policies that have finally been put to a well-deserved rest. Guriev and Ickes (2000) argue, however, that understanding the basics of the Soviet growth model is essential, since its legacies are important for both microeconomic incentives and growth performance in transition economies. See section 2 in Guriev and Ickes (2000) for a detailed discussion of the workings of a centrally-planned economy, which also applies to the South Asian scenario.

7   The paper also notes that a large part of savings in East Asia is corporate; this is consistent with the overinvestment story.

8   BMT see the move from one equilibrium to the other mostly as a matter of historical accident and good luck.

9   Strictly speaking, we should have average education of children. We are implicitly assuming, in the spirit of BMT, that countries are in a long-run equilibrium, in which case adult and child education would be correlated.

10 Remittances play a major role in many non-OECD countries, often being the single most important source of foreign currency. As shown in Abdel-Fadil (2000) and Guriev and Ickes (2000), in countries such as Egypt, Morocco, Syria, Albania and others, remittances account for tens of per cents of GDP and exports. In Egypt, the remittances actually exceed merchandise exports.

11 In many developing countries the exchange rate heavily depends on the current world prices for raw materials. As pointed out in the paper by Filer *et al.* (2000), natural-resource richness may therefore be a curse rather than a blessing. Given the non-diversified export structure, the whole economy is subject to an aggregate risk.

12 It is also interesting to compare the results of regional papers with a survey of 3,600 entrepreneurs in 69 countries on obstacles for doing business by Brunetti, Kisunko and Weder (1997). In general, the results are very similar: indeed, financing was not named as a major problem in any of the regions. Entrepreneurs were more concerned about lack of infrastructure (which as we discussed above is related to risk and volatility), corruption, taxes and regulation (and imperfect judiciary system). There is a substantial variation across regions: e.g. in Asia entrepreneurs trust government while in other regions they are very sceptical about both government policy and its implementation; in CEE, entrepreneurs ranked corruption below financing, which means that government predation is relatively weak. One should, however, be careful in comparing the results of this survey with the

regional papers: the survey included both small and large firms, and it is not clear to what extent the surveyed firms are representative of the respective countries and regions.

13 Protectionist policies create an additional burden on small businesses through increased costs of imported inputs.

14 This argument is especially valid when the share of large firms in employment is low, as it is the case in many poor countries (see section 2). At the top level of bureaucracy, policy choices are good for growth, but at the low level they are not implemented.

15 Also, Romania, that is similar to Russia in all respects except the small-business environment, has also been growing faster although not as fast as Poland.

16 One should bear in mind, however, the aforementioned bias due to the informal economy. The shadow sector is likely to be populated by smaller non-industrial firms that are not taken into account by official statistics.

17 The most striking case is of course the post-communist countries where firms' structure was driven by political and military rather than economic efficiency considerations (Guriev and Ickes, 2000). In Latin America and South Asia, high tariff and non-tariff barriers have protected firms from foreign competition (Edwards, 1993; Ranade and Siddiqui, 2000). See Balassa (1971) for estimates of the effective protection rates in the 1960s that ran well into double-digit and even triple-digit numbers. In East Asia, large firms have benefited from financial-repression policies that shifted investment supply into their favour (Kuncoro, 2000).

18 The regional papers on MENA and SSA focus on small firms, and the LAC paper does not consider firms at all so this section will only refer to CEE-FSU, South Asia and East Asia papers. However, most of this section applies to African and Latin American economies as well.

19 As Brown and Earle (2001) argue, endogeneity seems to be a lesser problem in transition economies than inherited industrial structure from a non-market system. Likewise, the market structure in Latin America and South Asia may also be exogenous because of high protection rates during the import substitution industrialization policies.

20 For a striking example of the difference between cross-section and panel-data estimates see Yudaeva *et al.*'s (2001) paper on the spillovers of FDI in Russia. The cross-section analysis suggests that FDI have negative spillovers on local firms' productivity, while the panel data prove that the spillovers are positive. The fact is that FDI are biased towards the industry with low productivity and therefore high growth potential.

21 One should be aware, though, that elimination of explicit subsidies may not be enough for hardening budget constraints. Soft budget constraints often come across as tax and inter-enterprise arrears, non-performing bank loans etc. (Djankov and Murrell, 2002; Gaddy and Ickes, 1998).

References

Abdel-Fadil, M. (2000) 'The Microeconomics of Growth in the MENA Region (1970–2000)', thematic paper for the Global Research Project, Global Development Network, Washington, DC.

Ahituv, A. (2001) 'Be Fruitful or Multiply: On the Interplay between Fertility and Economic Development', *Journal of Population Economics*, vol. 14, pp. 51–71.

Balassa, B. (1971) 'The Structure of Protection in Developing Countries' (Baltimore: Johns Hopkins University Press).

Banerjee, A. and E. Duflo (2000) 'Reputation Effects and the Limits of Contracting: A Study of the Indian Software Industry', *Quarterly Journal of Economics*, vol. 115(3), pp. 989–1017.

Banerji, R. (1978) 'Average Size of Plants in Manufacturing and Capital Intensity: A Cross-Country Analysis by Industry', *Journal of Development Economics*, vol. 5, pp. 155–66.

Becker, G. S., K. Murphy and R. Tamura (1990) 'Human Capital, Fertility, and Economic Growth', *Journal of Political Economy*, vol. 98, pp. s12–s37.

Behrman, J., S. Duryea and M. Székely (2000) 'Household and Economic Growth in Latin America and the Caribbean', thematic paper for the Global Research Project, Global Development Network, Washington, DC.

Behrman, J. R. (1997) 'Women's Schooling and Child Education: A Survey', Philadelphia, PA: University of Pennsylvania, mimeo.

Berglof, E. and G. Roland (1998) 'Soft Budget Constraints and Banking in Transition Economies', *Journal of Comparative Economics*, vol. 26, pp. 18–40.

Berglof, E. and L. von Thadden (1999) 'The Changing Corporate Governance Paradigm: Implications for Transition and Developing Countries', conference paper, Annual World Bank Conference on Development Economics, Washington DC.

Besley, T. J., S. Coate and G. C. Loury (1993) 'The Economics of Rotating Savings and Credit Associations', *American Economic Review*, vol. 83, pp. 792–810.

Bloom, D. E.; J. G. Williamson, (1998) 'Demographic Transitions and Economic Miracles in East Asia', *World Bank Economic Review*, vol. 12(3), pp. 419–55.

Boserup, E. (1965) *Conditions of Agricultural Growth; the Economics of Agrarian Change under Population Pressure*, Chicago: Aldine Publishing Company.

Brown, D. and J. Earle (2000) 'Competition and Firm Performance: Lessons from Russia', CFPR Discussion Paper no. 2444, London

Brunetti, A., G. Kisunko and B. Weder (1997) 'Institutional Obstacles to Doing Business: Region-by-Region Results from a Worldwide Survey of the Private Sector', World Bank PRD Working Paper no. 1759.

Caldwell, J. C. (1976) Toward a restatement of demographic transition theory. *Population and Development Review* 2 (3–4), 321–66.

Carlin, W., S. Fries, M. Schaffer and P. Seabright (2001) 'Competition and Enterprise Performance in Transition Economies: evidence from a cross-country survey', EBRD Working Paper no. 63.

Chen, Xiaomin (1997) 'Resource Reallocation, Productivity Dynamics and Industrial Evolution: Evidence from the Taiwanese Manufacturing Sector,1981–91', Unpublished dissertation, Pennsylvania State University.

Clerides, S., S. Lach and J. Tybout (1998) 'Is Learning-by-Exporting Important? Micro-Dynamic Evidence from Colombia, Mexico and Morocco', *Quarterly Journal of Economics*, vol. 113(3), pp. 903–47.

Collier, P. and J. W. Gunning (1999) 'The Microeconomics of African Growth 1950–2000', thematic paper for the Global Research Project, Global Development Network, Washington, DC.

De Soto, H. (1989) *The Other Path: the Invisible Revolution in the Third World* (New York: Harper & Row).

De Soto, H. (2000) *The Mystery of Capitalism: Why Capitalism Triumphs in the West and Fails Everywhere Else* (New York: Basic Books).

Djankov, S. and P. Murrell (2002) 'Enterprise Restructuring in Transition: A Quantitative Survey', *Journal of Economic Literature*, v.40(3), pp. 739–92.

EBRD (1999) *Transition Report: Ten Years of Transition* (European Bank for Reconstruction and Development, London).

Edwards, S. (1993) 'Openness, Trade Liberalization, and Growth in Developing Countries', *Journal of Economic Literature*, vol. 31(3), pp. 1358–93.

Filer, R., T. Gylfason, S. Jurajda and J. Mitchell (2000) 'Markets and Growth in the post-Communist World', thematic paper for the Global Research Project, Global Development Network, Washington, DC.

Friebel, G. and S. Gurlev (2000) 'Why Russian Workers Do Not Move', CEPR Discussion Paper no. 2368.

Fry, M. J. (1979) 'The Cost of Financial Repression in Turkey', *Saving and Development*, vol. 3(2), pp. 127–35.

Frydman, R., C. Gray, M. Hessel and A. Rapaczynski (1999) 'When Does Privatization Work: The Impact of Private Ownership on Corporate Performance in Transition Economies', *Quarterly Journal of Economics*, vol. 114 (4), pp. 1153–91.

Frye, T. (1999) 'Keeping Shop: The Value of the Rule of Law in Warsaw and Moscow', mimeo, Ohio State University.

Frye, T. and A. Shleifer (1997) 'The Invisible Hand and the Grabbing Hand', *American Economic Review*, vol. 87(2), pp. 354–8.

Gaddy, C. and B. W. Ickes (1998) 'Russia's Virtual Economy', *Foreign Affairs*, vol. 77(5), pp. 53–67.

Galor, O. and D.Weil (1994) 'The Gender Gap, Fertility, and Growth', *American Economic Review*, vol. 86, pp. 374–87.

Gersovitz, M. (1988) 'Saving and Development', in B. Hollis, H. B. Chenery and T. N. Srinivasan (eds), *Handbook of Development Economics* (Amsterdam: North Holland).

Guriev, S. M. and B. W. Ickes, (2000) 'Microeconomic Aspects of Economic Growth in Eastern Europe and the Former Soviet Union, 1950–2000', thematic paper for the Global Research Project, Global Development Network, Washington, DC.

Hanushek, E. (1992) 'The Trade-Off between Child Quantity and Quality', *Journal of Political Economy*, vol. 100(1), pp. 84–117.

Hanushek, E. and D. Kimko (2000) 'Schooling, Labor-Force Quality, and the Growth of Nations', *American Economic Review*, 90(5), pp. 1184–1208.

Higgins, M. (1998) 'Demography, National Savings, and International Capital Flows', *International Economic Review*, vol. 39(2), pp. 343–71.

Huffman, W. E. (2001) 'Human Capital: Education and Agriculture,' in B. Garnder and G. Rausser (eds), *Handbook of Agricultural Economics*, Vol. 1A (Amsterdam: Elsevier Science).

ILO (1999) *Trade Unions and the Informal Sector*, (International Labour Organisation. Geneva).

Johnson, S., J. McMillan and C. Woodruff (2002) 'Property Rights and Finance.' *American Economic Review* vol. 92(5), pp. 1335–56.

Karshenas, M. (2001) 'Economic liberalization, competitiveness and women's employment in the Middle East and North Africa', in D. Salehi-Isfahani (ed.), *Labour and Human Capital in the Middle East: Studies of Labour Markets and Household Behaviour* (Reading: Ithaca Press).

Kuncoro, A. (2000) 'Microeconomic Determinants of Economic Growth in East Asia', thematic paper for the Global Research Project, Global Development Network, Washington, DC.

Liedholm, C. and D. Mead (1987) 'Small Scale Industries in Developing Countries: Empirical Evidence and Policy Implications', International Development Paper 9, Agricultural Economics Department, Michigan State University.

Lewis W. A. (1954) 'Economic Development with Unlimited Supplies of Labour', *Manchester School*, vol. 22 (May), pp. 139–91.

Little, I., D. Mazumdar and J. M. Page, Jr. (1987) *Small Manufacturing Enterprises: A Comparative Analysis of India and Other Economies* (New York: Oxford University Press).

Lucas, R. E. (1988) 'On the Mechanics of Economic Development', *Journal of Monetary Economics,* vol. 21, pp. 3–42.

Lucas, R. E. (1998) 'The Industrial Revolution', manuscript, University of Chicago.

Lucas, R. E. B. (1997) 'Internal migration in developing countries', in *Handbook of Population and Family Economics*, vol. 1B, Amsterdam: Elsevier Science, pp. 721–98.

McKinnon, R. I. (1973) *Money and Capital in Economic Development* (Washington, DC: Brookings Institution).

Masson, P. R., T. Bayoumi and H. Samiei (1998) 'International Evidence on the Determinants of Private Saving', *World Bank Economic Review*, vol. 12(3), pp. 483–501.

Modigliani, F. (1970) 'The Life-Cycle Hypothesis of Saving and Intercountry Differences in the Saving Ratio', in W. A. Eltis, M. F. Scott and J. N. Wolfe (eds), *Induction, Growth, and Trade,* Oxford: Clarendon Press, pp. 197–225.

Morduch, J. (1998) 'The Microfinance Schism', HIID Development Discussion Paper 626, Harvard University.

Nickell, S. (1996) 'Competition and Corporate Performance', *Journal of Political Economy*, vol. 104(4), pp. 724–46.

Pissarides, C. (2000) 'Labor Markets and Economic Growth in MENA Region', thematic paper for the Global Research Project, Global Development Network, Washington, DC.

Pop-Eleches, C. (1998) 'Transition in Romaina: Three Essays on Private Sector Development', mimeo, Harvard University.

Pritchett, L. (1999) 'Has education had a growth payoff in the MENA region?' MENA Working Paper Series, no. 18, Washington DC: World Bank.

Pritchett, L. (1996) 'Where Has All the Education Gone?' Washington, DC: World, Bank mimeo.

Ranade, A. and R. Siddiqui (2000) 'Microeconomics of Growth in South Asia', thematic paper for the Global Research Project, Global Development Network, Washington, DC.

Razin, A. and E. Sadka (1997) 'International Migration and International Trade', in Handbook of Population and Family Economics, Vol. 1B, Amsterdam, Elsevier Science, pp. 851–87.

Rodríguez, F. and D. Rodrik (2000) 'Trade Policy and Economic Growth: A Skeptic's Guide to the Cross-National Evidence', in B. S. Bernanke and K. Rogoff (eds), *NBER Macroeconomics Annual* 2000, Cambridge, Mass., MIT Press, 2001.

Rosenzweig, M. R. (1995) 'Why Are There Returns in Schooling?' *American Economic Review,* vol. 85(2), pp. 153–8.

Sachs, J. D., J. L. Gallop and A. Mellinger (1999) 'Geography and Economic Development', CID Working Paper no. 1.

Salehi-Isfahani, D. (1999) 'Labor and the Challenge of Restructuring in Iran', *Middle East Report,* vol. 28, no. 210, pp. 34–7.

Salehi-Isfahani, D. (2000) 'Microeconomics of growth in MENA – the role of households', thematic paper for the Global Research Project, Global Development Network, Washington, DC.

Schultz , T. P. (1994) 'Human Capital, Family Planning, and Their Effects on Population Growth', *American Economic Review Papers and Proceedings,* vol. 84, pp. 255–60.

Schultz, T. W. (1975) 'The Value of the Ability to Deal with Disequilibria', *Journal of Economic Literature,* vol. 13(3), pp. 827–46.

Shaw, E. (1973) *Financial Deepening in Economic Development,* (New York: Oxford University Press).

Shleifer A. and R. Vishny (1994) 'Politicians and Firms', *Quarterly Journal of Economics*, vol. 109(4), pp. 995–1025.

Shonkoff, J. P. and D. A. Phillips (2000) editors, *From Neurons to Neighborhoods: the Science of Early Childhood Development,* National Research Council and Institute of Medicine Committee on Integrating the Science of Early Childhood (Washington, DC: National Academy Press).

Solow, R. (1956) 'A Contribution to the Theory of Economic Growth', *Quarterly Journal of Economics,* vol. 70, pp. 65–94.

Steel, W. (1993) 'Small Enterprises in Indonesia: Role, Growth, and Strategic Issues', DSP Working Paper 194, Jakarta Development Studies Project II.

Strauss, J. and D. Thomas (1995) 'Human Resources: Empirical Modeling of Household and Family Decisions', in J. R. Behrman and T. N. Srinivasan (eds), *Handbook of Development Economics,* Vol. 3A (Amsterdam: North-Holland), pp. 1883–2024.

Topel, R. (1999) 'Labor Markets and Economic Growth', in *Handbook of Labor Economics,* Vol. 3C (Amsterdam: North-Holland), pp. 2943–84.

Tybout, J. (2000) 'Manufacturing Firms in Developing Countries: How Well Do They Do, and Why?' *Journal of Economic Literature,* vol.39, pp. 11–44.

Woolcock, M. J. V. (1999) 'Learning from Failure in Microfinance *American Journal of Economics and Sociology,* vol. 58(1), pp. 17–42.

World Bank (1996) *Early Child Development: Investing in the Future,* Human Development Department (Washington DC: The World Bank).

World Bank (2001) World Development Indicators, Washington DC, The World Bank.

Young, A. (1995) 'The Tyranny of Number: Confronting the Statistical Realities of the East Asian Growth', *Quarterly Journal of Economics,* vol. 110(3), pp. 641–80.

Yudaeva, K., K. Kozlov, N. Melentieva, N. Ponomareva (2001) 'Does Foreign Ownership Matter? Russian Experience', CEFIR Working Paper no. 5, Moscow.

4
Markets and Growth

Štěpán Jurajda and Janet Mitchell

1 Introduction[1]

Markets are the mechanisms through which economic resources are channelled and where economic incentives are set. Hence, their functioning is critical to both static and dynamic efficiency as well as to the responsiveness of the economy to shocks. While both product and factor markets are important in allocating resources, factor markets also influence the rate of resource-creation.[2] This chapter affirms that markets are crucial to growth and combines suggestions of Topel (1999) and Pritchett (2000) to argue that country-specific markets should be a principal focus of future research on growth.

We study key markets (financial, labour, natural resource, and product) to assess how they are facilitating or constraining growth. First, we draw on the body of existing theoretical and empirical literature to provide a framework for discussing the links between markets and growth. Second, we summarize the findings of the six regional papers produced in the thematic area of 'Markets and Growth' for the Global Research Project (GRP) by presenting four stylized scenarios of the process of growth, relevant for some of the regions or phases of development.

Research agenda

Macro growth regressions, not to mention growth accounting, are, for the most part, uninformative about the mechanisms by which the studied sources of growth are working.[3] They are a useful data description tool, but are presently less able to provide a causal interpretation for the estimated growth effects.[4] Growth regressions have serious econometric problems, starting with the usual suspects of measurement error and endogeneity, and ending with (dynamic) misspecification.[5] While theory offers hypotheses about growth determinants and provides a description of some potential channels of effects, it is often surprisingly terse in many areas (see sections 2 to 5).

We believe that this lack of knowledge and testing methodology makes inquiry into mechanisms of growth effects crucial for the growth research agenda. We would like to accent the suggestion Topel (1999) made in his survey work on labour markets and growth, namely that the most important and productive future research on growth entails 'detailed empirical studies of the operation of labour markets and the impact of policies and institutions within individual countries'. We see this objective much in line with the idea of the GRP and would like to extend this suggestion to all factor and commodity markets. We propose that country-specific research can prove fruitful in distinguishing among existing growth theories and motivating new ones; it can provide a deeper perspective on growth, one focused on mechanisms by which the determinants of growth affect the process of growth.[6]

Yet, there are many possible interrelated determinants of growth working at different time horizons and this curbs the use of a single-country experience for study of growth determinants. The GRP country studies, however, can overcome this limitation by analysing external or internal shocks and episodes when growth patterns have changed. Pritchett (2000) shows that periods with large shifts in growth (up or down) are characteristic for most developing countries and constitute the bulk of panel-data variation in growth rates; hence, they are likely to provide important insight into the process of growth. The country-specific GRP research can focus on such episodes and study what caused them (for example policies or institutions or politics), and why some countries have been able to overcome shocks with little impact on growth while others have been completely overwhelmed.

However, it is not clear how to cumulate knowledge from the country-specific studies. While theorists can model relationships that appear important in certain regions, systematically relating case studies of growth–change episodes and of market functioning to the macro aggregate measures of growth may be an issue.[7] We find it useful to cumulate the preliminary evidence of the regional thematic papers into stylized *growth scenarios* of the process of growth (section 6). These scenarios are linked to specific market mechanisms of growth (discussed in sections 2 to 5) and are aimed to provide a tentative framework for country-specific research.

General organizational structure

As we motivated ourselves above, our discussion of markets and growth evolves around mechanisms by which markets may affect the process of growth. Hence, each market-specific section will begin by identifying the relevant market-specific mechanisms. However, in order to provide a structure for our discussion of the ways in which markets can affect economic growth, and to support identification of variables for subsequent analysis, we use a simple classification of market dimensions. Specifically, we focus on three dimensions: (1) *infrastructure*, which refers to the institutional underpinnings, including laws and courts; (2) *price wedges or distortions* due to policy interventions; and (3) *participants*, or the relevant players, which are determined by competition policy, ownership structure and so on. Market infrastructure aids processing of information and allocating resources. Removal of price distortions from policy wedges increases economic activity by eliminating deadweight losses. Finally, different types of participants in a given market may have differing incentives and objectives, and the different objectives across types of participants can impact market outcomes (often through a political economy channel). In each market the three dimensions are interrelated (for example, the market infrastructure may determine the type of participants); however, treating each dimension separately permits us to better distinguish between the effects of institutions and of policies on economic growth.[8]

2 Financial markets

The positive association between financial-sector development and economic growth is now a well-documented stylized fact. Since Goldsmith (1969) found that the level of financial development, defined as financial intermediary assets divided by GDP, was positively associated with economic growth, numerous authors have reconfirmed positive correlations between differing indicators of financial development and growth, and several have included tests for causality.[9]

Growth mechanisms

Links between financial systems and economic growth occur through one or more of three basic functions served by the financial sector in an economy: (1) the provision of adequate instruments for saving; (2) the channelling of resources from savers to borrowers (the resource-allocation function); and (3) the reallocation of resources when their current uses are no longer the most profitable.[10]

Savings

Savings flowing into the financial sector may be increased by improvements in the liquidity and breadth of financial assets, reductions in information asymmetries between firms and outside investors, increases in the returns on financial instruments, and by reductions in transactions costs related to financial assets. An increase in savings can increase growth by permitting an increase in investment.

Channelling of funds

The efficiency with which the financial sector performs the allocation function – that is, the selection and monitoring of firms and projects receiving external finance – will also affect a country's growth rate. Theory offers some indications of the ways in which financial-sector development could result in more efficient channeling of resources from savers to borrowers and in higher growth. Diamond (1984) suggests that financial intermediaries can perform monitoring and screening at lower cost than individual investors; Greenwood and Jovanovic (1990) argue that financial intermediaries are better able to identify investment opportunities than are individuals; and Harrison, Sussman and Zeira (1999) assume that the costs of monitoring borrowers are a function of the distance between banks and their borrowers. Therefore, as more banks enter the financial system, regional specialization occurs, monitoring costs fall and investment increases. Bencivenga, Smith and Starr (1996) show that a beneficial effect of the increase in liquidity of financial assets arising from the development of secondary securities markets, which allow transfer of financial assets across individuals, is to permit short-term savings to be directed into long-gestation production technologies, which may generate greater long-run returns than short-gestation technologies.

Reallocation of funds

Finally, the efficiency with which the financial system reallocates resources from unprofitable to profitable uses will affect economic growth. For example, the existence and terms of bankruptcy provisions can influence the degree of effort that firm managers exert, the point at which unprofitable firms are closed down, and the efficiency with which a liquidated firm's assets are channelled to more profitable uses.[11]

Market dimensions

Each of the dimensions of infrastructure, policy wedges and participants in financial markets can influence economic growth through their impact on any or all of the three functions that the financial system performs. We consider each of the dimensions in turn.

Market infrastructure

Elements of financial-market infrastructure that are important for financial-sector development and growth include institutions such as courts that facilitate contract enforcement; accounting rules requiring firms to disclose adequate information to outside investors; and laws (such as bankruptcy laws) protecting the rights of outside investors. Well-developed financial market infrastructure will increase the supply of savings flowing to firms by ensuring that financial contracts are honoured and the rights of outside investors are protected. Accounting rules requiring adequate information disclosure by firms should improve the efficiency of resource allocation. As suggested above, bankruptcy laws (and other guarantees of creditors' and shareholders' rights) could be expected to improve the efficiency of the reallocation of resources.

Little theory exists relating financial-market infrastructure to growth. Numerous empirical studies involving cross-country growth regressions have, however, included variables representing infrastructure.[12] To the extent that the results of these studies capture causal relationships, infrastructure indeed appears to be important. Variables focused on in such studies include indicators of creditors' and/or shareholders' rights,[13] an indicator of the degree of law and order, an indicator of contract enforcement, an indicator of accounting standards, and indicators of corruption or government interference in financial markets. A variable indicating the origin of the legal system (English common law; French civil law; German civil law; or Scandinavian civil law), constructed by La Porta *et al.* (1997, 1998), is also sometimes used as an instrument for infrastructure variables.

Whereas results of cross-country regressions suggest a potential role for legal and accounting institutions in increasing growth, it may be useful to distinguish – under the rubric of financial infrastructure – between general indicators of a commitment to the rule of law or to contract enforcement and more targeted measures, such as improvement of accounting standards or of shareholders' and creditors' rights. An important question is whether the general commitment to law and order (which may also represent the elimination of corruption) is a stronger determinant of financial-sector development and of growth than are more specific measures aimed at protecting creditors' or shareholders' rights. The significance of the commitment to law and order is that it guarantees that the government will not expropriate the assets or profits of private owners and investors. Once a minimum commitment to the rule of law has been established, the implementation of more specific protections for shareholders and creditors may become more important.[14] Within-country analysis of data relating to the commitment to the rule of law versus specific infrastructure reforms would shed light on this question and could feed into cross-country analysis.

Policy wedges

Typical distortions created by financial-sector policy relate to restrictions on interest rates and reserve requirements on bank deposits. Financial repression, which results in imposition of interest-rate ceilings on bank deposits or on rates charged on loans to certain sectors, can reduce savings and can also distort the allocation of resources. In addition, politically motivated directed lending represents an implicit form of policy wedge, which leads to 'soft budget constraints' for firms benefiting from the lending and, therefore, to poor performance of the financial sector in reallocating resources.

Financial liberalization policies may eliminate the distortions created by financial repression. It is a well-recognized theoretical result, however, that financial liberalization has an ambiguous effect on saving, due to the presence of income and substitution effects following an increase in the interest rate. There is also some evidence (Demirgüç-Kunt and Detragiache, 1998, cited in Caprio and Honohan, 1999) that banking crises often follow financial liberalizations. However, this outcome may reflect more a weak financial market infrastructure, which leaves regulators ill-equipped to adequately supervise newly liberalized financial intermediaries.

Participants

Important participants in financial markets include financial intermediaries and individual investors providing outside finance to firms through stockmarkets. Recent cross-country empirical research that attempts to assess the relative importance of financial intermediaries and stockmarkets concludes that the relative weight of each in the financial system does not appear to matter.[15] Since the typical path of financial-sector development is for the banking sector to develop first, followed later by the stockmarket, we focus our attention here on financial intermediaries. Potentially important distinctions between types of financial intermediaries are state versus private banks, differences in the qualifications of owners of private banks, and foreign versus domestic banks.

The nature of bank ownership and management can significantly affect the efficiency of resource allocation by the banking sector. Banks must have both the ability and the incentives to identify and invest in profitable firms and to halt lending to unprofitable firms. Conditions that would be expected to lower banks' incentives to allocate (or reallocate) resources efficiently include:

(1) government pressure on banks to lend to particular firms or sectors for political reasons;
(2) pressure on banks by governments to purchase government debt;
(3) too few constraints on banks' activities, either because supervision is inadequate or restrictions on entry into banking are too lax; and
(4) banks that are themselves in financial distress, in which case limited liability results in excessive risk-taking and hiding of bad loans.

Conditions (1) and (2) may be more likely to hold when banks are state-owned. In any case, government interference in bank lending is common in developing countries (Caprio and Honohan, 1999). Conditions (3) and (4) have a negative effect on the financial sector's resource-allocation functions through inefficient investment behaviour on the part of banks, and banking regulations will influence the extent to which conditions (3) and (4) hold. Regulations that would be expected to guard against inefficient investment behaviour include regulation of entry into the banking sector, capital adequacy requirements, rules relating to loan classification and loan–loss provisions, restrictions on bank activities, and adequate handling of banks with high levels of non-performing loans.

A high rate of entry into the banking sector can sometimes cause more harm than good, despite the fact that entry increases competition.[16] Two sources of danger arising from lax entry policies are difficulties in regulating a large number of banks and the increased riskiness of loans made by banks faced with competition-induced declining spreads between interest rates on loans and deposits. Banking-sector problems arising from poor banking supervision or from excessive entry into banking by unqualified bankers are thus potentially harmful to growth. Several transition economies and Sub-Saharan African economies have suffered banking crises as a result of excessively lax restrictions on entry into the banking sector.

Research examining links between conditions such as (1)–(4) and growth is sparse. Some empirical evidence relating to state ownership of banks is offered by Barth, Caprio and Levine (2000), who report preliminary results from an ongoing research project in which data on bank regulation and ownership have been collected from over 60 countries. They find that state ownership of banks is significantly and negatively correlated with financial-sector development.[17] La Porta *et al.* (1997, 1998) collected data on state ownership of the 10 largest banks in over 90 countries, including 12 transition economies. They found that their measure of government ownership is significantly and negatively correlated with subsequent financial development, measured by the growth in the ratio of private credit to GDP.

3 Labour markets

In contrast to financial markets, the role of labour *markets* in affecting growth has not yet become a major topic of empirical analysis. This is especially surprising given the extended empirical research linking financial markets to growth performance. Furthermore, the existing empirical work, including a 1999 survey on labour markets and growth by Robert Topel, studies only one aspect of labour markets: the effect of human capital accumulation on growth. This reflects the almost exclusive focus of labour-market-related growth theory on human capital (HC). We will take a broader view, building also on a large body of empirical literature on labour-market flexibility, which is, if only implicitly, related to growth.

Growth mechanisms

The economic links from labour markets to growth are likely to occur through the allocation (and mass reallocation) function of labour markets and through their role in supporting the production and efficient use of HC. The links from growth to labour markets, on the other hand, are likely to occur though the build-up of infrastructure as a result of economic growth.

Production of human capital

Human capital is the 'engine' of workhorse growth models and lies at the heart of the revival of growth economics. There are two important causal links from HC to growth in the theory: first, in the neoclassical growth models, increases in HC cause growth as HC is one of the main inputs to the production; second, Nelson and Phelps (1966) suggest that a higher stock of HC makes technological innovations and therefore growth more likely. The first channel suggests that an increase in

HC leads to a one-time increase in production, while the second implies that the effect of increasing HC on output is permanent.[18] Neither theory implies how labour markets can impede or foster HC-creation and use.

There is only limited empirical evidence on the *process* that relates HC and growth. At the micro level, schooling increases productivity when included in an estimated production function (see, for example, Griliches, 1997, for references) and schooling is a causal determinant of individual income (Card, 1999). However, the definition of HC used in growth theory covers not only schooling, but also accumulation of knowledge or abilities to conceive and implement new ideas, labour-augmenting technology, and possibly even social capital. It is hard to measure these concepts and they do not differentiate the ability to apply knowledge in productive ways from technical progress. Still, the measure of HC used in macro empirical work is typically educational attainment, capturing only one form of knowledge,[19] and the hard existing empirical results based on educational attainment measures of HC are mixed at best.[20] Yet, given the overwhelming (causal) evidence from micro studies, and the strong theoretical foundation of growth in HC, one is pressed to ask how HC is created (and what affects its use).

Is the tentative evidence of the regional papers on markets and growth consistent with the view that HC should be the centerpiece of growth research? The evidence is puzzling since school attainment measures grow consistently in most countries, but output does not. While in the East Asian countries and in some Latin American coun-tries large investments in HC by youth coincide with dramatic increases in growth rates, there are other countries – for example in the Middle East and North Africa (MNA) region – where a growing stock of HC was associated with little productivity growth. The Eastern Europe and Central Asia (ECA) region has a highly-educated work force and an enormous potential for technology adoption and imitation, yet this potential is far from being realized in many ECA countries.[21]

Hence, at first glance, HC does not appear to be the main determi-nant of differences in growth rates across countries. At second glance, however, one can consider HC a necessary but not sufficient condition for growth and look at labour markets for an explanation why (growing) HC stock was not put to its best use in some countries. This perspective stresses the role of HC allocation as opposed to HC produc-tion. We take up this issue within the context of the following two subsections, focusing on labour allocation and reallocation.

Allocation of labour

The ability to allocate existing resources (that is, labour, HC) across economic sectors, occupations or regions is, at an intuitive level, crucial for static efficiency. Further, one can hypothesize that the apparent lack of explanatory power of HC for growth may be related to misallocation and therefore to the functioning of labour markets. The allocation function of labour markets would then be as important as the key theoretical role of HC in driving growth. The country-specific question is then not only how Korea increased its stock of HC, but how did it also increase its labour utilization and non-agricultural labour force (Topel, 1999). In contrast, one must also ask why are most degree holders entering the labour market in Egypt hired by the public sector and how much this affects growth.

The effect of misallocation is twofold: first, present-day efficiency of allocation is lower; second, misallocation may lead to the build-up of political economy obstacles to reallocation – that is, pressure groups that benefited from misallocation rents will oppose efficiency-enhancing reforms and this opposition to reform may form a long-term obstacle to growth.

A strong effect on growth through allocation of resources probably comes through high labour taxation. This issue is of primary concern only in developed industrialized economies (see, for example, Tabellini and Daveri, 1997, and the references therein) as direct labour taxation is low in most developing countries. Yet, labour taxation is important in many ECA post-communist countries where the welfare-state commitments, inherited from the communist era misallocation of resources, result in high statutory contribution rates and excessive labour taxation.

Labour reallocation

A tightly related issue is the ability of labour markets to undertake massive reallocation, that is the ability to successfully deal with extensive (initial) misallocation or with external shocks. It is crucial for transitional growth of countries off the steady-state path. For example, extensive reallocation of labour appears to be needed in the ECA region as a result of communist misallocation, in the SAS (South Asia) region as a result of the doctrine of economic nationalism, or in the MNA region as a result of misuse of high oil revenues in the 1970s.

Large shocks often occur in less-developed countries and often appear to establish turning points differentiating between multiple growth equilibria. For example, the initial misallocation of labour in communist countries resulted in workers moving from overstaffed heavy industries to services, finance and trade in the European transition economies. In contrast, Russia and parts of the former Soviet Union were not that successful and the initial transition often resulted in an increase in agricultural employment, reversing the process of economic development. This distinction is likely to drive long-term growth prospects.

Market dimensions

Let us now draw on the preceding discussion and on the GRP regional papers to consider the labour-market dimensions that may affect the three labour-market growth mechanisms.

Market infrastructure

The important labour market *infrastructure* includes: (i) transportation, housing (and mortgage) market, and residency restrictions; (ii) schooling systems; (iii) market-clearing mechanisms such as channels of information on vacancies; (iv) protection against diversion; (v) labour code and regulations; and (vi) social security. While there is extensive empirical research on the effects of (v) and (vi) on many labour-market outcomes and some theoretical research on growth effects of (ii) and (iii), many of these issues appear to be not covered at length in the existing growth research agenda.

Functioning *housing market and transportation infrastructure* clearly improve the allocation function of labour markets. Further, closely related mortgage markets improve the ability of workers to reallocate from regions with high unemployment to thriving areas. The latter is likely to be especially important in geographically dispersed (large) developing countries; for example, in Russia where massive misallocation under central planning led to non-viable industrialization of far-north isolated regions. (Note that the proposed growth effects lead to specific research questions. For example, to study whether territorial mobility restrictions curb growth through an effect on human capital allocation, one can relate region and time-specific labour-market outcomes such as unemployment, education–occupation match or productivity to variation in housing-market regulation and/or residential permit policy.)

Schooling systems produce human capital; hence, their direct effect on the HC growth mechanism. Reforms promoting the quality and supplied quantity of education are likely to improve the chances of a country to grow. An important related issue of HC accumulation has to do with social returns to education being higher than private returns. Existence of positive externalities and spillover effects of education calls for government support of schooling.[22] Finally, the ability of schools to adjust their focus (curricula) to market needs also affects the allocation of labour and HC on the labour market.

Poor quality of *market-clearing mechanisms* (such as information channels used in hiring) will clearly negatively affect the allocation function of labour markets. Labour-market segmentation (along, for example, ethnic dimensions) also negatively affects market-clearing. However, it also alters schooling and HC accumulation. Since students will expect their class status to determine their careers, segmentation will also affect HC production. If innovative activity and social mobility play an important role in determining growth, policy should support equal schooling and innovations (entrepreneurs).[23]

Rule of law and protection against diversion are likely to play an important role in both creation and use of HC on labour markets: if the benefits of innovations are not protected by law, few will invest in research; if benefits of entrepreneurship are grabbed by either organized crime or the state, few will become (innovative) entrepreneurs. The regional papers indeed suggest that extensive diversion (grabbing hands)[24] will preclude a rise in productive types of self-employment and force even well-educated (ECA) workers to self-subsistence agriculture.[25]

The ability to reallocate labour is likely to be related to the popular notion of labour-market flexibility (lack of rigidity). *Labour codes and regulations*, that is labour-market flexibility (and its effect on worker mobility), has become a major object of empirical research.[26] Much of this research focuses on job security regulation (for example, high firing costs and limited part-time or fixed-term contracts). While there are undisputed benefits to recipients of job protection, there is disagreement over the extent to which regulation is responsible for the difference in equilibrium (un)employment rates and worker mobility: Blank (1994) and Freeman (2000), among others, argue that regulations are not harmful, while for example OECD (1994), Burgess (1994) and Michie and Grieve-Smith (1997) claim that they matter. Heckman and Pagés-Serra (2000) analyse the role of job-security provisions using natural experiments from the recent history of Latin American countries, and establish that such regulations have a substantial negative impact on the level of employment and especially on youth. Looking both across countries (Burgess, 1994) and US states (Dertouzos and Karoly, 1993) the evidence is that employment protection legislation slows down structural adjustment and the reallocation of labour from declining industries to innovative, growing industries. To the extent that structural reallocation is an important growth ingredient, labour-market regulation affects growth.[27] However, the evidence from the regional thematic papers appears to suggest that an important empirical question related to regulations in developing countries is the degree to which they are enforced.

While labour-market segmentation, impediments to labour mobility and other rigidities have been recognized as obstacles to growth and studied in developing countries (for example Collier and Gunning, 1999; Agenor, 1996), there is relatively little research looking at the importance of social safety for massive reallocation and growth.[28] The ability to deal with large shocks may be improved if workers can rely on *social safety nets* while searching for new jobs and do not plunge into poverty (and subsistence home plots). On the other hand, social safety nets require high levels of labour taxation, which appears harmful to economic growth. Finally, an important related ingredient of many recent growth stories is labour-force participation. It is shaped by demography, but to a large extent also by incentives set in the labour market including social safety nets and unconstrained wage-setting (see below). Output per capita increases even if bad macroeconomic policies remain in place as long as participation increases.

Policy wedges

The most important price wedge on the labour market occurs through wage-setting distortions (minimum wage, centralized compressed wage structure, massive taxation and redistribution). Compressed wage distribution adversely affects HC accumulation in a stylized theoretical growth scenario. In the Lucas–Uzawa framework, recently surveyed by Topel (1999), HC is accumulated endogenously as a result of individual optimal investment decisions sacrificing present consumption for future returns. Incentives to invest in HC are related to rewards to such investments, which are carried by a flexible wage structure.[29] In a market-driven scenario of (Kuznets) growth, exports propel the demand for industrial output, which in turn raises the demand for skilled labour and consequently the skill-wage premium. This leads to investment in HC and consequently growth. This growth story requires, among other conditions, a flexible (regulation-free) wage structure and an elastic response of HC investment (see also pp. 214–17).[30]

Participants

The relevant participants in labour markets are government-sector employees and other pressure groups as opposed to employees in small firms, home production and the shadow economy.[31] The first type of participants (pressure groups, labour unions) is likely related to political-economy constraints on growth. If those who would lose from efficient restructuring block reforms, this surely affects the labour markets' ability to support efficient reallocation.

A strand of theoretical models called Optimal Speed of Transition theory (for example Aghion and Blanchard, 1994; Castanheira and Roland, 2000) relates to the political-economy problems of massive reallocation. These models are motivated by the transition of post-communist economies, but are relevant for extensive reallocation in other regions, for example for a situation in which an overstaffed public sector puts a heavy burden on the private sector, which is thus incapable of creating large numbers of 'good' jobs. They model the reallocation of labour (and capital) from an inefficient oversized (state) sector to a growing efficient (private) sector. This strand of literature advocates gradual phasing out of the inefficient sector as optimal, partly based on political-economy constraints. Too fast a downsizing of the inefficient sector creates obstacles to successful reallocation and slows down growth.

Indeed, the tentative evidence from the regional thematic papers suggests that the establishment of pressure groups (as a result of initial misallocation of resources) is a major obstacle to successful reallocation.[32] Buying out workers who are harmed by first-choice economic reforms may be one solution to this obstacle to growth (for example, in MNA).

4   Natural-resource markets[33]

So far we have discussed the factor markets for capital and labour. As it is common to view natural resources, including land, as an additional factor of production, we will consider the relevance of natural-resource markets for economic growth. The current consensus is that natural-resource abundance depresses economic growth (for example Sachs and Warner, 1995). The main upshot of the literature is twofold: first, natural resources, if not well-managed in well-built markets, will impede growth through rent-seeking; and second, an abundance of natural resources leads to serious policy failures: for example, if the windfall from a natural-resource boom is poorly invested, it can have long-run detrimental effects.

Natural-resource abundance tends to induce *rent-seeking* behaviour that can take many forms, including corruption and looting, and consequently increase the degree of diversion in the whole economy. The interaction of markets with this growth mechanism is very strong in that the ability to circumvent or thwart markets is often a precondition of rent-seeking. A natural consequence of rent-seeking control of valuable resources (for example oil) is the buildup of interest (pressure) groups, which may further impede efficient allocation of resources and which often directly influence politics. Rent-seeking is therefore both a consequence and a source of market failure. What fails is primarily market infrastructure: property-rights protection. Rent-seeking appears present in all resource-rich areas, including ECA, and in Sub-Saharan Africa (SSA) it takes the extreme form of looting. For example, Collier and Hoeffler (1998) find that a dependence on natural resources strongly increases the risk of civil war.

An abundance of natural resources also often leads to *policy failures* and results, typically, in a serious misallocation of resources, high inflation and a build up of pressure groups. When the windfall from natural resources is captured by the state, it is often used to (i) offer highly-paid jobs in a bloated public sector (as for example in Côte d'Ivoire or Egypt), (ii) finance extensive public projects or state-owned industrial enterprises (Nigeria or Trinidad and Tobago), and (iii) support import-substitution policies and/or subsidies to non-natural-resource industries (Venezuela). Such increases in government spending are hard to reverse when oil prices drop as pressure groups lobby for their subsidies. Next, excessive foreign borrowing results in inflation and indebtedness. The country becomes highly dependent on the (fluctuation in) raw material prices in world markets, which results in large external shocks to the economy as it is difficult for the government to smooth revenues and even harder to cut down on spending programmes started during natural-resource boom periods. When the windfall is distributed to the population, wrong policies are often in place, such as restricted access to foreign capital markets. This leads to the windfall being invested in construction or other activities leading to little increase in productivity.

The market dimension playing an important role here is players: governments and public employment. One of the apparent reasons for policy failure is a false sense of security of governments of resource-rich countries. The country-specific research question is why, given the high propensity to misallocate oil windfalls, did Indonesia apparently manage its windfall well, while for example Venezuela invested in growth-impeding import substitution (Gelb *et al.*, 1988). The policy response to natural-resource booms may have to do with market infrastructure before the boom, which is testable.

There are also other mechanisms potentially relating natural resources to lower growth, which consider the trade-off between manufacturing and natural-resource extraction. It is argued that manufacturing contributes larger positive externalities compared to the natural-resource sector. A reallocation of resources away from the manufacturing sector then impedes learning by doing, while, say, mineral production occurs without any linkages to the rest of the economy. This argument is at the heart of the Dutch-disease or linkage theories. When the high-rent natural-resource-based industries thrive in the presence of high real exchange rates and wages, other industries are smothered with the Dutch disease: this lowers the growth of high-tech capital-intensive or high-skill labour-intensive industries, which typically offer large growth externalities, such as learning, R&D and technology adoption. The disease is a consequence of a general market failure, not that of particular market dimension. An effective cure may involve distortion-free resource rent fees or subsidies to high-externality industries.

Finally, resource abundance in agriculture leads to an overemphasis on low-skill education. However, low-skilled labour is not versatile and becomes less useful in other industries; workers with few options tend to oppose reallocation when resource prices plummet and reallocation is needed (see section 3).

5 Product markets

Product markets affect growth through the efficiency of the mix of goods and services produced, the rate at which productivity-enhancing innovation occurs, and the ease of firm-creation. A mix of goods that does not reflect an economy's comparative advantage does not allow exports to grow at the rate that they otherwise would. Production of goods for which the production process generates positive externalities with respect to growth (such as learning-by-doing or acquisition of 'tacit' knowledge) can also enhance growth.[34] The ease with which new firms may be created may also influence the amount of innovation in an economy and the ability of markets to reallocate resources from unprofitable to profitable sectors.

Market infrastructure: important elements of market infrastructure with respect to product markets include public infrastructure, such as transportation and telecommunications networks, and the prevalence of patents. Adequate public infrastructure lowers transaction and production costs for firms and increases production. The quality of infrastructure may also influence the level of foreign investment. The prevalence of patents influences firms' incentives to innovate, and the greater the ease of obtaining a patent for an innovation, the greater are firms' incentives to innovate and the higher the resulting rate of growth.

Policy wedges: policies such as preferential taxes and subsidies to particular sectors, quotas or tariffs on imports, and laws governing export and import licensing may influence growth through their effect on the mix of goods produced. For example, import-substitution policies adopted in South Asia have been cited as one of the key explanations for the low growth rates of this region from the 1960s to the 1980s.[35]

Participants: elements of what was described above as financial-market infrastructure, such as a commitment to private property rights and to contract enforcement, can influence the types of participants in product markets. The commitments to contract enforcement and to property rights ensure that firms' profits will not be seized by the government or corrupt officials, and these commitments can affect the willingness of private and foreign firms to enter into differing markets.

Another element of infrastructure with a potential impact on the amount of innovation concerns restrictions on the creation of firms. If regulations regarding the formation of new firms are very strict, then innovative entrepreneurs may be discouraged from forming firms, thereby slowing the rate of innovation and economic growth. Regulations restricting entry and the formation of new firms will also affect the proportion of private firms in a market and the distribution of established versus new firms. Governments that implement restrictive entry policies may do so in order to protect state-owned firms or firms whose managers wield political influence.[36] The potentially negative effects of such policies on productivity, innovation and growth are clear.

These observations lead to the question of whether an increase in product-market competition promotes growth. The theoretical relationship between competition and growth is in fact ambiguous; on the one hand increased competition lowers incentives for managerial effort or innovation because of the lower level of profit that can be sustained from the extra effort, on the other hand increased competition motivates managers of inefficient firms to exert more effort in order to avoid being driven out of the market.

Several theoretical papers have played on the ambiguous relationship between product-market competition and managerial effort. Hart (1983) and Scharfstein (1988) show that managerial effort is not only a function of the level of potential profit (or of competition), but also of the nature of firm managers' objectives. Aghion, Dewatripont and Rey (1999) take this idea further and analyse a model where managerial objectives, combined with financial-market efficiency, play a significant role in determining which effect dominates. When firm managers are profit-maximizers, an increase in competition will lower profit and, consequently, innovation and productivity (and growth). When firm managers care about their private benefits of control, competition will discipline the managers (by removing financial 'slack') and force them to innovate more often, thereby increasing economic growth.[37] Given the prevalence in many developing economies of state-owned firms, firms benefiting from special government protection, and a generally weak legal protection of outside creditors and shareholders, we see these results as highlighting the important role that increased competition can play in disciplining firm management and enhancing growth.[38]

Openness, which represents a removal of policy wedges linked to international trade, can also influence the types and behaviour of participants in product markets. Openness may generate benefits from any of the following: economies of scale (possibly arising from learning by doing) due to the increase in the size of the market; the disciplinary effect of competition on inefficient firms; or more rapid diffusion of technology, as entry of foreign firms or products makes transfer of technology easier.

According to Ahn and Hemmings (2000), results from empirical studies on the impact of openness on growth are mixed, although recent studies seem to have confirmed a positive relationship between trade and growth. Two caveats to these results should be noted. First, causality probably runs in both directions; therefore, the question of causality needs to be addressed. Second, many studies make use of a binary openness indicator constructed by Sachs and Warner (1995), which includes a number of differing dimensions relating to policy wedges, nature of market participants, and market infrastructure.[39] Such an indicator makes it difficult to identify the exact mechanism by which openness might be affecting growth. For example, Rodríguez and Rodrik (1999) suggest that two of the components of this indicator (size of the black-market premium and the existence of a state monopoly on exports) are primarily responsible for its statistical power. The black-market premium could be an indicator of macroeconomic policy as much as of openness. Similarly, a negative relationship between the existence of a state monopoly on exports and growth may be more directly attributable to state ownership than to openness.

6   Four growth stories

In this section we present four scenarios or growth stories coming from the regional growth papers. Each relates to the experience of one or more regions during some period and highlights what seems to emerge as a key theme in explaining growth performance. These scenarios should be interpreted as tentative and exploratory. We use them, first, as an expositional device in our discussion of regional growth experience, but at the same time the scenarios also embody hypotheses that could be explored in future country-level and regional research. Such a focus is in line with the research agenda outlined in the introduction. By distilling patterns of growth from both past, we seek to identify both past pitfalls and future policy implications. Within each scenario, we highlight the involved market mechanisms of growth discussed above.

After discussing each scenario and the region(s) to which it applies, we raise caveats and unresolved questions. The four stories focus on the following themes:

1   the importance of openness policies;
2   market flexibility in response to major shocks;
3   the influence of high natural resource endowments; and
4   consistently low growth (the 'everything's wrong' story).

Scenario 1 identifies a theme arising from experience in the East Asia and Pacific (EAP) region and SAS; scenario 2 characterizes experience in ECA in the 1990s, in some MNA countries in the 1980s, in Latin America and the Caribbean (LAC) in the 1980s, and possibly in some SSA countries in the 1970s and 1980s. Scenario 3 describes the MNA region and may tell part of the story in SSA; while finally scenario 4 describes several countries in SSA that have exhibited consistently low growth rates over very long periods.

Openness

East Asian countries, which started with comparable rates of income per capita as South Asia in the 1960s, consistently improved their growth rates from 1960–97, whereas South Asia did not. East Asia switched from import-substitution policies to export-oriented policies earlier. This, in short, motivates our first story.

The first scenario is essentially a story of market-driven Kuznets-type growth, in which openness policies raise the potential of a developing country to export and therefore attract investment into manufacturing. Rising exports then propel the demand for industrial output, which in turn raises the demand for skilled labour. A higher skill-wage premium leads to investment in human capital (and/or a higher participation rate in a country with many educated non-participants) and movement of labour force from agriculture (villages) to manufacturing (cities). The story involves a significant increase in the level of human capital (of youth) and an expansion of employment in high-skill industries (manufacturing), accompanied by increasing technology adoption, positive externalities spilling from manufacturing into other industries, and the concurrent development of financial markets.[40] This process of growth also entails a large movement of labour force from rural to urban areas, and an initial increase in inequality which may later be reversed by a growing supply of degree holders. Real wages grow together with productivity (but not faster).

This success scenario hinges on (i) openness, (ii) the ability of a country to accommodate industrial production (perhaps including easy start-up procedures, little corruption and diversion), (iii) a flexible wage structure, and (iv) the ability of workers to move and to invest in human capital (alternatively, state support of such investment). Governments' pro-export policies (a shift from import substitution to active export promotion) may trigger this scenario; hence, while international trade is a key element of this story, the trigger may deserve a separate political economy analysis.

Note that the openness scenario is a market-driven story of growth: it starts with a removal of a market barrier/wedge. To reap the benefits of this market opening, other factor-market mechanisms must be invoked, including human-capital production and labour reallocation. Market infrastructure must be able to support the accommodation of industrial production, and so on. At a more fundamental level, this scenario regards openness (and its immediate implications for product markets) as the causal force behind growth. The causality may run in two directions: first and foremost, international trade expands the size of the local market, which may have growth-promoting effects of fostering productivity and labour reallocation to manufacturing. Trade provides demand for manufacturing output in low-income labour-abundant countries and therefore fosters labour reallocation and schooling. The effect on productivity may come from technology adoption, returns to scale, positive externalities, and international competition's disciplinary effect. Second, in this scenario import-substitution policies lead to product-market distortions. These distortions (or the lack thereof) in turn feed into the workings of factor markets, thereby reinforcing the growth effect of openness.

East Asia and Pacific (EAP).

Characteristic features of this region (and apparently that of the long-term economic programmes of the region's governments) are early export-oriented policies, high levels of human capital, and high rates of growth. The central hypothesis of the scenario is that the steady and high rates of growth of most of the countries of East Asia were a result of policies of export promotion (and technology adoption in some cases), perhaps combined with high levels of human capital which facilitated acquisition of tacit knowledge following the adoption of foreign technology.[41] Related questions, however, are the importance to the EAP growth story of the role played by large-scale labour reallocation and the fact that political economy constraints did not prevent useful product-market interventions. Both may have to do with a relative weakness of interest groups, in which case it would be interesting to study why protected industries and labour unions did not become important.

Another question concerns whether any *preconditions* are necessary to drive this scenario. This question comes to the fore upon comparison of EAP's growth with the low growth of the SAS region, which was characterized by anti-openness policies. Although openness policies represent a major difference between SAS and EAP, it appears that SAS countries also suffered from a number of other factor and product-market distortions which may have contributed to their low growth. Did EAP avoid these imperfections? To the extent that there do exist necessary preconditions for the success of openness policies, likely candidates on the basis of EAP experience would include: low levels of natural resources, which do not suffocate manufacturing and which may imply or coincide with weak labour unions and low corruption; a threshold level of initial human-capital stock; high savings; and macro-economic stability.

One dissenting view with respect to the description of EAP growth offered by this scenario is that the causality runs in the opposite direction: economic growth promoted exports (Rodrik, 1994). If the latter hypothesis is correct, the sources of the initial growth need to be identified. The above list of potential preconditions would appear to offer a natural point from which to begin searching. Alternatively, high savings and investment may have offered the original stimulus for the high growth rates.

South Asia (SAS)

This region may present a converse case of the EAP openness-and-success story. Here, governments favoured inward-oriented policies: import substitution, not export promotion. This was apparently not optimal, as no South Asian country reported high growth in any decade from 1950 to 1980 (Reynolds, 1985). SAS governments implemented centrally-planned public-sector-oriented industrialization programmes based on an economic nationalism doctrine. This raises the political economy question of how and why this ideology was conceived. In particular, were mistrust of markets and belief in state intervention related to the former British colonial status of SAS?

The economic nationalism programmes called for restrictive trade and exchange-rate policies, which gave rise to overvalued exchange rates and product-market distortions (that is, protection of specific industries). Furthermore, public firms and publicly financed investment projects faced soft budget constraints; priority was given to basic, heavy industries; and employment in the public sector expanded fast, without regard to productivity. The anti-export policies resulted in balance-of-payments deficits leading to a cycle of further import controls.

While even mild forms of central planning (mild in comparison to pre-transition ECA) beget misallocation of resources and low growth, the driving force of low growth in SAS may be related to the issue of openness. This conjecture, however, leads to a number of more specific questions related to openness in the SAS context. In particular, how important are product-market distortions relative to factor-market distortions in explaining SAS growth? For example, Tendulkar and Sen (2001) note that legislative restrictions on employers led to the hiring of contract labour and to adoption of capital-intensive technology. These authors also suggest that progress in SAS in the 1980s in eliminating trade distortions was not matched by liberalization in factor markets.

A second question relating to the importance of openness for SAS is whether inward-oriented policies such as trade restrictions inhibit growth through their negative effect on demand for exports (and hence investment), distortionary effect on product mix, or by encouraging rent-seeking? Alternatively, do they hamper growth through the reduction in foreign direct investment, which would then imply less capital and less transfer of productivity-improving technology? Trade restrictions in SAS countries actually correlate with higher growth, whereas the absence of foreign investment is associated with lower growth.

Additional, largely unexplored potential explanations for lower growth in SAS than in EAP are related to the importance of restrictions on the expansion of private enterprises, the apparent underinvestment in human capital combined with high fertility rates, the quality of market infrastructure (corruption, commitment to contract enforcement, and so on), and the functioning of financial markets (for example the apparent attempts of the governments to control banks and/or interest rates). Initial conditions in SAS that could also be considered include a high proportion of agriculture in GDP and a potentially lower initial level of human capital.

Finally, the persistence of inward-oriented policies in SAS is likely to be related to a political-economy argument of path-dependence.

Responsiveness to shocks

In this scenario a shock to the economic system either generates or reveals the need for a major reallocation of resources from low-productivity to higher-productivity firms or sectors. The extent to which the economy succeeds in reallocating resources will determine growth rates in the short and medium term and may also have a significant impact on long-term growth rates. Examples of such shocks include decreases in terms of trade for a country dependent upon commodity exports, a financial crisis, or a change in the political regime, such as the beginning of transition from a socialist to a capitalist economic system.

What is significant about this scenario is the need to reallocate massive quantities of resources from existing to new uses. The required reallocation often involves significant labour movement (across regions as well as industries), restructuring or closing of firms in low-productivity sectors, and creation of firms in high-productivity sectors. The new equilibrium to which the economy will move may either be a 'high-growth' equilibrium in which market imperfections are sufficiently low to permit an efficient reallocation of resources, or a 'low-growth' equilibrium in which market development is inadequate. Typical outcomes in a low-growth equilibrium include expansion of the public sector to absorb workers displaced by the shock (some MNA countries), retreat of displaced workers from industry to agriculture (some ECA countries), or movement of labour from the formal to the informal sector (SSA). Each of these outcomes may exert negative long-term effects on growth.

Market mechanisms that will determine the outcome of the shock are those that are cited above in sections 2–5 as relating to the reallocation of resources in labour, financial and product markets. In terms of market dimensions, whereas infrastructure, policies and types of participants all play an important role, infrastructure is crucial to achieving efficient resource reallocation. Bankruptcy and collateral laws determine the likelihood that unprofitable firms are liquidated or restructured, freeing capital to move to more profitable activities. Restrictions on hiring and firing affect both the probability that firms release redundant labour and the degree of labour mobility across regions. The ease with which new firms can be created influences the speed at which resources can be reallocated to profitable activities.

Although adequate market development appears to be a necessary condition for efficient resource reallocation in response to a shock, it may not be sufficient: political economy factors may also push the economy in the direction of the low-growth equilibrium. For example, groups benefiting from the existing allocation of resources (such as firm owners or workers in particular sectors) may put up strong resistance to reallocation. The degree of political will to tolerate (or compensate) losers may be important in determining the new equilibrium after the shock. In addition, government responses to the shock can influence the movement to a particular equilibrium by influencing agents' beliefs regarding government credibility: if agents believe, for example, that the government is not committed to reform, then entrepreneurs may be unwilling to create new firms, thereby slowing movement to the high-growth equilibrium or pushing the economy toward a low-growth equilibrium.

Eastern Europe and Central Asia (ECA)

The countries of the ECA region have all faced the shock imposed by the transition from socialism to capitalism, initiated in these countries at the beginning of the 1990s.[42] The transition, which was motivated in part by a grossly inefficient allocation of resources during the socialist regimes, created the need for resource reallocation on a massive scale. This task, which would be enormous in any economy, has been made even more difficult in the ECA countries by the virtually complete absence at the beginning of transition of infrastructure in all types of markets and by the dominance of state participation in all markets.[43] The ECA countries have had to put into place market infra-structure while at the same time reallocating resources throughout the economy.

All of the ECA countries suffered a large fall in production at the beginning of the 1990s as a result of the dissolution of the Soviet Union, the abandonment of central planning and, in some countries, macroeconomic stabilization policies. One market variable that appears to correlate with more rapid turnaround in growth rates following the declines is the commitment by government to the rule of law and to contract enforcement.[44] Commitments such as these foster financial-sector development and encourage entry of private firms into product markets.

With respect to the response to the shock of transition, there is a marked contrast between most of the former Soviet republics (exclud-ing the Baltic countries) and the countries in Central and Eastern Europe. The former have made noticeably less progress in developing markets and have suffered low growth rates and significant increases in poverty, forcing a retreat of much of the active population from indus-try to agriculture.

The distinction between the former Soviet republics and Central and Eastern Europe also applies to financial markets, especially to the com-mitment to the rule of law, which is sorely missing in some of the former Soviet republics. These countries also exhibit smaller and more poorly developed financial sectors and weak banking regulation. At the same time, all of the ECA countries (with the exception of Hungary) have been slow to implement workable bankruptcy laws, although the countries in the former Soviet Union have moved even more slowly than other ECA countries. In addition, in all of the ECA countries newly-created small and medium-sized firms have had difficulty obtaining bank finance. High quantities of inherited bad debt on the balance sheets of state-owned banks and inexperience in lending on the basis of market criteria are features of banking sectors that have contributed to this problem.

Labour-market imperfections that have affected labour mobility in the ECA countries include administrative restrictions on moves between regions, the tie of provision of social services to the employer, and underdeveloped housing markets and rent controls for much of the existing housing. As before, elimination of such barriers has pro-ceeded much more slowly in the former Soviet Union than in the other ECA countries.

Product-market imperfections that are likely to have played a role in differential responses to the shock of transition are barriers to entry of new firms and the form and pace of privatization of state-owned firms. Whereas rising self-employment has helped channel labour from previous to new uses and has lowered unemployment rates, high barriers to entry and corruption in Russia have translated into low self-employment rates.[45] Success in privatization has varied across countries, with the former Soviet republics still reporting much greater shares of the state-owned sector in GDP as late as 1999.

Interestingly, the degree of openness does not appear to explain much of the variation of growth rates across ECA countries (although the level of foreign direct investment does correlate with growth). Most of the ECA countries have adopted policies of openness, and many have reoriented exports to countries outside the region. The determinants of foreign direct investment appear to depend more on success in development of market infrastructure, commitment to the rule of law, and political stability.

One caveat that must be raised with respect to the argument that market infrastructure and market development are important for determining the growth performance of ECA countries is the observation that the commitment to the rule of law – in addition to representing development of market infrastructure – may also signal political commitment to the transition process. This political commitment may encourage foreign direct investment and the creation of private firms and, therefore, accelerate growth. The ECA countries that are lacking in a commitment to the rule of law have also exhibited lack of progress in virtually every dimension of the transition, suggesting the absence of political commitment.

A second caveat to our analysis of markets in ECA is the question of the role of initial conditions. ECA countries that have reported poor growth performance throughout the 1990s also faced weaker initial conditions, which included high proportions of agriculture and natural resource extraction activities in GDP, lower levels of human capital, high proportions of trade to the Soviet bloc, smaller initial private sectors, and less historical experience with democracy or capitalism. The importance of initial conditions versus policies has been a continuing source of debate with respect to ECA countries.

Sub-Saharan Africa (SSA)

While the long-term growth performance of most SSA countries has been poor in relation to that of developing economies in other regions, half of the SSA countries experienced reasonable growth rates throughout the 1960s but then suffered drastic falls in the 1970s (Ndulu and O'Connell, 1999, 2000; Prichett, 2000). A question raised by this experience is whether the sharp declines in growth followed a major shock. Information regarding any shocks preceding the growth declines and the specific responses of different countries to the shocks could provide valuable insight into the fall in growth of these countries.

One observation that appears to hold at a very general level for all of SSA is that these countries have failed to develop their manufacturing sectors sufficiently to reallocate labour from agriculture to manufacturing, or from the informal to the formal sector. Agricultural production remains a very high proportion of GDP, and, furthermore, significant imperfections exist across all types of markets in SSA. Therefore, it is difficult to point to any one area that might be responsible for the failure to develop the manufacturing sector. Our account (pp. 147–9) of the many market imperfections in the SSA region does not allow us to distinguish between the SSA countries that experienced respectable growth rates in the 1960s and then suffered setbacks, from those countries that have shown consistently weak growth since 1960.

Middle East and North Africa (MNA)

Growth rates in MNA countries are more volatile than in other regions, and the growth trends appear to follow trends in oil prices. Much of the long-term growth experience of the MNA region is related to the theme of the natural-resource scenario (pp. 145–7). However, negative oil price shocks in the 1980s appear to have had different effects across countries within the MNA region.

Public sectors are disproportionately large in MNA countries, implying that the government is a major participant in labour markets. As the discussion of the natural-resource scenario suggests, the size of the public sectors may have contributed to a misallocation of human capital. Whereas some of the MNA countries responded to negative oil-price shocks in the 1980s by drawing on foreign reserves to maintain government spending, countries that were more financially constrained were forced to limit government expenditures in response to the price shocks. An important question is whether the latter group of countries was forced to reduce public-sector wages or the extent of government hiring of skilled workers and whether there was an indirect, positive effect on the allocation of labour or capital through movement into the private sector. Did negative oil-price shocks push financially constrained economies in the direction of a 'high-growth' equilibrium in response to the shock?

South Asia (SAS)

While the SAS region has been characterized by policies of import substitution described above (pp. 133–9), recently the region experienced a considerable reduction in inward orientation and a move towards product-market liberalization. According to Tendulkar and Sen (2000), the liberalization was caused by the necessity of reacting to external shocks and economic crises, rather than by long-term strategy. Tendulkar and Sen (2000) argue that measurable progress in eliminating trade distortions has not been matched by liberalization in factor markets. This may be attributable to political-economy problems originating in the past strategy of inward orientation: the bloated state-owned sector and the protected industries oppose reforms, which would curtail their rents. Market distortions introduced by inward-oriented policies may be reinforcing themselves beyond product markets.

Latin America and the Caribbean (LAC)

Like a number of SSA countries, Latin American (LA) countries exhibited reasonable growth rates during the 1960s and 1970s, but suffered severe declines in growth (exhibiting negative growth rates) during the 1980s. Several LA countries suffered financial crises during the 1980s, raising the question of the extent to which these crises constituted shocks that may have been followed by movement to a 'low-growth' equilibrium. The growth rates of some LA countries recovered in the 1990s, and observers have suggested that market reforms may have played a role in the recovery. The extent to which shocks to the financial sector in the 1980s may have contributed to low growth and the extent to which reforms leading to improvements in factor or product markets in the 1990s may have resulted in increases in growth rates remain open questions.

   Market imperfections in LAC that have been suggested to have exerted negative effects on long-term growth include policies of financial repression, lack of openness, and low rates of human-capital accumulation in some countries. The pervasiveness of financial repression and financial crises in LA suggests that financial markets may have had an important influence on growth in this region. However, as discussed in section 2, the effect of financial repression on growth is ambiguous due to the uncertain response of savings to interest rate changes. In addition, some research has indicated that financial crises have followed financial liberalization in some LAC countries. Weak financial market infrastructure and banking supervision may have allowed newly-liberalized banks to take on excessively risky investment, leading to a crisis.

The role of a lack of openness in explaining LA growth performance also remains an open question. Although many LA countries rated poorly on indicators of openness, some of these countries nevertheless exhibited relatively high growth rates. Again, the question of explanations for the sharp declines in LA growth rates in the 1980s arises. Information on terms-of-trade shocks or changes in openness would be useful for providing an answer to this question.

One caveat to the claim that market imperfections may have heavily influenced the growth performance of LA is that macroeconomic policy may be potentially important relative to market imperfections in explaining growth in this region. Poor macroeconomic policy has been reflected in very high inflation rates and has been cited as contributing negatively to growth in LA.

Natural resource curse

In this scenario, motivated by the MNA region (and potentially also by LAC and SSA), high natural-resource endowments are present in a developing country that exhibits weak markets, weak democracy or myopic governments. Comparative advantage leads to dependence on natural-resource extraction, which in turn naturally makes economic policies and growth depend on commodity prices (and their volatility). A more damaging problem, however, is that poor market infrastructure or bad governments interact with natural resources: either rent-seeking related to extraction becomes pervasive or high resource revenues are misallocated, typically into supporting bloated public sectors.

Rent-seeking during natural-resource booms may be related to pre-boom quality of market infrastructure, which is a question for country-specific research. The policy failure of overstaffing the public sector may be a result of a false sense of security ensuing from high oil revenues. It leads to buildup of pressure groups opposing reallocation and negatively feeds back into growth. This is where the growth mechanism of human-capital accumulation may break down because of extensive inefficient allocation of human capital.

While the above-mentioned market mechanisms appear important, the analysis of natural-resource policy failure is primarily a task of political economy. High natural-resource endowments pose a significant policy challenge for governments of developing nations.

Although it would appear relatively easy to propose appropriate growth-enhancing policy,[46] the political economy question that arises is why these policies are not being implemented.

Middle East and North Africa (MNA)

The region is rich in its endowment of natural resources. High oil-export revenues have permitted the oil-producing countries to undertake significant public investment, including improvement in education. Yet, one of the key puzzles raised by the experience of this region is the observation that steady increases in human capital have not translated into increases in growth. Measures of total factor productivity reveal an average decline in TFP growth in the region during the period 1960–90.[47]

One hypothesis explaining the weak link between human-capital acquisition and growth in this region is that labour has been misallocated as a result of swollen public sectors, which absorb a high fraction of the skilled workforce and jeopardize the ability of private sectors to attract skilled workers.[48] Public-sector wages appear to be higher in this region than in any other region, which makes it difficult for the private sector to create jobs, which further increases the pressure on the public sector to absorb labour-market entrants. What is less clear is whether labour-market infrastructure or labour market policies reinforce the misallocation of labour. Country studies could yield insights into this issue via the gathering of information on labour-market infrastructure, policies, and the extent of government hiring.

While the dependence on oil is a consequence of comparative advantage, several of the countries of this region have maintained low degrees of openness, which would tend to strengthen the dependence on oil. A caveat to the natural-resource scenario therefore depends on the extent to which the lack of openness may have contributed to low growth rates independently of any effect via oil-export dependence. A fruitful avenue of research along these lines would be a comparison of openness policies across the countries of the region, in relation to the presence of oil.

Just as human-capital accumulation does not seem to have increased growth rates in the MNA region, high savings rates and investment ratios similar to those of East Asia do not seem to have translated into growth rates similar to those of the latter region. A potential explanation relates once again to the size of the public sector, the hypothesis being that investment has been directed to low-productivity projects, such as housing. Another potential explanation, however, is that financial systems are not attracting savings or allocating them efficiently. Information relating to the infrastructure, policy, and the functioning of financial markets across countries of this region would be valuable for assessing the role that financial systems have played in attracting savings and directing them to their most productive uses.

Finally, initial conditions that are likely to have played a role, in addition to the endowment of oil, in explaining the historical growth performance of this region are low literacy rates, arising in part from the bias against educating females. Country-specific shocks that also may have contributed to variability in growth include civil and regional wars.

Consistently low growth

As noted above, roughly half of the SSA countries have exhibited low growth rates over very long periods of time. Market imperfections that could be expected to limit growth are severe and pervasive in the SSA economies, yet because so many problems exist it may be difficult to identify one key explanation for low growth. Complementarities in market reforms may yield convexities in outcomes, which would imply that growth performance is significantly poorer in countries where problems exist in most market dimensions, as opposed to a few. Perhaps, as Collier and Gunning (1999) suggest, initial low growth may lead to a self-reinforcing, low-growth trap.

A fruitful approach to understanding the poor growth performance of SSA countries would be to identify policy or institutional variables that differentiate the group of SSA countries that performed reasonably well during the 1960s from the group of low-growth countries. As suggested in the scenario above on the responsiveness to shocks, growth rates of the countries with initially good performances may have dropped as a result of negative shocks. A related question with respect to the consistently low-growth countries is whether these countries experienced a series of negative shocks. If not, market imperfections offer a potentially convincing explanation for the persistence of low growth rates.

Severe product-market imperfections in SSA include lack of infrastructure and heavy use of policy wedges. Among the deficiencies in infrastructure are restrictions on entry of new firms and weak transportation and communications infrastructure. Weak infrastructure leads to uncertain input supplies, to which firms respond by inefficiently producing their own inputs. For example, many firms react to uncertain electricity supply by producing their own electricity (Collier and Gunning, 1999).

Poor product-market infrastructure has increased the costs of production and trade, thereby reducing the potential for growth.

Policy wedges in product markets include import-substitution policies, protection for certain firms, heavy regulation of trade, overvalued exchange rates, and other trade barriers. In addition, an urban bias on the part of governments has resulted in heavy taxation of agriculture in some countries.

With respect to the types of participants in product markets, few foreign firms are present and rates of foreign investment in SSA are very low. The proportion of global private capital flowing into SSA declined from the 1970s to the 1990s. Potential market explanations for the exceptionally low rates of FDI include policy wedges relating to international trade (that is, lack of openness), as well as extensive corruption among public officials and lack of commitment to contract enforcement.[49] The latter two factors have also undoubtedly discouraged domestic investment. In 1995, SSA was ranked the riskiest region in the world for investors. Rates of return on private capital have been very low, probably reflecting the severe product-market imperfections.

Labour markets are also fraught with problems.[50] They are highly segmented in SSA; formal and informal markets coexist, and informal markets are large. Informal and agricultural labour markets have served as the 'sponge' for absorbing high numbers of otherwise unemployed. Unemployment rates among educated youth are high in SSA. Although the size of informal labour markets probably reflects weak demand for labour by the formal sector – itself a result of low rates of investment – an interesting question that could be pursued in country-specific studies is to what extent imperfections in labour markets limit labour mobility from the informal to the formal sector. For example, Adenikinju and Oyeranti (1999) argue that lack of formal information on job openings results in most of the hiring in the formal sector occurring primarily through relations with family and friends.

Government participation in labour markets in SSA has been extensive, with governments often serving as the employer of last resort. According to Adenikinju and Oyeranti (1999), public-sector employment accounts for as much as 60 to 80 per cent of non-agricultural employment in several African countries. High levels of public-sector employment translate into high levels of government expenditure and lower average productivity, as skilled labour is discouraged from moving into manufacturing. In addition, Adenikinju and Oyeranti (1999) suggest that declines in real wages in the public sector have contributed to corruption by government employees.

Financial-market imperfections in SSA are severe, and they must certainly have contributed to low growth through the failure to stem the high flow of savings out of the region. Financial-market infrastructure is extremely weak: legal institutions and credible means of enforcing contracts are severely lacking in many countries.[51] Informal credit markets characterize the financial sector in rural areas; formal financial intermediaries are concentrated in urban areas.

The appearance of informal credit markets may actually have a positive effect on growth, as an efficient response to costly information problems arising in rural lending. However, as funds do not appear to flow from the formal to the informal sector, informal money-lenders' funds are limited. This in turn limits the extent to which capital may be efficiently allocated in rural areas.

Costly policy wedges are prevalent in the formal financial sector: interest rates have been regulated; high requirements placed on banks' reserves; and much bank lending has been directed to state-owned or otherwise favoured firms. Implicit taxation of unremunerated required reserves has been estimated to exceed banks' value-added in some SSA countries. Extensive use of directed lending has resulted in very high rates of loan defaults on banks' balance sheets; percentages of bad loans have reached as high as 40 per cent to 95 per cent. Directed lending and weak banking regulation have led to protracted or repeated banking crises in many countries. Nigeria and Kenya offer examples where banking crises resulted from weak regulation following financial-sector liberalization. Both low interest rates and frequent banking crises are likely to have exacerbated the flight of capital from the region.[52]

Despite the plethora of market imperfections that could potentially lead to low rates of growth in SSA countries, an open question relating to the poor SSA performance and an issue of debate has concerned the role of initial conditions relative to policies. Initial conditions that have been linked to weak growth performance include a large agricultural labour force, high fertility rates, low levels of human capital, geography (a large number of land-locked countries), and a high degree of ethnic diversity (see Collier and Gunning, 1999).

6   Conclusion

We argue in this chapter that market policies and institutions have a crucial impact on economic growth. We explore the dimensions through which product, labour, financial, and natural-resource markets may affect growth, then we develop four growth scenarios through which we summarize the findings of six regional papers dealing with markets and growth.

Several observations emerge from our analysis. First, financial market 'infrastructure' is important. Commitments to law and order and to contract enforcement are potentially significant determinants of financial-sector development and economic growth. We speculate that other features of financial market development may be of only secondary magnitude in comparison. Financial-market infrastructure can also affect the outcome of financial liberalization policies; liberalization in the face of weak banking regulation, for example, can result in a financial crisis.

A second observation relates to the lack of research on the relationship between labour markets and growth, as opposed to the relationship between human-capital production and growth. We highlight the need to fill this gap, pointing to the importance of labour markets in the efficient allocation of human capital in addition to its production. Human-capital production may be a necessary condition for growth, while an efficient allocation of human capital (related, for example, to political economy) may constitute a sufficient condition.

A third observation concerns the importance of efficient factor reallocation in response to shocks: unsuccessful reallocation following a shock can lead to a low-growth equilibrium with negative long-run effects. The presence of social safety nets and the strength of pressure groups may affect the speed and efficiency with which labour can be reallocated across sectors or regions.

Finally, our examination of financial and labour markets suggests that factor markets are important for growth. A question that nevertheless remains open is whether factor markets serve more as facilitators of product-market reforms or of positive responses to shocks, or whether labour or financial market reforms alone can generate large increases in economic growth.[53]

The country studies of the GRP project have a unique opportunity to verify or reject important growth theories by focusing their detailed investigation on the relevant mechanisms of growth.[54] Finally, our growth scenarios also offer testable hypotheses about causality links upon which country-specific analysis can shed light.

Notes

1   The authors drew upon the regional papers on markets and growth by Adenikinju and Oyeranti (1999), Ersel and Kandil (2000), Filer, Gylfason,

Jurajda and Mitchell (2000), Pissarides (2000), and Tendulkar and Sen (2000).

2 Conditions in labour markets influence the extent of acquisition of human capital. Financial markets determine the amount of savings available to be transformed into domestic physical capital.

3 To give one major example, it is not clear yet from the existing empirical work whether human capital affects the level of output or its growth rate.

4 The regressions are often specified *ad hoc*, without a link to an underlying structural model. Recently, however, Hall and Jones (1999) use variation in a country's colonization language to instrument for social infrastructure in a regression explaining the differences in levels of income. For a similar approach see Levine *et al.* (2000).

5 For example (moderate) inflation may have positive effects on growth in the short run, but negative effects in the long run. More generally, growth can be decomposed into its steady state, transitional (off-steady-state), and cyclical components, which each may have different determinants (Pritchett, 2000).

6 One avenue of research would first relate, e.g., markets infrastructure to measurable market-specific outcomes (i.e. labour reallocation), and second relate the measured ability of markets to support the hypothesized channels of growth to the aggregate outcome. This would allow for differentiating among competing hypotheses about growth mechanisms. For example, is the level of human capital causing the ability to implement R&D as in the imitation model of Rivera-Batiz and Romer (1991)?

7 One way to cumulate knowledge is to use the country-specific studies to identify exogenous variation in the determinants of growth or detailed changes in policy, which can later be used in a regression framework.

8 It also allows us to identify potential links between the types of actors in each market and the potential effects on economic growth, an issue which bridges the theme of markets and growth with that of the microeconomics of growth.

9 See, for example, Atje and Jovanovic (1993), Beck, Levine and Loayza (2000), Harris (1997), King and Levine (1993), Levine (1997, 1999), Levine, Loayza and Beck (2000), Levine and Zervos (1996, 1998), Rajan and Zingales (1998), and Wurgler (2000). Techniques used to test for causality consist of the use of instruments for variables whose values are believed to be determined simultaneously with growth.

10 We focus here on the functions of the financial system that are most influential for growth. In reality, the financial sector performs more than these three functions: for example, the financial sector serves a critical role in the payments system and in risk transformation of assets. (For a broad description of the functions of financial systems, see Levine, 1997.)

11 See, for example, Aghion and Bolton (1997) and Gertner and Scharfstein (1991).

12 See, for example, Demirgüç-Kunt and Maksimović (1998), Filer, Campos and Hanousek (1999), Levine (1999), Levine *et al.* (2000), Rajan and Zingales (1998) and Wurgler (2000).

13 These variables were constructed and originally used by La Porta *et al.* (1997, 1998).

14 Empirical evidence from economies in transition suggests that a commitment to law and order may be a precondition for financial development. See Filer *et al.* (2000).

15 Variables that appear in cross-country regressions to be more correlated with growth than the structure of the financial system *per se* include laws protecting stockholders and creditors, accounting standards, and overall financial-system development. (See Beck, Demirgüç-Kunt and Levine, 2000, Levine, 2000, and Demirgüç-Kunt and Maksimović, 2000.)

16 As we point out in section 5, an increase in competition in product markets can also have ambiguous effects on growth.

17 Perhaps surprisingly, Barth *et al.* (2000) also find that restrictions on the range of bank activities, such as laws preventing banks from operating in real estate, insurance or securities markets, have no beneficial effect on financial-sector development and are even positively correlated with banking-sector instability.

18 The second channel is supported by micro-evidence (e.g., Welch, 1966).

19 Further, while increases in years of schooling at low levels of human capital in less-developed countries are likely to correspond to an actual increase in the amount of human capital, in developed economies additional human capital is often produced even if educational attainment grows only slowly (i.e. quality of education; e.g., use of computers). In fact, education policy in the more developed countries has recently turned attention towards pre-primary schooling, transition from school to work, and adult education. Indeed, Hanushek and Kimko (2000) recently show that human-capital quality is strongly related to growth.

20 However, Topel (1999) and Krueger and Lindahl (2000) recently find macro returns to schooling in line with those estimated in the Mincerian wage regressions.

21 One explanation for the puzzle could be differences in HC quality, but this only appears potentially important in the ECA region where cognitive skills test reveal low ability of workers to process and analyse information.

22 Schooling is also affected by the difference between private and state schools (Glomm and Ravikumar, 1992), decentralized and centralized school finance, or segregation of students with heterogeneous ability (Benabou, 1996).

23 E.g., Hassler and Mora (2000) focus on the interaction of intelligence (HC channel) and social mobility (allocation channel) in affecting growth. In their model, higher growth entails new technology adoption which makes intelligence more important (as opposed to social position of parents). As a result, growth makes intelligence better rewarded, which again feeds back into easier adoption of technology and more growth.

24 See, e.g., Djankov, La Porta, Lopez-de-Silanes and Shleifer (2000).

25 This may be particularly important given that self-employed and small firms appear to be the driving force of growth in ECA (see, e.g., Jurajda and Terrell, 2000; or World Bank, 2001).

26 Yet, there appears little applied theoretical work on the issue, unless we note that reallocation also means transfer of innovation and/or organizational practices across sectors. In the Schumpeterian models (e.g., Romer, 1990a, b) growth depends on the rate of innovation generated in the economy.

27 A related issue is entry into self-employment/entrepreneurship and the amount of red tape. The issue of firm closings and startups is taken up on p. 133.

28 Much Western research also suggests that the design of a country's unemployment system can have a major effect on the equilibrium level of unemployment (e.g., Mortenson and Pissarides, 1998a, 1998b). The issue of unemployment benefits disincentives and more generally welfare traps in developing countries is probably only relevant for the more successful ECA countries and we do not dwell upon it here due to space constraints.

29 Hence, to verify the effect of wage-setting policy wedges on human capital production in a country-specific context, one can relate measures of returns to education to HC investment.

30 Artificially high wages in the public sector represent another important growth-detrimental policy wedge, but this issue is discussed on pp. 145–7 on natural resources.

31 Another set of players are ethnic groups since market-clearing mechanisms, one of the components of market infrastructure, are affected by segmentation arising from ethnic or class identity of groups of workers/players.

32 E.g., in the MNA region. Supporting this observation, Forteza and Rama (2000) study the implications of labour-market rigidity for the success of economic reforms and conclude that the political dimension of rigidity is important, i.e. the size of organized labour and public employment.

33 This section draws heavily on the natural resource part of the ECA 'Markets and Growth' paper written by Thorvaldur Gylfason and on McMahon (1997), both of which include an extensive list of references.

34 Schumpeterian models of growth (as discussed in Aghion and Howitt, 1998) emphasize growth as occurring through product (or capital) improvements via innovation. New capital or products render old technology or products obsolete (creative destruction).

35 See Tendulkar and Sen (2001).

36 Djankov *et al.* (2000) collect data on the regulation of entry of start-up firms in 75 countries and find a correlation of entry restrictions with corruption.

37 Note that the assumption that financial markets adequately perform the function of eliminating unprofitable firms is crucial to these results. This implies that the efficiency of financial markets, together with firm managers' objectives, plays a role in determining the effects of increased product-market competition on innovation and growth.

38 Empirical studies that have reported a positive correlation between competition and productivity growth include Nickell (1996) and Blundell *et al.* (1995). See Ahn and Hemmings (2000) for a discussion of studies reporting a negative relationship between market regulation and growth.

39 Sachs and Warner define an economy to be open if all of the following conditions holds: (1) average tariffs less than 40 per cent; (2) quotas and licensing cover less than 40 per cent of imports; (3) the black-market premium is less than 20 per cent; (4) non-socialist economy; and (5) state does not have a monopoly in major exports.

40 We have little information on financial markets in the EAP and SAS regions, which motivate this scenario, and hence it is hard for us to evaluate the role of financial markets in this process.

41 Cross-country regressions show that the Sachs–Warner openness index is highly correlated with a regional dummy for East Asia; the countries of this region score high on this index relative to other developing countries. Yet, more country-specific investigation of performance along the individual dimensions of this index, together with description of the specifics of export-promotion policies, might provide a better idea of the potential relationship between openness and growth. For example, were there different implications for growth of the 'technology policy' pursued by South Korea from the policies adopted by other countries. The South Korean government directed funds to particular firms for technology adoption in return for export production quotas.

42 The discussion of ECA countries draws heavily on Filer *et al.* (2000).

43 Private sectors accounted for less than 10 per cent of total production in most ECA countries prior to the transition.

44 Successful macroeconomic policies also appear to correlate with growth increases.

45 Self-employment plays an important role in job-creation in ECA countries; job-creation in small newly-established private businesses appears to be the driving force of successful transition (see, e.g., Jurajda and Terrell, 2000).

46 For example, to prevent corruption, governments should allocate resources by market prices rather than by fiat.

47 Comparing EAP and MNA should prove useful in explaining the puzzle: as we noted in the discussion on 'Openness', high levels of human capital are often cited as contributing to the growth rates of East Asia. Contrary to the MNA region, it appears that human-capital acquisition may well have contributed positively to growth.

48 In Egypt the government alone employs more than one-half of university degrees holders in the economy.

49 An issue of debate relating to SSA performance has been the importance of openness relative to other market-related policies. See Collier and Gunning (1999) for an excellent discussion.

50 Our discussion of labour and financial markets draws liberally on Adenikinju and Oyeranti (1999).

51 For example, Adenikinju and Oyeranti (1999) report that bankruptcy procedures in Kenya are said to last from four to ten years.

52 Adenikinju and Oyeranti (1999) note that much of the capital flight involves money stolen from the government – another indication of the pervasiveness of corruption.

53 For example, in the 'openness' growth scenario, there are necessary conditions on the factor markets that support growth, but the sufficient stimulus is coming from product markets.

54 They can also consider the dependence of policy choice (in product and factor markets) on initial conditions.

References

Adenikinju, A. F. and O. Oyeranti (1999) 'Characteristics and Behaviour of African Factor Markets and Market Institutions and Their Consequences for Economic Growth', paper prepared for GDN global research project on 'Explaining Growth'.

Agenor, P.R. (1996) 'The Labour Market and Economic Adjustment', *International Monetary Fund Staff Papers*, vol. 43(2), pp. 261–335.

Aghion, P. and O. Blanchard (1994) 'On the Speed of Transition in Central Europe', NBER *Macroeconomics Annual*, pp. 283–320.

Aghion, P. and P. Bolton (1997) 'A Theory of Trickle-Down Growth and Development', *Review of Economic Studies*, vol. 64(2), pp. 151–72.

Aghion, P., M. Dewatripont and P. Rey (1999) 'Competition, Financial Discipline, and Growth', *Review of Economic Studies*, vol. 66, pp. 825–52.

Aghion, P. and P. Howitt (1998) *Endogenous Growth Theory* (Cambridge, MA: MIT Press).

Ahn, S. and P. Hemmings (2000) 'Policy Influences on Economic Growth in OECD Countries: An Evaluation of the Evidence', OECD Working Paper.

Atje, R. and B. Jovanovic (1993) 'Stock Markets and Development', *European Economic Review*, vol. 37, pp. 632–40.

Barth, J., G. Caprio and R. Levine (2000) 'Banking Systems Around the Globe: Do Regulation and Ownership Affect Performance and Stability?', World Bank Working Paper no. 2423.

Beck, T., A. Demirgüç-Kunt and R. Levine (2000) 'A New Database on the Structure and Development of the Financial Sector', World Bank Economic Review, vol. 14, pp. 597–605.

Beck, T., R. Levine and N. Loayza (2000) 'Finance and the Sources of Growth', *Journal of Financial Economics*, vol. 58, pp. 261–300.

Benabou, R. (1996) 'Heterogeneity, Stratification, and Growth: Macroeconomic Implications of Community Structure and School Finance', *American Economic Review*, vol. 86(3), pp. 584–609.

Bencivenga, V., B. Smith and R. Starr (1996) 'Equity Markets, Transaction Costs, and Capital Accumulation: An Illustration', *World Bank Economic Review*, vol.10, pp. 241–65.

Blank, R. M. (ed.) (1994) 'Social Protection versus Economic Flexibility: Is There a Trade-Off?', University of Chicago Press for the NBER.

Blundell, R., R. Griffiths and J. Van Reenen (1995) 'Dynamic Count Data Model of Technological Innovations', *Economic Journal*, vol. 105, pp. 333–44

Burgess, S.(1994) 'The Reallocation of Employment and the Role of Employment Protection Legislation.' London: London School of Economics, Centre for Economic Performance, Discussion Paper no. 193.

Caprio, G. and P. Honohan (1999) 'Restoring Banking, Stability: Beyond Supervised Capital Requirements', *Journal of Economic Perspectives*, vol. 13(4), pp. 43–64.

Card, D. (1999) 'The Causal Effect of Education on Earnings', in O. Ashenfelter and D. Card (eds), *Handbook of Labour Economics* (Amsterdam: North Holland).

Castanheira, M. and G. Roland (2000) 'The Optimal Speed of Transition: A General Equilibrium Analysis', *International Economic Review*, vol. 41(1), pp. 219–39.

Collier, P. and J.W. Gunning (1999) 'Explaining African Economic Performance', *Journal of Economic Literature*, vol. 37, pp. 64–111.

Collier, P. and A. Hoeffler (1998) 'On Economic Causes of Civil War', *Oxford Economic Papers*, vol. 50(4), pp. 563–73.

Demirgüç-Kunt, A. and E. Detragiache (1998) 'The Determinants of Banking Crises in Developing and Developed Countries', *International Monetary Fund Staff Papers*, vol. 45(1), pp. 81–109.

Demirgüç-Kunt, A. and V.Maksimović, (1998) 'Law, Finance, and Growth', *Journal of Finance*, vol. 53, pp. 2107–37.

Demirgüç-Kunt, A. and V. Maksimović (2000) 'Funding Growth in Bank-Based and Market-Based Financial Systems: Evidence from Firm-Level Data', World Bank Working Paper.

Dertouzos, J. and L. Karoly (1993) 'Employment Effects of Worker Protection: Evidence from the United States', in C. F. Büchtemann (ed.), *Employment Security and Labour Market Behavior: Interdisciplinary Approaches and International Evidence* (Ithaca, NY: Cornell University Press).

Diamond, D. (1984) 'Financial Intermediation and Delegated Monitoring', *Review of Economic Studies*, vol. 51(3), pp. 393–414.

Djankov, S., R. La Porta, F.Lopez-de-Silanes and A. Shleifer (2000) 'The Regulation of Entry', *Harvard Institute of Economic Research Paper* no. 1904.

Ersel, H. and M. Kandil (2000) 'Markets and Growth for MENA Countries: Financial Markets', paper prepared for the Global Research Project on 'Explaining Growth'.

Fershtman, C., KM. Murphy and Y. Weiss (1996) 'Social Status, Education, and Growth', *Journal of Political Economy*, vol. 104(1), pp. 108–32.

Filer, R., N. Campos and J. Hanousek (1999) 'Do Stock Markets Promote Economic Growth?', CERGE-EI Working Paper (Prague: CERGE-EI).

Filer, R., T. Gylfason, S. Jurajda and J. Mitchell (2000) 'Markets and Growth in the Post-Communist World', paper prepared for the World Bank Global Research Project.

Forteza, A. and M. Rama (2000) 'Labour Market "Rigidity" and the Success of Economic Reforms Across More Than One Hundred Countries', mimeo, Development Research Group, World Bank.

Freeman, R. B. (2000) 'The US Economic Model at Y2K: Lodestar for Advanced Capitalism?', *Canadian Public Policy*, vol. 26, pp. S187–200.

Gelb, A. and associates (1988) *'Oil Windfalls: Blessing or Curse?'*, Oxford University Press and the World Bank.

Gertner, R. and D. Scharfstein (1991) 'A Theory of Workouts and the Effects of Reorganization Law', *Journal of Finance*, vol. 46(4), pp. 1189–222.

Glomm, G. and B. Ravikumar (1992) 'Public versus Private Investment in Human Capital: Endogenous Growth and Income Inequality', *Journal of Political Economy*, vol. 100(4), pp. 818–34.

Goldsmith, R. (1969) 'Financial Structure and Development', New Haven, CT, Yale University Press.

Greenwood, J. and B. Jovanovic (1990) 'Financial Development, Growth, and the Distribution of Income', *Journal of Political Economy*, vol. 98(5), pp. 1076–107.

Griliches, Z. (1997) 'Education, Human Capital, and Growth: A Personal Perspective', *Journal of Labor Economics*, vol. 15(1), pp. S330–S334.

Hall, R. and C. I. Jones (1999) 'Why Do Some Countries Produce So Much More Output Per Worker Than Others?', *Quarterly Journal of Economics*, vol. 114(1), pp. 83–116.

Hanushek E.A. and D.D. Kimko (2000) 'Schooling, Labor-Force Quality, and the Growth of Nations', *American Economic Review*, vol. 90(5), pp. 1184–208.

Harris, R. (1997) 'Stock Markets and Development: A Re-assessment', *European Economic Review*, vol. 41, pp.139–46.

Harrison, P., O. Sussman and J. Zeira (1999) 'Finance and Growth: Theory and New Evidence', mimeo, London Business School.

Hart, O. (1983) 'The Market Mechanism as an Incentive Scheme', *Bell Journal of Economics*, vol. 14, pp. 366–82.

Hassler, J. and J. Mora (2000) 'Intelligence, Social Mobility, and Growth', *American Economic Review*, vol. 90(4), pp. 888–908.

Heckman, J. and C. Pagés-Serra (2000) 'The Cost of Job Security Regulation: Evidence from Latin American Labor Markets', *Economia*, vol. 1(1), pp. 109–54.

Jurajda, S. and K. Terrell (2000) 'Optimal Speed of Transition: Micro Evidence from the Czech Republic', William Davidson Institute Working Paper no. 355.

King, R.G. and R. Levine (1993) 'Finance, Entrepreneurship, and Growth: Theory and Evidence', *Journal of Monetary Economics*, vol. 32, pp. 513–42.

Krueger, A. and M. Lindahl (2000) 'Education for Growth in Sweden and the World', *Swedish Economic Policy Review*, vol. 6(2), pp. 289–339.

La Porta, R., F. Lopez-de-Silanes, A. Shleifer and R. W. Vishny (1997) 'Legal Determinants of External Finance', *Journal of Finance*, vol. 52, pp. 1131–50.

La Porta, R., F. Lopez-de-Silanes, A. Shleifer and R. W. Vishny (1998) 'Law and Finance', *Journal of Poitical. Economy*, vol. 106, pp. 1113–55.

Levine, R. (1997) 'Financial Development and Economic Growth: Views and Agenda', *Journal of Economic Literature*, vol. 35, pp.688–726.

Levine, R. (1999) 'Law, Finance, and Economic Growth', *Journal of Financial Intermediation*, vol. 8, pp. 8–35.

Levine, R. (2000) 'Bank-based or Market-based Financial Systems: Which Is Better', mimeo, University of Minnesota.

Levine, R., N. Loayza and T. Beck (2000) 'Financial Intermediation and Growth: Causality and Consequences', *Journal of Monetary Economics*, vol. 46, pp. 31–77.

Levine, R. and S. Zervos (1996) 'Stock Market Development and Long-Run Growth', *World Bank Economic Review*, vol. 10, pp. 323–39.

Levine, R. and S. Zervos (1998) 'Stock Markets, Banks, and Economic Growth', *American Economic Review*, vol. 88, pp. 537–58.

McMahon, G. (1997) 'The Natural Resource Curse: Myth or Reality', World Bank, mimeo.

Michie, J. and J. Grieve-Smith (1997) *Employment and Economic Performance: Jobs, Inflation and Growth*, (Oxford: Oxford University Press).

Mortenson, D. and C. Pissarides (1998a) 'Job Reallocation, Employment Fluctuations, and Unemployment Differences', in M. Woodford and J. Taylor (eds) *Handbook of Macroeconomics* (Amsterdam: North Holland).

Mortenson, D. and C. Pissarides (1998b) 'New Developments in Models of Search in the Labor Market', in O. Ashenfelter and D. Card (eds), *Handbook of Labor Economics*, vol. 3 (Amsterdam: North Holland).

Ndulu, B. and S. A. O'Connell (1999) 'Governance and Growth in Sub-Saharan Africa', *Journal of Economic Perspectives,* vol. 13(3), pp. 41–66.

Ndulu, B. and S. A. O'Connell (2000) 'Background Information on Economic Growth', Paper prepared for the AERC Explaining African Economic Growth Project, April.

Nelson, R. and E. Phelps (1966) 'Investment in Humans and Technological Diffusions', *American Economic Review*, vol. 61(2), pp. 69–75.

Nickell, S. (1996) 'Competition and Corporate Performance', *Journal of Poitical Economy*, vol. 104, pp. 724–66.

OECD (1994) 'The OECD Jobs Study: Evidence and Explanations, Part II: The Adjustment Potential of the Labour Market'. Paris: Organization for Economic Cooperation and Development.

Pissarides, C. (2000) 'Labor Markets and Economic Growth in the MENA Region', paper prepared for GDN global research project on 'Explaining Growth'.

Pritchett, L. (2000) 'Understanding Patterns of Economic Growth: Searching for Hills among Plateaus, Mountains, and Plains', *World Bank Economic Review*, vol. 14(2), pp. 221–50.

Rajan, R. and L. Zingales (1998) 'Financial Dependence and Growth', *American Economic Review*, vol. 88(3), pp. 559–86.

Reynolds, L.C. (1985) *Economic Growth in the Third World: 1950–1980* (Yale University Press, New Haven).

Rivera-Batiz, L. A. and P. M. Romer (1991) 'Economic Integration and Endogenous Growth', *Quarterly Journal of Economics*, vol. 106, pp. 531–55.

Rodríguez, F. and D. Rodrik (1999) 'Trade Policy and Economic Growth: A Skeptic's Guide to the Cross-National Evidence', mimeo, Harvard University.

Rodrik, D. (1994) 'Getting Interventions Right: How South Korea and Taiwan Grew Rich', National Bureau of Economic Research Working Paper: 4964, p. 46.

Romer, P. M. (1990a) 'Are Nonconvexities Important for Understanding Growth?', *American Economic Review*, vol. 80, pp. 97–103.

Romer, P. M. (1990b) 'Endogenous Technological Change', *Journal of Political Economy*, vol. 98(4), 571–102.

Sachs, F. and A. Warner (1995) 'Economic Reform and the Process of Global Integration', *Brookings Papers on Economic Activity*, no. 1, pp. 1–18.

Sachs, J.D and A. M. Warner (1995) 'Natural Resource Abundance and Economic Growth', NBER Working Paper no. 5398.

Scharfstein, D. (1988) 'Product Market Competition and Managerial Slack', *Rand Journal of Economics*, vol. 14, pp. 147–55.

Tabellini, G. and F. Daveri (1997) 'Unemployment, Growth and Taxation in Industrial Countries', Centre for Economic Policy Research, Discussion Paper no. 1681.

Tendulkar, S. D. and B. Sen (2000) 'Markets and Economic Growth in South Asia, 1950–97: An Interpretation', paper prepared for GDN global research project on 'Explaining Growth'.

Topel, R. (1999) 'Labor Markets and Economic Growth', in O. Ashenfelter and D. Card. (eds), *Handbook of Labor Economics*, vol. 3 (Amsterdam: North Holland).

Welch, F. (1966) 'Education in Production', *Journal of Political Economy*, vol. 78, pp. 35–59.

World Bank (2001) *Transition–The First Ten Years: Analysis and Lessons for Eastern Europe and the Former Soviet Union*, Washington, D.C., World Bank.

Wurgler, J. (2000) 'Financial Markets and the Allocation of Capital', *Journal of Financial Economics*, vol. 58, pp. 187–214.

5

The Political Economy of Growth: Lessons Learned and Challenges Ahead

Micael Castanheira and Hadi Salehi Esfahani

1 Introduction

This chapter examines the lessons of recent research on the political economy of growth in light of regional survey papers commissioned by the Global Research Project on Growth.[1] We develop a relatively general framework that encompasses a variety of issues highlighted in those papers based on regional experiences. We then review the existing evidence and assess the hypotheses put forward in those papers. In the last section, we present conclusions and offer suggestions for further research on critical issues in the political economy of growth that are not yet well-understood. The purpose of this exercise is to assess current findings and identify the theoretical and empirical work needed at the country and cross-country levels in order for the political economy of growth analysis to provide a deeper perspective on the process of growth.

The political-economy literature studies the role of collective action processes (interest-group activity, policy-making institutions, and the like) in resource allocation and rent distribution. The part of that literature that is concerned with economic growth examines the impact of such processes on the incentives of economic agents to invest and to improve productivity in the long run. That is, the key political-economy question from a growth perspective is how much of an economy's potential surplus (that is, rents and quasi-rents or the value produced in excess of the recurrent costs of production) is realized and guided towards growth-enhancing activities. While political economy in general concerns surplus distribution, from a growth standpoint, distribution matters only to the extent that it affects the surplus available for investment in productivity-enhancing factors.

In this survey we analyse several reasons why the resources mobilized for economic growth vary across political systems. Among others we shall highlight how interest-group interactions and public policies depend on the ability of a country's institutions (that is, rules that structure interactions in the society and assign roles) to facilitate information flow, coordination and commitment among diverse interest groups in the society. We identify a host of factors that render some political systems less efficient than others in regulating collective action, and we also argue that inefficiencies caused by institutional weaknesses tend to persist over time because reforming institutions itself requires effectiveness in collective action. In section 2 we briefly review the theoretical issues concerning the growth consequences of political institutions; in section 3 we examine these issues in light of country and regional experiences around the world, and in section 4 we present our conclusions.

2   Theories of the political economy of growth

Overview of existing theories

To keep things simple, we identify three groups of agents that influence policy-making in different manners: *the public* (or the population at large who act as *voters* when there are elections or other opportunities to show public approval or disapproval of policies or policy-makers), *interest groups* (organized groups that influence policy decisions on a systematic basis but do not control it directly), and *political elites* (or, for short, *politicians*: elected or self-proclaimed policy-makers, administrators and political parties).[2] Politicians are interested in expanding their control over the government apparatus, which requires public and/or interest-group support. Each member of the public and each *interest group* wants to maximize its net benefits from the economy, and can offer its support to politicians in exchange for receiving the benefits induced by policy. This implies that in choosing economic policies, politicians are largely motivated by the relative ability of interest groups and various segments of voters to support them. Struggles to capture a larger share of the economic surplus can arise both *within* and *across* interest groups and voter segments, and the eventual allocation is determined by the rules of the political game.

The interactions described above can be quite complex and the 'rules of the game' may themselves be subject to change as a result of political activity. These problems have prevented the current literature from developing a comprehensive theoretical framework for political-economy analysis. In the literature, we can distinguish at least three different approaches to explain economic policy; these strands will certainly evolve and converge into a more unified view in the future, but the literature is not there yet. In this survey, we shall try to combine these approaches and exploit their relative strengths.

One approach to the political economy of public policy is to focus on the interactions among *voters*. Different voters have different preferences over policy outcomes; politicians propose a variety of policy platforms and the one supported by a majority of the electorate is implemented (Hotelling, 1929; Downs, 1957; Black, 1958). This view of the policy-making process in a democratic setting can be combined with different models of economic growth to explain the links between voter diversity and the growth orientation of public policies. Indeed, this has been the dominant approach in the literature on the role of inequality in the growth process, with the typical result that the median voter's interest in redistribution in unequal societies tends to discourage investment and productivity.[3] The difficulty with this approach is that its applicability is essentially limited to single-issue votes. Once more than one issue is on the agenda, those voting models may fail to have a stable equilibrium and may require additional institutional specification for full determination (Shepsle, 1979).

An alternative approach is to focus on the role of *interest groups*. In this view, interest groups influence policy-making beyond their roles as voters. They do so by offering block political support or financial contributions to the politicians' favourite causes, or by delivering bribes and personal favours. The politicians' decision is then based on a weighted average of the preferences of different interest groups and voters (Olson, 1965, 1982; Becker, 1983; Baron, 1994, among others). The weights of those groups can also be endogenized and explained by their relative cohesiveness at the election stage (Lindbeck and Weibull, 1987), their level of organization (Olson, 1982), and by their institutional or relational advantages. Adverse growth effects in such models arise when lobbies fail to coordinate and induce inefficient policy mixes (Grossman and Helpman, 1994) or when rents are dissipated in the lobbying process (Krueger, 1974). However, when interest-group activity is considered in tandem with electoral competition, the inefficiency result loses its strength because the public may be able to neutralize the effects of lobbying by voting for politicians with offsetting policy preferences (Besley and Coate, 2001).[4]

The third approach to political economy modeling is to concentrate on the struggle between the *public* and the *ruling politicians*, who tend to abuse their power to divert resources towards their private interests. Here, the main issue is the role of institutional arrangements that allow the public to constrain the ruling politicians. One obvious application of this approach is the analysis of the role of democracy versus autocracy in the process of economic growth. For example, McGuire and Olson (1996) compare the policy outcomes generated by such systems and argue that autocrats who have long-term horizons in office and expect to reap the benefits of investment tend to enhance growth, though generally not as much as ruling majorities in democracies, especially majorities with more encompassing interests. McGuire and Olson's (1996) analysis is interesting and simple, but abstracts from the endogeneity of time horizons in autocracies and from agency problems in representative democracies. In order to explain political outcomes, one needs to analyse more detailed games played between politicians, the public and interest groups. In dictatorships, autocrats may be concerned about the rise of opposition to their regimes and may deliberately prevent investment in 'developmental goods' such as education and infrastructure that facilitate the rise of an organized and effective opposition (Robinson, 1997; Bourguignon and Verdier, 2000). Interestingly, having access to abundant natural resources and better control over government policy may induce autocrats to be even more anti-development. In democracies, there are possibilities that permit incumbent politicians to divert some rents away from the public, even though it hurts the country's growth prospects and the public has a chance to vote them out of office (Persson, Roland and Tabellini, 1997, 1998). In these situations, institutional factors such as separation of powers and the degree of proportionality in the representation system play important roles.

As this brief overview of the literature suggests, despite the diversity of approaches and apparent contradictions in results, we already have a fairly good understanding of the tensions among and between the players in political economy games, and hence how and why policy outcomes can differ among countries and regions. Furthermore, the review shows that there is a unique force behind all these actions and interactions: gaining control over larger rents.[5] This force leads to inefficient outcomes and low growth when the institutional context does not enable them to overcome agency problems and coordination failures. The approach that we follow here is based on these premises. All agents are interested in gaining greater access to rents and, in choosing their strategies, take account of the costs and benefits of possible ways to extract and distribute rents. The rules that govern their interactions may induce them to overlook the externalities that they impose on each other and may thus prevent opportunities for long-run growth from being grasped. We develop this theme in the rest of this section.

Rent generation and appropriation

To simplify our exposition of the problems posed by rent appropriation, we start with a simple model analysed by McGuire and Olson (1996), where an autocrat who faces no risk of losing power chooses a tax rate to fund public goods and to allocate part of the nation's income to himself. The tax is distortionary and the public good contributes to production. Expressed formally, the autocrat's problem is:

$$\max_{\tau,G} \tau \cdot Y(\tau, G) - G \tag{1}$$

where Y is the economy's output, τ is the tax rate, G is the supply of public goods (measured in output units), and $\tau Y(\tau,G) - G$ is the rent extracted by the autocrat. The first-order conditions of this problem are:

$$-\tau Y_\tau = Y \qquad \text{and} \qquad \tau Y_G = 1 \tag{2}$$

As taxes are distortionary, we have $\partial Y/\partial \tau < 0$, and because G is productive, we have $\partial Y/\partial G > 0$. It is also reasonable to assume that $\partial^2 Y/\partial \tau^2 < 0$ and $\partial^2 Y/\partial G^2 < 0$. Then, if $\partial^2 Y/(\partial \tau \partial G)$ is sufficiently small, problem (1) will have a solution, which we assume to be the case. Conditions (2) show that, at the margin, the autocrat equates *his* gain from an increase in public good provision, τY_G, with the marginal cost of the public good, 1. In addition, he equates *his* marginal benefit from a percentage point increase in the tax rate, Y, with his share of the consequent deadweight loss, $-\tau Y_\tau$. As a result, when deadweight losses rise quickly with the tax rate – that is, when the elasticity of income with respect to tax is larger at each tax rate – the autocrat will find it optimal to leave a larger share of the surplus to the public.[6] Similarly, when the marginal productivity of public goods is higher, the autocrat increases spending, and total surplus increases.

The solution to (2), τ_A and G_A, can be contrasted with τ^* and G^* that maximize aggregate welfare, $Y - G$, subject to $G = \tau Y(\tau,G)$. First, note that welfare maximization and the allocation of all tax revenues towards public goods obtains only in a consensual democracy. Second, observe that t^* and G^* solve:

$$G = \tau Y(\tau,G) \qquad \text{and} \qquad (-Y_\tau /Y)(\tau Y_G - 1) = \tau Y_\tau /Y + 1 \tag{3}$$

It can be shown that $\tau_A > \tau^*$ and $G_A < G^*$. That is, in his attempt to max-imize extracted rents, the autocrat will choose an inefficiently high tax rate and a sub-optimal level of public goods provision. However, the supply of public goods will still be positive and some surplus, $(1 - \tau_A)Y$, will be left in the hands of the public. Interestingly, if the autocrat has opportunities to impose lump-sum taxes, he can extract more rent with less deadweight loss and, therefore, will have a stronger incentive to spend on public goods. This can raise output, but reduces the surplus captured by the public and, thus, lowers their welfare.

It is important to note that the same economic elements determine both τ_A and G_A on the one hand, and τ^* and G^* on the other hand. Namely, and as equations (2) and (3) show, the responsiveness of income, Y, with respect to τ and G is a key factor in determining tax and public goods supply in both autocracies and democracies. The key difference between the outcome of an autocracy and that of a democ-racy, is that in the latter rents are not diverted by the autocrat. Instead, they are entirely spent on public goods, so that no additional dead-weight loss is imposed on the economy for redistribution purposes. That is, economic forces are not the sole determinant to potential income and growth; political and redistributive forces also play impor-tant roles. This also implies that when democracies use part of their public resources for redistribution, their behaviour becomes more similar to the autocrat's, especially when the groups that win the contest over policy choices have narrow interests. However, as McGuire and Olson (1996) show in the context of this simple model, as long as the interests of the winning coalition are sufficiently encom-passing, policy choices become more similar to those of the consensual democracy. We will discuss the role of redistribution concerns in more detail below.

There are several ways one can modify the above model in order to capture the variety of outcomes that are observed in actual situations. First, when there is a time lag between expenditure on public services and its impact on output, policies become sensitive to the time horizon of the autocrat or of the winning coalition in democracies. The higher the expected turnover rate of the policy-makers, the greater will be the policy bias towards the short run and away from long-run concerns, which means more rent extraction/diversion and slower growth.

Secondly, when there is a multiplicity of economic activities with different rent-extraction costs, an autocrat or a ruling coalition with narrow interests will have an incentive to invest public resources more in sectors where it is easier to extract rents and capture the returns at the expense of other sectors where rent extraction is more difficult. This effect is likely to be harmful to growth because sectors with greater growth potentials often have more elastic supplies and respond more strongly to taxation. For instance, take a country that is abundant in natural resources (say, land) which can be taxed easily. While natural resources bring some wealth to the country, enhancing growth calls for policies that help develop some type of industry with more value-added and growth potential (say, electronics). However, the development of the latter typically requires financial and intangible assets (skills, technological and managerial know-how, marketing connections, and so forth) that have opportunities in other countries. For this reason, those resources are much more responsive (that is, elastic) to tax rates and to the availability of physical and institutional infrastructure. Moreover, the development of that industry would induce workers to move out of the traditional sector, thereby diminishing the amount of extractable rents. Quite intuitively, under these circumstances, the autocrat or the narrow winning coalition has an incentive to focus on the exploitation of natural resources and refrain from spending government resources on the development of more productive activities.[7]

Thirdly, the ruling coalition or individual may avoid growth-enhancing public expenditures and policies that diminish their power *vis-à-vis* other groups and the public. An example that springs to mind is that of education. A common view is that education has significant positive externalities and contributes to long-run growth. However, education may also increase political awareness and thus reduce the relative political power of an already wealthy and educated minority. Bourguignon and Verdier (2000) analyse this issue and show why such a minority may have strong incentives to restrict education (and hence economic growth) in order to prevent increased redistribution. Clearly, such perverted incentives may also apply to other types of developmental goods (for example, infrastructure) that are essential for productivity growth, but may provide the poor with the means to organize and become politically influential (Robinson, 1997). However, it should be kept in mind that other effects may complicate the picture or even work in the opposite direction. For example, extensive poverty may create a risk of upheaval against the system (Roemer, 1985; Perotti, 1996b; Alesina and Perotti, 1996). If that effect is strong, then the rich may actually want to *promote* education at least in some segments of the population to appease the poor or divide them into groups with opposing interests (divide-and-rule tactics). Sharing power with a middle class created in this way may have some costs, but the costs may be even higher if the poor were to take control of policy levers.[8] As this illustrates, there is no clearly dominant strategy for the ruling minority, but the result remains that in order to maintain their grip over power they must manipulate the distribution of rents and generally limit growth below its optimal level.

The above discussion suggests that several aspects of both *available* and *potential* rents must be taken into account to understand the policy choices in autocracies and democracies. In particular, the *size* of different rent sources, their respective *deadweight losses* of rent extraction, and their responsiveness to the provision of public goods all greatly matter. Also, the characteristics of the *groups* that benefit from each of the rent sources are important in the choice of policies. When there is a congruence of interests between the autocrat or the ruling coalition and the population at large – that is, when the population is most in need of an expansion in the sector where rents are large and have a low elasticity with respect to taxation – the autocrat or the ruling coalition will 'naturally' promote relatively good policies. If instead the needs of the population potentially hurt the autocrat or the ruling coalition (or the groups that the autocrat needs to please), then it is more likely that the adopted policy will not promote growth.

While there are differences across countries with respect to the structure of resources and socio-economic groups that cause variations in policy efficiency and growth performance, differences in the 'rules of the game' governing the interactions among politicians, interest groups and the public also have a major role. We turn to this issue in the following sub-section.

Rents and institutions

Paying attention to the role of institutions is important for at least two reasons. First, there is a great deal of evidence that institutions play a significant part in economic performance. Secondly, institutions are subject to change through collective action and, if their functions are well-understood, reform movements can make better-informed choices and become more successful. In other words, institutions comprise an area in which bringing about change may be practical and productive in terms of growth enhancement. However, this endogeneity feature also makes it hard to study institutions and arrive at definitive results. Some rules of social and political engagement seem to be less enduring than others, and there it is easier to study the conditions under which they change. But, the more consequential institutions are often the ones that change less frequently and, as a result, make it difficult to uncover the particular constellations of factors that lead to their transformation. Studying institutions has been further complicated by the fact that they are difficult to specify and measure. Nevertheless, the crucial role of institutions on economic performance has stimulated both empirical and theoretical research, which has blossomed in recent years.

On the empirical side, the most common type of variables used to explain growth are measures showing the 'outcomes' of the functioning of institutions such as the degree of corruption, the 'rule of law', political instability (revolutions, civil wars), the perceived level of commitment of the state ('can you trust the government's promises?'), and so on. These variables have proven to be highly correlated with growth, confirming that research on institutions is likely to be very fruitful. Accordingly, the results have encouraged researchers to go beyond the role of such *outcome* measures and examine the detailed institutional ingredients that *determine* the rule of law, political instability, and the like. In this endeavour, there is also the promise that some of the identified ingredients may be subject to reform and offer opportunities for improving growth potential in poor countries. For example, recent research has tried to discern the impact of various aspects of representation systems, separation of powers, budget procedures and so forth on economic and institutional performance (for example, Svensson, 1997; Tanzi, 1998; La Porta *et al.*, 1999; Persson and Tabellini, 2000; Persson, Tabellini and Trebbi, 2001; Treisman, 2000; von Hagen and Harden, 1994, 1995).

By way of creating a framework that allows one to put the studies of the innumerable institutional aspects into perspective, we identify three key functions of institutions that contribute to economic performance – namely, the effectiveness in *representation, commitment* and *coordination*. Effectiveness in *representation* refers to the capability of the public to align the incentives of policy-makers with its broad interests. Much of the work using the third approach to political economy modeling discussed above, especially research on the role of limitations on political competition, electoral systems and separation of powers focuses on this aspect of institutions. In a series of papers, Persson, Roland and Tabellini have explored the tradeoffs of presidential versus parliamentary systems and majoritarian versus proportional representation (see Persson and Tabellini, 2000, for a survey). They show that in countries with parliamentary regimes and proportional electoral rules, government expenditure tends to be efficient but politicians are allowed to extract too much in rents. Majoritarian electoral rules and presidential systems instead stiffen competition among politicians, which curbs their rents but induces a suboptimal allocation of public goods. These tradeoffs imply that parliamentary and proportional-representation systems may be conducive to increased growth in countries with a greater shortage of public goods, whereas presidential-majoritarian systems perform better in countries where political agency problems are more serious.[9]

Commitment is the second institutional function essential for supporting efficient policies. It consists of any cost that policy-makers must bear if they decide to reverse an adopted policy. The presence of such costs is crucial for economic growth because otherwise the ruling politicians will have a time-inconsistency problem, which could discourage investment. The reason is that most investments become sunk once they are in place, so their quasi-rents can be easily taxed without much economic consequence in the short run. This creates an incentive for the politicians to renege on *ex ante* promises that they make to encourage investment and to redistribute the returns to investment *ex post*. Of course, the possibility of reneging has obvious adverse effects: if investors know that their quasi-rents are likely to be redistributed, they may not invest in the first place. We should, therefore, expect to observe suboptimally low growth in countries where the government cannot commit to follow its announced policies. The importance of this issue in infrastructure development has become quite obvious (Levy and Spiller, 1996). The role of the time-inconsistency problem in macroeconomic performance has also been long-recognized. Kydland and Prescott (1977), Rogoff (1985) and Chari and Kehoe (1999), among others, show that unless there are mechanisms that ensure fiscal and monetary discipline, the interest group or even public demands for expenditure may give rise to expectations of high public debt and high inflation, which will make it difficult for the policy-makers to maintain macroeconomic stability. The significance of commitment in many other policy areas is also quite visible. For example, export expansion is known to involve some sunk costs for becoming established in international markets (Roberts and Tybout, 1995). Thus, export-promotion policies cannot be successful without a minimum level of commitment to such policies that minimizes the probability that the government will reverse its policies and implicitly or explicitly tax exporters in favour of other agents in the economy. Reneging on policies can be made costly by imbedding them in laws, constitutional clauses or contracts that are difficult to change. Obviously, the stability of the political system, strength and independence of the judiciary, and the rule of law in general are important ingredients that can enhance a government's ability to commit.

Finally, *coordination* is another crucial institutional feature needed for minimizing resource waste. Distributive struggles typically create a 'tragedy of the commons' problem where the parties involved tend to overexploit the source of rents over which they compete or overuse their own resource to secure a larger share (Persson and Svensson, 1989; Aghion and Bolton, 1990; Alesina and Tabellini, 1990; Chari and Cole, 1993). For example, when government budgets are made in parliaments where the lawmakers can independently and freely propose amendments, total expenditure and the deficit tend to be inefficiently large (von Hagen, 1992; Alesina and Perotti, 1995; Velasco, 1999). The reason is that in such a situation the cost of an additional dollar spent on the favourite project of each policy-maker is shared by the population at large and, as a result, is not fully internalized. Similar problems can exist in trade-policy formation and many other public policies. To avoid such commons problems, policy-makers must be able to coordinate their actions and some institutional settings are more conducive to coordination than are others. For example, in some countries coordination over some policies is achieved through *ex ante* rules (for example, constitutional clauses, enduring laws, or cultural values), *ex ante* agreements, or long-term plans that constrain the actions of political players and rule out some uncooperative behaviours (for example, 'golden' and balanced budget rules in the fiscal policy area, constant money growth rules or currency-board arrangements in the monetary policy area, and free-trade agreements in the trade policy area).[10] Alternatively, decision powers over some features of policy can be delegated to specific politicians or institutions that have broader interests in the system than individual decision-makers (von Hagen and Harden, 1994, 1995; Alesina and Perotti, 1995, 1999). This is the idea behind assigning the monetary policy to an independent central bank and giving the finance minister or the chief executive an upper hand in setting budget aggregates.

While we have discussed the three main institutional functions – *representation*, *coordination*, and *commitment* – separately, it should be clear that these functions are likely to be interrelated and interacting within each institutional system. In particular, to have effective representation and coordination, an institutional setup should have reasonable commitment capability. Better representation and coordination may also help a system reach commitment more easily. However, there may be tradeoffs between representation and coordination. For example, more democratic conditions and arrangements help larger segments of the population to be represented, yet this may make the task of coordination more difficult and reduce the quality of policy outcomes. While many studies abstract from the coordination problem to make the analysis focused and manageable (for example, Persson, Roland and Tabellini's work on separation of powers), this approach is not always feasible. For example, the extensive and rapidly growing literature on decentralization shows that the trade-offs between representation, coordination and commitment are difficult to ignore when analysing the pros and cons of power devolution in each situation (Bardhan and Mookherjee, 2000). It is becoming increasingly evident that we need to better understand the tradeoffs and complementarities between those main three functions, and the role of administrative capability in allowing countries to achieve those functions ought to be further studied as well (see Rauch and Evans, 2000).

The above discussion shows that several important results have emerged in the literature on institutions and growth. We have come to know the key institutional functions that are essential for growth, and we have learned about some institutional mechanisms that render those functions in certain settings. However, we still know very little about the role of the wide variety of institutions that exist around the world. We also know very little about how a particular mechanism interacts with other elements in a system of institutions, and hence how 'good' institutions can be transposed from country to country. This is important because most economic reforms focus on modifying a limited range of institutional mechanisms and try to adapt those changes to the rest of the system that remains unchanged. Such endeavours have sometimes succeeded in improving economic performance, but have failed in other situations. Institutional structures and the interactions among their elements are extremely complex and we are still far from a general understanding of what works and what does not in each particular setting. This has made the adoption of new institutions based on theoretical designs or on the experience of other countries very difficult and risky.[11] However, past research on the political economy of growth has shown that there can be enormous rewards from reforming institutions to enhance investment incentives. This message should encourage intensive research on how institutions can be reformed to help improve economic performance.

Reforming rent-allocation mechanisms

As institutions are crucial to explain growth, it is important to understand how institutional deficiencies can be corrected. History tells us that institutions evolve – but why and when? Could knowledge of the process help shift the direction of change towards mechanisms that are more effective in raising economic efficiency? Though systematic studies of the process of institutional change are rare, our previous analysis of the role of voters, interest groups and politicians suggests possible perspectives. While some changes such as cultural developments are largely spontaneous, some other changes (especially those in political and economic institutions) can arise through prior plans and interactions of identifiable actors. The latter changes can be viewed as policy reforms that require much more challenging collective action. Therefore, a country may fail to improve its institutions if it already lacks basic mechanisms for aligning the interests of key political actors with economic growth and for ensuring effective *representation, coordination* and *commitment*. Instead, countries initially benefiting from some basic mechanisms of this kind can initiate reforms more easily and ultimately develop institutional systems that are able to continually improve and adapt to changes in economic and social conditions. This perspective may explain the vast diversity of outcomes that we observe today.

Over the past decade, a number of studies have formally modelled the *status quo bias* effects – that is, the mechanisms that prevent the adoption of Pareto-efficient policy changes (changes that increases *ex ante aggregate welfare*). Two prominent views are those of Alesina and Drazen (1991) and Fernandez and Rodrik (1991). The first one offers an explanation based on *coordination* failure. Alesina and Drazen (1991) argue that when interest groups do not know each other's costs and benefits from reform, they may engage in a holdup (or a 'war of attrition') and reforms are delayed while each group tries to assess how much costs the other groups are willing to bear through policy adjustment. Fernandez and Rodrik (1991), on the other hand, suggest that the status quo bias may be due to the presence of known minority winners from reform that leaves the majority of the population pessimistic about their potential gains and turns them against the new policies. In this case, the reform may become acceptable if the winners commit to pass on part of their gains to others. So, in this case, *commitment* deficiencies can be identified as the source of the problem.[12]

While the models of status quo bias show that institutional deficiencies may prevent the polity from implementing reforms whose efficiency gains exceed their costs, they can also be turned on their heads and interpreted as theories of reform. From this perspective, these models imply that reform may come about when institutions change in ways that help coordination and commitment or when the efficiency gains from policy change exceed the costs by a sufficiently large margin. Rodrik (1994) has employed the latter effect to analyse macroeconomic and trade policy reforms. He argues that trade policy reforms are often more difficult because, compared to macro reforms, their efficiency gains are small relative to the costs of the large redistributions needed to ensure political support. This also implies that reforms may become more likely during a crisis, that is when the cost of maintaining the status quo increases (Drazen and Grilli, 1993).

Another implication of the above perspective on reform is that the existing division of surplus and institutional capabilities determine the *types* of reforms that are feasible in the country. In particular, different countries facing the same scope for reforms may experience strikingly different successes because of their differences in their institutional characteristics or the initial distribution of surplus. A further implication is that the packaging of reforms may also be crucial for its success. For example, Rodrik (1994) suggests that the reason why macroeconomic reforms are sometimes combined with trade reform is that the package may make the latter more palatable. Dewatripont and Roland (1992a, 1992b, 1995, 1996) and Dehejia (1997), among others, point to a different direction; they argue that in some situations it may be better to split the overall reform into steps that individually benefit a majority of the population. In that case, each increment may become acceptable, possibly with the help a different majority, and the whole reform may eventually go through in a chain of policy changes. Of course, such a gradualist approach slows down the pace of reforms and delays its fruition.[13]

3   Applications and empirical evidence

The theoretical overview of section 2 suggests that several elements determine whether political interactions inside the country lead to fast or slow growth. We identified three groups of agents (the public, the lobbies, and the politicians) and three broad elements that influence their incentives and interactions (namely, the sources of rents, the heterogeneity of interests across socio-economic groups, and the institutional structure within which they interact). These elements have been repeatedly stressed in the literature as well as in the regional survey papers to explain actual policy and growth outcomes. In this section, we review the existing evidence regarding these factors. Of course, as may be seen, regional and national peculiarities make different elements of the political economy framework more salient in different countries.

In our presentation of evidence, we distinguish between two components of economic growth that are driven by different forces. One component is long-term growth, which is determined by factors that persist over time and shape the opportunities and constraints for the economy to continue expanding over many decades. Some institutions, resources and geographic conditions are examples of such factors. The other component is transitory growth that is caused by factors and circumstances that do not persist. For example, a country experiencing a shock that destroys parts of its physical capital stock may experience a drop in income and find that, given its other assets, the returns to rebuilding the stock are quite high. This may induce an excess investment effort and lead to high rates of growth for a while. But, as the capital stock is rebuilt over time, growth is likely to taper off towards its long-run component. Similarly, a country facing credit constraints in international markets and experiencing an unusually favourable terms of trade may have extra resources to invest and grow faster for a while, but when the terms of trade return to their normal level, the higher growth will not be sustainable. Because of its temporary nature, transitory growth is often viewed as less important than long-term growth. However, empirical growth studies indicate that transitions may take a few decades, and therefore it is important to consider both components. Below, we first focus on long-run growth, and in the next sub-section we review the empirical evidence concerning the role of institutions, endowments, geography and external factors. Following that, we analyse the effects of initial conditions in the transition process, and use the framework developed above to examine specific government interventions as policy links between country characteristics and growth performance. The final sub-section deals with the determinants of policy and institutional change which can allow a country to move to higher long-term growth paths.

Political-economy determinants of long-run growth: institutions, resources and external factors

The role of institutions

As North (1990) observes, succeeding in piracy takes as much skill and knowledge as good performance in manufacturing. The incentives of individuals to develop their skills in piracy or in manufacturing hinges on the relative payoffs of the two activities, which in turn decisively depend on the institutional framework of the economy. This connection has been confirmed in growth regressions, but comes through vividly in all regional survey papers.

The statistical relationship between growth and some institutional capability measures – such as the rule of law and political stability – is quite robust (see, among many others, Barro, 1991; Barro and Sala-í-Martin, 1995; Keefer and Knack, 1995; Rodrik, 1999). In fact, these were found to be among the few variables that could be systematically related to GDP growth in the regional growth-accounting studies carried out as part of the GRP project (Perry, 2000). However, these measures mainly reflect the extent of commitment capability, while the role of coordination and representation aspects of institutions have not been examined to the same extent in the empirical literature. A number of studies have found indicators of democracy to have ambiguous effects in growth regressions (Barro, 1997), and the reason seems to be that while those indicators are intended to measure representation, they are also associated with increased coordination problems. This is because reaching agreements in democratic polities tends to be more difficult than in autocracies. This effect has been ignored in many empirical studies and the role of democracy has been examined without controlling for coordination problems. Interestingly, Collier (1998) and Esfahani and Ramírez (2001), who interact democracy measures with indices of ethno-linguistic heterogeneity and in this way control for some coordination problems, find that democracy tends to raise long-term incomes, especially through mitigating the adverse effects of heterogeneity. The regional survey papers offer additional evidence and concrete examples in support of this view.

The institutional failures that underlie stagnation in Africa have been widely documented. As Bates and Devarajan (2000) observe, political parties in Africa are typically based on regions and ethnic groups, which are themselves quite heterogeneous. The parties that come to control the government face little constraint redistributing the economy's rents towards their own supporters. Groups outside the government also use whatever means at their disposal to push the ruling parties out of power and replace them with their own parties. This gives rise to short horizons for the politicians and eventual political instability. The consequence is that governments in most African countries are hardly representative of broad segments of the population, have little ability to commit, and rarely achieve coordination. All this breeds policies that can hardly be conducive to long-term growth.

Interestingly, when such countries manage to bring about broader representation, coordination and commitment also improve and long-term growth rates rise (Collier, 1998).

Other regions also have their own share of ethnic disparity and political instability, though probably not as much as Africa. Kelegama and Parikh (2000) stress how ethnic conflicts and the lack of representativeness of governments led to vicious, growth-depleting circles in South Asia. After independence, some minorities in those countries gained access to power and (ab)used their position to maintain their grip over power. In turn, the gap between the ruling class and the population broadened and internal tensions and divisions intensified, leading to even more adverse policies. Countries that are abundant in natural resources used their wealth to delay needed reforms, and industrial policies were mainly oriented towards protecting existing industries from foreign competition. Rodríguez (2000) tells a similar story about Latin American countries, with colonist–native divisions being the starting point. Though the countries in that region gained independence at the about same time as the United States (and with similar levels of development), their subsequent growth has been noticeably slower. Here again, institutional failures, strong internal inequalities (both in terms of assets and education), and uneven access to power fuelled internal tensions and prevented development.

By contrast, Krongkaew (2000) stresses the positive role of institutional arrangements and of the limited internal divisions in East Asian countries in shaping their successes. Most of the countries in that region managed to contain ethnic conflict and reduce income inequalities (mainly through land reforms) early on. This prepared the ground for implementing the right combination of incentives and institutions that rendered those countries 'investor-friendly'. As an example, one can contrast Malaysia with Nigeria, both of which are former British colonies, have major ethnic divisions, and are well-endowed with natural resources. In Malaysia, the political parties representing the three main ethnic groups (Malays, Chinese and Indians) formed an Alliance before independence under the leadership of the Malay-based party, UMNO, to campaign for an end to colonial rule. After independence tensions among the poorer Malays who were the majority of the population, and the more prosperous Chinese and Indian minorities who dominated business, grew.[14] But, the Alliance and the parliamentary system that it established served as an effective mechanism for representation, coordination and commitment. To quell tensions, the parties in the Alliance created an explicit distributive system and granted the Malay majority a set of economic privileges. In effect, the rich minorities agreed to share part of its surplus with the poorer majority in exchange for economic and political security. The result was that all parties involved found a stake in increased output and supported growth-enhancing policies (Campos and Root, 1996). In Nigeria, on the other hand, the three major ethnic groups had not formed institutions that could help them coordinate and be represented. As a result, a party representing mainly one group came to dominate after independence and, before long, other groups resorted to violence and coups to claim power. The result has been predatory policies and falling standards of living despite enormous oil resources.

In the Middle East and North Africa (MENA), ethnic tensions within countries have typically played a less-prominent role. Still, the lack of institutional constraints on the use of arbitrary power by the ruling politicians has restricted representation and commitment capability in many countries of the region (Esfahani, 2000a). Abundance of resource rents in the region has exacerbated these problems because it gave the elite an easy control over large funds that could be distributed to some parts of the population without any need to be extracted from other parts. To varying degrees, the ruling elite in each country has appropriated parts of such funds and has used some other parts for controlling markets and buying political support in various ways. The remaining funds have been applied to investment, but the productivity of such investments remained relatively low since they have mostly helped expand inefficient public enterprises. Inadequate commitment has largely deterred the private sector from contributing to economic growth and lack of representation has made many public enterprises sources of rent for narrow interest groups. These effects have been stronger in some countries such as Algeria and less significant in some others, especially the small states of the Persian Gulf where traditional rulers remain more representative of the citizen population.

For transition economies, the key issue has been institution-building in ways that would allow countries to implement successful reforms and align the preferences of the government with those of the public (Castanheira and Popov, 2000). At the time when the transition began, some countries (especially Central European ones) already had better institutional infrastructure than others and managed to quickly develop minimum capabilities to ensure coordination and commitment. Predictably, most Central European countries experienced milder and shorter transformational recessions than Eastern European countries, and certainly fared far better than the Central Asian republics of the former Soviet Union. These sharp differences usually appear in regressions as a 'distance from Brussels' effect, and many Central European economists now attribute it to differences in the populations' prior exposure to Western-like institutions, which are more hospitable to a market economy.

The above sketchy account focuses mainly on the overall role of institutions. Since institutions structure interactions and incentives within the economy, their role is visible when the effects of other factors are examined. Below, in our discussion on exogenous factors and policy outcomes, we see more specific examples of how institutions matter in the process of growth.

The role of natural resources

Abstracting from political-economy problems, natural resources should be a blessing for any country. Discovering additional resources on the territory should increase revenues (static gain), relieve the foreign-exchange constraint, ease borrowing, and provide funds for increased spending on public goods. Therefore, one should also expect natural resources to increase the growth potential of the country. Surprisingly, natural resources are empirically associated with *slower* growth (Sachs and Warner, 1995).

One thus has to question how such a blessing can be turned into a curse. We can identify three factors. First, the well-known 'Dutch disease' tells us that natural resources may have a negative externality on the other sectors of the economy, mainly through an increase in the real exchange rate. However, there are reasons to believe that such a problem is not as salient as it may seem (see Jurajda and Mitchell, chapter 4 in this volume, for a discussion). Second, if most value-added is concentrated in one single sector, the country as a whole might become more exposed to price fluctuations. Here again, one should doubt that this problem is at the roots of slower growth: the availability of those resources should enable the country to create a diversified portfolio of assets (through cross-holdings for instance) that *reduces* aggregate risk. The third (and main) suspect is that political-economy factors prevent the country from obtaining the benefits of increased natural resources.

In contrast to the other factors, there are strong reasons to believe that political-economy factors consistently and strongly depress economic growth in the presence of abundant natural resources. As discussed earlier (p. 162), ruling politicians have an incentive to focus their attention on sectors in which rents are large and inelastic to taxation, which is precisely the case of natural resources. When such rents are concentrated in the hands of a minority, the incentive becomes particularly strong to bias policy against the development of factors that bring about growth in other sectors. Moreover again, as discussed earlier (pp. 166–70), institutional deficiencies (whether it is lack of representation, commitment or coordination) play crucial roles in preventing the implementation of efficient, growth-enhancing policies.

These conjectures are largely confirmed by the observed pattern of growth across regions. At one extreme, most high-performance East Asian countries have few natural resources; a fact that seems to have induced their governments to encourage surplus generation through growth-enhancing policies, especially educational development and export promotion. Many of these countries (for example Korea, Taiwan, Singapore) are good examples of 'naturally-aligned' preferences between the government and the population. Of course, other characteristics helped such developments. Still, the absence of natural resources is a notable characteristic of these countries. At the other extreme, one finds countries that are extremely well-endowed in natural resources, but suffer from low and stagnant incomes – for example Republic of Congo, Nigeria, and Yemen (all endowed with oil and gas) and Zaire (now Democratic Republic of Congo) and Sierra Leone (both endowed with minerals). The poverty of these countries despite their riches has a close link to their institutional deficiencies because discovery of large natural resources in countries with strong institutions (such as Norway and the United Kingdom) does not seem to have had any negative effect on growth. The point can also be seen in the comparison of Malaysia and Nigeria, discussed above. Both countries are major oil exporters and share other characteristics such as being former British colonies and having major ethnic divisions. Still, Malaysia has long had much stronger judicial and political institutions and has performed far better than Nigeria in terms of using its oil revenues and developing its non-oil sectors.

Exogenous uncertainty

Some countries are exposed to external and natural shocks much more than others, and high uncertainty in such exogenous conditions is often viewed as an adverse influence on long-run growth. The issue here is not the effect of adverse natural conditions on factor productivity, which we examined above; instead, the question is whether the variability of conditions matters and, in the context of the political economy of growth, how institutions (especially fiscal and capital- and insurance-market institutions) interact with those shocks. With appropriate institutions, shocks should not be a major impediment to growth: market and fiscal failures, as well as the weakness of political incentives to address those problems, are the main reason why such shocks may slow down growth in the long run.

In developing countries, policy-makers often blame their economic problems on terms-of-trade fluctuations in international markets, which are beyond their control; but this claim is not as obvious as it may sound. In fact, some countries – most notably Kuwait – have solved major terms-of-trade problems by creating portfolios of international assets that insure them against external shocks. Thus, the real question is why some countries cannot save part of their additional income during booms to create stabilization funds. Interestingly, the problem is not limited to exporters of raw materials and agricultural products. Indeed, government expenditure in most developing-countries is strongly pro-cyclical (IADB, 1998). During expansion periods, when the country's creditworthiness rises, developing-country governments tend to borrow and spend as much as they can, saddling the country with huge short-term debts and serious liquidity constraints during downturns when it is in greatest need of borrowing or drawing on its assets to smooth out consumption and investment. This pattern has also fuelled inflation throughout the business cycle due to overly expansionary public expenditure during booms and the need for monetization of inevitable budget deficits during busts. The consequence has been unnecessary macroeconomic instability.

Clearly, mitigating the adverse effects of exogenous uncertainty requires policies with a long-term horizon. The government needs to plan for downturns and adverse shocks by restraining expenditure and setting aside resources during upturns and favourable shocks, which calls for strong coordination and commitment capabilities. When a country lacks the institutions that provide such capabilities, internal or external shocks can become quite costly. For instance, if political turnover is high, politicians will have a stronger tendency to capture as much resources as they can while in office, regardless of the long-term consequences for the economy. Economic volatility reinforces this tendency because in this situation the main determinant of borrowing becomes the creditors' willingness to extend credit, which will be necessarily short-term and pro-cyclical. When the economy experiences a favourable shock, the creditors perceive some chance of recouping loans to the country in the short run and credit and expenditure booms. On the other hand, when an adverse shock hits, the prospect of loan repayment dims, and all sources of credit dry up. This seems to be the sad story of many politically unstable countries such as Nigeria (Bates and Devarajan, 2000). In contrast, countries with secure political leadership, such as Kuwait, seem to have pursued much more long-term policies (Esfahani, 2000a). Statistical work by Haggard and Kaufman (1992) also indicates that developing countries with authoritarian governments tend to be economically less stable when regime changes are more frequent. Put differently, in authoritarian regimes, the political horizon is limited to the autocrat's own horizon, which prevents long-run goals from being followed.

However, the problem of pro-cyclical public expenditure and foreign borrowing is not limited to countries with insecure leaders with free hands to shift resources toward narrow interests. Even if representation is strong, the same pattern may arise in the absence of effective institutional mechanisms that help various interest groups reach coordination (Tornell and Lane, 1999; Perotti, 1996b). This phenomenon again creates incentives for creditors to be forthcoming with short-term loans when shocks are favourable, and to withhold credit when adverse shocks hit. Stein, Talvi and Grisanti (1998) provide empirical support for this idea in the correlation they find between the degree of proportionality of the electoral system and the pro-cyclicality of public expenditures in Latin America.[15] Haggard and Kaufman (1992) also find a positive correlation between macroeconomic instability and party fragmentation or other indicators of conflict among social forces. Lack of ability to commitment can also exacerbate the effects of coordination failures. When a country cannot manage to commit itself to a long-run course of action, it becomes difficult to arrange *long-term* loans and smooth out consumption and investment. Rodrik's (1999) empirical study supports this view. He finds that an economy's capacity to react to external shocks is particularly deficient when there is a coincidence of social conflict and poor institutions (such as weak rule of law) that impedes commitment.

Some of the regional surveys touch on these issues and offer further evidence. Kelegama and Parikh (2000) offer a detailed description of how South Asian governments responded to adverse external shocks such as the oil price hike of the 1970s by moving to protect various interest groups through subsidies and market controls. This created growing obligations for the government that came at the cost of long-term investment and greater vulnerability to future shocks. Krongkaew (2000), on the other hand, presents a contrasting picture of the situation in East Asian countries, where policy-makers could coordinate and commit effectively. In that region, governments came up with long-term solutions to terms-of-trade shocks, including creative policies to restructure the economy toward industries that could deal with the shocks more effectively. The situations in other regions with weaker institutions resembled more the ones that prevailed in South Asia. While uncertainty is of major concern for households and firms in Africa (Collier and Gunning, 2000), unstable and narrowly-based governments of the region are hardly concerned about long-term policies that can address the problem (Bates and Devarajan, 2000). In the case of Latin America, Rodríguez (2000) observes how institutional weaknesses stifled the ability of the governments to deal with the external shocks of 1970s and 1980s, and led to long-term stagnation in the region. Finally, Esfahani (2000a) compares the ability of MENA countries to cope with their terms-of-trade fluctuations and suggests that those with less political stability suffered most from the problem.

To summarize, the view that exogenous shocks are harmful to growth is consistent with empirical evidence. However, the effect is conditional on a lack of those institutional capabilities that allow interest groups to coordinate themselves or commit to a long-term course of action. The adverse effects of shocks are also strong when there are deficiencies in the representation system and the ruling politicians have short time horizons. In the absence of such institutional weaknesses, shocks can be weathered out at little cost through insurance, timely borrowing and stabilization funds.

Transitory growth and the role of initial conditions

Initial conditions – the history of a country and the existing endowment and distribution of factors of production at each point in time – weigh a lot on the subsequent growth path, at least for some time. Growth regressions invariably confirm that there is an 'error-correction' process that takes economies towards their long-run growth paths when there are deviations from the path due to shocks and shifts in the underlying conditions. Transitions often take decades and their lengths depend on the institutional and economic characteristics of the country (Esfahani and Ramírez, 2001). To review the evidence regarding such effects, in this sub-section we focus on three major factors: human capital, physical capital, and initial inequality in income and asset ownership. In our discussion of these factors, we also point out the role of institutions and other persistent factors in the transition process.

Initial human capital

Unlike natural resources, high initial endowments of human capital are viewed as a positive force for growth. In fact, this is part of the explanation for the rapid growth of Germany and Japan after the Second World War (Becker, Murphy and Tamura, 1990), the success of the 'Asian Tigers' (Krongkaew, 2000), or the strong potential of transition countries (Castanheira and Popov, 2000). At the other extreme, low initial endowments of human capital are seen as part of the factors responsible for the growth failure of African and South Asian countries (Bates and Devarajan, 2000; Kelegama and Parikh, 2000).

The cross-section growth regressions also confirm the positive influence of initial education levels on growth (for example, Barro and Sala-í-Martin, 1995; Easterly and Levine, 1997). However, surprisingly, concurrent expansion of schooling does not seem to show much significance in typical growth regressions (see Pritchett, 1999, and other studies cited there). This is also clear from cursory observations across regions. For example, as Table 5.1 shows, there is no obvious connection between regional growth rates and average school enrolment rates over the past two decades. Most obviously, Eastern Europe and Central Asia has had among the highest education rates and the lowest growth rate (see also Campos and Coricelli, 2000). Latin America has also generated many years of schooling with little output growth to show for it (see also Rodríguez, 2000).

Pritchett (1999) suggests that the latter result could be due to the enormous heterogeneity in the *returns* to education among countries. In many developing countries, poor quality of schooling, wrong economic incentives and adverse institutional conditions have caused all the education to go to waste. Misspecification of the lag structure and

Table 5.1   School enrolment rates and economic growth, averages for 1980–99(%)

	Primary	Secondary	Tertiary	Per capita GDP growth
Sub-Saharan Africa	78.59	22.64	2.09	–0.91
South Asia	89.86	38.86	5.54	3.42
Middle East & N. Africa	94.18	54.23	12.22	0.08
E. Europe & Central Asia	100.64	85.12	33.73	–1.87
Latin Am. & Caribbean	106.61	48.69	15.47	0.34
East Asia & Pacific	117.16	49.72	6.20	5.98
High-income OECD	102.70	96.20	46.86	2.02

inadequate instrumenting for education growth may also be additional reasons for the finding. This might in fact be part of the explanation because the initial level of education seems to matter. In other words, there appears to be a long-run relationship between education and income levels, with the short-run interactions between the two being very noisy. Indeed, this is what Esfahani and Ramírez (2001), who specify the growth equation as an error-correction process, observe. Their results show that higher levels of schooling are associated with higher levels of steady-state per capita income, which implies that a higher initial level of education tends to raise the target towards which the economy is moving and induces a higher transitory growth for a few decades. They also find that this effect is stronger when the country enjoys better institutions. Duflo's (2000) analysis of Indonesia's educational system offers a concrete example of the way such an effect may come about. She shows that a massive expansion of education in Indonesia had limited benefits, in part because the country failed to coordinate policies and ensure that sufficient increases in the supply of *physical* capital would accompany the adjustment in the supply of *human* capital.

The positive long-run association between education and long-term growth might be due to a variety of factors. The most basic view is that education generates human capital, which in turn raises workers' productivity. The endogenous growth literature typically points to possible economic externality effects of education (Lucas, 1988). Schooling may also affect the relative value of different rents. Human capital indeed offers a growing source for direct taxes without large deadweight losses (Pechman, 1985; Dao and Esfahani, 1995). Consequently, when a larger stock of human capital exists, the government has access to a less costly source of public funds, can spend more on public goods, and is less tempted to abuse policy levers.[16] However, education may also significantly affect the political balance inside a country and may help explain other, complementary, effects. First, better-educated people typically participate more in elections (see, for example, Leighley and Nagler, 1992) and other areas of politics, which contributes to improving the representation function of the government. These effects together tend, among other things, to constrain the government to maintain higher levels of education. At the other extreme, for low initial levels of human capital, governments may have little incentive to expand the educational programmes, hence perpetuating the status quo (see section 2). Another consideration is that the initial level of education may positively interact with other institutions and socio-economic factors. In particular, institution-building requires education and, in turn, the ability of the government to increase the quantity and quality of schooling depends on the effectiveness of institutions. As a result, this interaction may give rise to a virtuous circle under favourable initial conditions, and to a poverty trap when the initial conditions are adverse. Such interactions have been recognized in the literature but remain largely unexplored, especially in empirical terms.

To conclude, there are many reasons why the initial level of education matters for the long-run level of income and transitory growth. Evidence from regression analysis and observations across countries and regions also confirm this view. However, empirical observations also show that the benefits of education are not automatic. Specifically, the contribution of initial educational levels to growth hinges upon good institutions.

Initial physical capital

The idea of transitory growth and error correction (or *convergence*) has been examined more extensively in the literature in the context of capital formation. As the neo-classical models of economic growth show, decreasing returns to capital imply that countries initially poorly endowed should accumulate more capital and grow quicker than better-endowed countries (see, for example, Aghion and Howitt 1998, ch. 1). Therefore, initial deviations from the steady state should fade out over time.[17] Using initial capital stock per capita (often substituted by initial GDP per capita, for which better data are available) in growth regressions typically yields significant negative coefficients and confirms this implication of growth theory, which is known as β-convergence. The literature has not attempted to explain this effect through any alternative hypothesis.

Another issue that remains largely unexplored is the role of capital with obsolete technologies. A great deal of difficulties in transition countries stems from the fact that most of the existing equipment and skills are badly outdated and must be replaced (Castanheira and Roland, 2000). However, adjustment costs are high and interest groups controlling such assets or possessing such skills fiercely resist structural change (Castanheira and Popov, 2000). This problem is not limited to transition countries. In most of the developing world, industries created behind protective walls resist liberalization and shifts toward comparative advantage (Bates and Devarajan, 2000; Esfahani, 2000a; Kelegama and Parikh, 2000; Rodríguez, 2000). By contrast, most high-performance economies of East Asia managed to develop fast-growing, export-oriented industries at an early stage and created a countervailing force against protectionist temptations (Krongkaew, 2000). Though the resistance to restructuring is well-documented, the conditions under which it tends to be a bigger burden on policy reform and overall economic growth remains understudied.

Initial inequality

The discussion in section 2 suggests that essentially two types of inequality can affect the political economy of growth: economic disparity (in terms of asset ownership and income) and unequal access to political power. These two dimensions often overlap, but they are separate and each has a different impact on policy-making.[18] The literature on inequality and growth generally assumes that wealth and political power go together and shows that high inequality is detrimental to developmental policies (especially education) and impedes growth (for example Bourguignon and Verdier, 2000). While this coincidence of wealth and political power is not uncommon, there are also many cases where, in economically unequal societies, the representatives of the poor or the middle class have managed to take control of political power and to coexist with a separate economic elite, at least for some years. This may happen as a result of a coup (as in Egypt in 1952 and in Korea, 1961), following the defeat of a colonial power (as in Zimbabwe in 1979), or through a democratic process (as in Chile in 1970 and Portugal in 1975). Such situations do not seem to have unique outcomes in terms of interactions among political and economic elites; rather, there appear to be many different equilibria and growth paths. We will review all such cases and offer a taxonomy of possible outcomes based on empirical evidence.

Before we start, it is worth noting that early growth models such as that of Kaldor suggested a positive link between inequality and growth. The argument in those models is based on the observed correlation between income and savings across households, which implies that concentrating income should increase total saving and, therefore, investment. This argument, of course, ignores the complexities in the saving–income relationship that may nullify the effect (Schmidt-Hebbel and Serven, 2000). The political-economy models have tended to generate the opposite effect, though they do not agree about the actual mechanisms at work. Median voter models depict the connection as the consequence of redistributive taxes imposed on the rich by the poorer majority, which discourages capital accumulation and efforts at enhancing productivity. The interest-group models suggest that the effect may be due to efforts by the wealthy ruling groups to avoid redistributions that help the poor enhance their human capital formation. Such redistributions are often needed for growth because the poor face insurance and capital-market problems that keep their education low and fertility high. More generally, as the marginal productivity of wealth held by the poor may be higher than that held by the rich, income concentration may reduce productivity (Benabou, 1996). Extensions of these models further imply that inequality may breed political instability, which is harmful to growth. More recently, Banerjee and Duflo (2000) have argued that other effects may make the relationship between initial inequality and growth more complex. By turning to panel data, they distinguish the effect of initial inequality from that of *changes* in inequality (that is, changes in the redistribution scheme). As they show, such changes prove to hinder economic growth, regardless of whether it generates redistribution from the rich to the poor or vice versa. Put differently, it seems that reforming redistribution schemes in itself bears a growth cost. Under that assumption, a rise in inequality that increases distributional conflicts may reduce growth, but the opposite can also happen if the costs of conflicts are low and even relatively equal interest groups engage in them too frequently.

The empirical evidence on the impact of initial inequality on growth is as mixed as the theories at hand. A host of cross-country studies have found a negative relationship, while some other studies reached different conclusions depending on the choice of measures, the sample used and the specification of the regressions. Figini (1998) surveys this literature, runs further cross-country regressions, and explores more detailed, structural transmission mechanisms from inequality to growth. His results confirm that the linkages between inequality and growth are not monotonic and do not pertain to only one channel. More recent studies that use new data sets, new techniques, and new specifications also collectively confirm this result (see, for example, Forbes, 2000; Barro, 1999; Banerjee and Duflo, 2000).

The contribution of Figini (1998) is that he examines the interactions of institutions with the effects of inequality and shows that they are quite important. For example, he finds that in the presence of capital market imperfections, the relationships between inequality, redistribution, and growth become non-linear, following the predictions of Benabou (1996). Another interesting finding is that the negative relationship between inequality and growth disappears if one runs the regressions on the sample of democratic countries alone (see also Barro, 1999). This is an interesting result because it suggests that when inequality occurs in a democratic society, the demands for redistribution may reduce the welfare of the upper class, but the *form* of public expenditure helps maintain the growth potential of the country. By contrast, in non-democratic societies, redistribution pressures from the poor and efforts by the rich to resist and reverse them end up wasting growth opportunities. The result can also be related to the point made by Collier (1998) concerning the interaction between democracy and ethnic heterogeneity mentioned above. One can view income inequality as another form of heterogeneity that can be made less costly under democratic conflict-resolution mechanisms. Esfahani and Ramírez (2001) test this hypothesis and find support for it.

The regional survey papers examine these issues and offer richer anecdotal or historical evidence. In particular, Rodríguez (2000) presents extensive evidence that, historically in most of Latin America, considerable economic and political powers were concentrated in the same hands.[19] He argues that this fact was a major determinant of development policies and a significant cause of political and economic instability in the region. Krongkaew (2000) offers similar evidence for the case of the Philippines. However, in most other countries, the story is somewhat more complex. While the absolute majority of developing countries have had high power concentration (especially in the form of autocratic regimes), wealth distribution has varied and fortunes have not always been in the hands of the groups represented by the ruling elite. In situations where political power and wealth have been concentrated, but in different hands, four broad patterns appear to have emerged. In some, such as Indonesia under Suharto, the ruling political elite used policy levers to take over or share economic resources and turn the system into one of joint concentration of economic and political power. As in the case of many Latin American countries, these systems experienced growth for a while, followed by major instability due to the lopsided nature of the policies they pursued (Rodríguez, 2000). However, some countries following this pattern, such as Nigeria and Zaire, did not even experience the temporary growth. The second pattern is that of Malaysia after 1970, where the ruling politicians managed to strike deals with groups holding significant economic power so that their incentives to help develop the country remained strong while the fruits of growth were shared (Krongkaew, 2000; Campos and Root, 1996). Korea in the 1960s and 1970s may be viewed in line with the same pattern. However, the land reforms of the 1950s had made income distribution much more equal in that country. This feature brought Korea closer to the third pattern, which was initial redistribution of land by the political elite, followed by capitalist incentives for the growth of new industries, as in Taiwan and, more recently, in China.[20] The final pattern is one of massive expropriation of assets and establishment of public enterprises to run the economy through direct political control. As the reviews by Bates and Devarajan (2000) and Esfahani (2000a) indicate, this pattern has been much more prevalent in Africa and the MENA countries (for example Egypt, Algeria, Iran after the Islamic Revolution, Ghana, Senegal, Myanmar, Zambia and, most recently, Zimbabwe). In this group, inequality initially diminishes, but growth could not be sustained and eventually inequalities returned while low growth continued at least for some time. Eastern European countries under communism were also examples of such regimes *par excellence* (Castanheira and Popov, 2000).

It should be emphasized that the above categorization of country experiences with inequality is based on a broad reading of the thematic regional surveys and has not been explored in depth in the literature. Much more extensive and intensive work is needed to produce a deeper understanding of how economic and political inequality interact and why redistribution works in some countries and not in others.

Given these ambiguities, it is clear that recommending redistributive policies, especially massive asset redistributions, as a blanket cure for any perceived detrimental effect of inequality is unwarranted. Evidence from regional surveys suggests that populist policies of heavily taxing the rich to subsidize the consumption of the poor only tend to aggravate instability, as in Latin America (Rodríguez, 2000). Asset redistribution such as land reform seems to have worked for Korea and Taiwan, but in many other countries it has brought about little prosperity or has been outright disastrous, especially when the government has ended up as the *de facto* owner.[21] In many cases, even though the ownership of the distributed land or asset remains private, for a variety of reasons landlords and entrepreneurs are replaced by heavy-handed bureaucrats who have even less incentive to care about poor farmers' needs or about investment and productivity (Binswanger and Deininger, 1997; Esfahani, 2000a). Even when the landlords and entrepreneurs are allowed to remain engaged under certain conditions, their reactions to evade loss of ownership and rent often introduces a different set of distortions with adverse impact on growth (de Janvry and Sadoulet, 1989; Waterbury, 1993).

If reduced inequality in a country seems helpful for growth and is desirable for its own sake but massive redistribution does not work well, is there any way that income distribution could be changed for the better? To address such a problem, more successful countries seem to have focused on policies such as improving access to education and infrastructure that not only reduce inequality but also boost growth. Since in a political-economy setting such policies are endogenous, one may naturally wonder if they are feasible under adverse initial conditions with high inequality. This is a well-placed concern, but it should be kept in mind that inequality and other initial conditions are not the only determinants of government policy. Policy-makers always have some room for manoeuvre, which they may use more effectively if there is a more knowledge about what works and what does not. There are also external players that can influence the outcome.

Government policies: actions and interventions

Our review of the empirical findings has until now focused on very broad and general aspects of government policies and state institutions. However, when it comes to analysing the problems of economic policy in a given country, one faces a host of different interventions and concrete analyses of specific policies are required. What explains the use of inefficient government interventions that are costly in terms of growth? Can the political-economy framework developed above shed light on why governments intervene in inefficient forms? These questions are our concerns in this sub-section. We first examine the balance between state and markets in running the economy, and then analyse the patterns of interventions in financial, product and labour markets.

The determinants of the balance between state and markets

There is a vast theoretical and empirical literature showing that private firms perform more efficiently than their public counterparts (see Megginson and Netter, 2000, for a recent survey). Regional surveys of political economy of growth confirm this finding and invariably refer to substantial inefficiencies and resource waste in public enterprises (PEs). Nevertheless, PEs exist in all countries and, indeed, many developing countries maintain sizable PE sectors.[22] Given the demonstrated costs of PEs in terms of productivity and growth, why do many governments continue to maintain direct control over enterprises? Why are some governments so much keener to keep and expand PEs than other governments?

One often-cited motive behind establishing a large public sector is the ideological orientation of the government. There has certainly been an association between nationalist/socialist rhetoric and government takeover of enterprises and extensive control of markets (Esfahani, 2000a; Kelegama and Parikh, 2000; Krongkaew, 2000). However, in most such cases, the policy has persisted long after ideological dispositions have shifted (as in Egypt and Iran during the past couple of decades). In addition, not all governments that promoted the public sector showed anti-market orientation (for example Turkey in the 1930s and Taiwan in the 1950s). In any event, ideology may have played a role in the creation of PE sectors in some countries, but other motives must also be at work.

Political economy factors provide the complementary, if not more prominent, motives behind government control of firms. Bates and Devarajan (2000), Kelegama and Parikh (2000) and Krongkaew (2000) provide detailed accounts of how governments in Africa and Asia have used PEs to help certain regions or interest groups receive investment, jobs and other benefits. For example, as Krongkaew (2000) puts it, in South East Asian countries such as Malaysia, 'one could see widespread establishment of state enterprises in the postwar periods as an attempt by the government to counter the economic influence of the Western companies and the Chinese minorities' and eventually help increase 'Malay participation in the ownership and control of the corporate wealth in the country'. Once these enterprises were established, their employees, customers and suppliers gained vested interest in maintaining them as sources of rent and economic security. Interestingly, in some cases, the political leaders seem to have extended public ownership not so much in response to interest-group demands than for the purpose of creating an interest group that would serve as their base of support (see, for example, Waterbury's, 1983, account of expropriations and nationalizations in Egypt in the late 1950s and early 1960s).

While the above political-economy arguments explain the motives behind government interventions, they are not sufficient for explaining the form of intervention. Public ownership is a very costly form of intervention and may be particularly detrimental to growth of productivity and output. So, the question still remains as to why this form is used and why it is more prevalent in some countries than in others. The answer that has emerged from the recent literature on public ownership points to contracting problems. For example, Hart, Shleifer and Vishny (1997) and Rajan and Zingales (1998) show that incomplete contracting between the government and the firms supplying goods and services to it may lead to public ownership if there are possibilities of holdup or the quality of the product cannot be specified *ex ante*. This idea can also be extended to the contracting problems that the government may face when it wants to provide services to firms – for example, when the government wants to fill in for the failure of private markets to offer insurance and credit services due to agency problems. In other words, the government may be better off vertically integrating with the suppliers of some of the products it purchases and the recipients of some of its services. Since institutional capabilities vary across countries, the extent of public ownership also varies, albeit inversely.

Another major contracting problem is deficiency in commitment capability on the part of the government, which can discourage private investment and force politicians to resort to PEs as a means of reaching their policy goals (Levy and Spiller, 1996). Esfahani (2000b) stresses that a higher marginal cost of public funds may make commitment more difficult and exacerbate the problem. This is important because other institutional factors such as coordination problems may increase the demand for (or reduce the supply of) public funds, hence creating incentives for the politicians to extract more rents from firms through direct controls. Hou and Robinson (2000) test these hypotheses and find them consistent with country panel data. Further evidence can be found in Knack and Keefer (1995) and La Porta *et al.* (1999).

To conclude, examination of political-economy factors is essential for understanding government interventions in markets. However, to explain PEs as the preferred mode of intervention, one must take account of institutional factors, particularly commitment, coordination and administrative capabilities.

Financial-market interventions

Some financial-market regulations are useful policies that help mitigate imperfections in information and contracting. But, many pervasive credit-market interventions – such as interest rate ceilings and directed credit programmes that target industries or even individual firms – do not have obvious efficiency-enhancing effects. In fact, such interventions often act only as instruments of redistribution. The low elasticity of savings with respect to interest rates may indeed render parts of the resources in the financial markets an easy target for redistribution. This can explain the omnipresence of interest rate controls in developing countries where, at the margin, taxation is generally very costly.

As such, interventions on the supply side of the financial markets may not be particularly costly to growth. Even on the demand side they need not be costly if the interventions help address credit-market inefficiencies. In fact, as Krongkaew (2000) points out, financial-market interventions in East Asia may have helped accelerate growth. Allocation of funds as part of a conscious and coordinated plan to bring about social peace and stability, as in Malaysia under the New Economic Policy drawn in the early 1970s, can also be seen as a positive force that can help growth. However, the more recent experience of East Asian countries also demonstrates that such arrangements cannot work forever and eventually give rise to misallocations and abuses that can be very costly to the economy. In many other countries, the costs of misallocation have overshadowed the benefits from the start. When institutions are weak (in terms of representation, coordination and commitment), the specific uses to which the government puts the rents extracted from depositors depend not so much on market correction needs than on the nature of the interest groups that are in a position to borrow the funds (Bates and Devarajan, 2000). For example, in contrast to Malaysia where direct credit allocations have at least partially contributed to social stability and economic growth, interventions in Nigerian banks have mainly led to massive embezzlement of funds, capital flight, and economic decline (Ayittey, 1995).

Product-market interventions

As in capital markets, some state interventions in product markets can be welfare-enhancing by targeting potential market imperfections (such as standardization and quality controls). However, as in capital markets again, there are hosts of interventions that essentially target redistribution and introduce heavy distortions (like monopolization and price controls), which prevent or hinder long-run investment and factor reallocation (Parente and Prescott, 2000). The political-economy rationales for such interventions also follow the same lines: in the absence of efficient institutions, firms and workers can be protected through trade or market restrictions, especially if import demand is not too elastic to cause sizable deadweight losses. Of course, as the empirical trade policy literature finds, this phenomenon does not preclude the use of trade policy for supporting well-organized and highly concentrated industries.

A feature that seems to distinguish the more successful systems with monopolies and trade and credit-market interventions is export orientation (Krongkaew, 2000). Participating in export markets can turn the monopoly aspect of domestic firms into a competitive asset in world markets and allows them to generate additional surplus with domestic resources. Since developing countries typically face a foreign exchange constraint, export earnings also provide resources for greater imports of intermediate and capital goods and the new technologies embodied in them (Edwards, 1993; Rodrik, 1996). The export surplus can also be the basis of a deal between the government and large business groups in which the latter develop specific industries in exchange for government support in terms of credit provision and other business and economic incentives (Rhee, 1994; Lim, 1998). There is, of course, still much to be learned about why some developing countries manage to concentrate on the export promotion policy, coordinate their policies accordingly, and enjoy higher growth, while others instead get stuck in import-substitution and growth-depleting policies.

Labour-market interventions

Interventions in labour markets have important consequences for labour allocation and human-capital formation. As Topel's (1999) survey of the growth consequences of labour markets shows, labour policies and institutions play pivotal roles in economic performance and studying them should be a central part of research on growth. Naturally, a key issue in this respect is why governments intervene in the ways they do. Unfortunately, there has been very little systematic research on this topic beyond documenting the costs and benefits of interventions and identifying the gainers and losers. Here, we review the existing work and suggest hypotheses that are worth exploring.

The typical forms of intervention in the labour market are wage controls, employment quotas, restrictions on layoffs and unemployment insurance. The players in the market are private and public firms, labour unions (when present), and workers with different socio-economic characteristics (that is, skills, geographic location, ethnic affiliation, and so on). In public firms, the government often has sufficient leverage to set policies as it wants. Therefore, we mainly focus on unemployment provisions and employment and wage regulations for private firms.

As the thematic reviews of regional evidence suggest, the use of employment quotas is closely associated with the presence of ethnic divisions in the country, which is common in Africa as well as Asia. Employment quotas, especially the explicit ones, are typically justified based on affirmative action principles as attempts to rectify historical injustices and misfortunes (as in Malaysia). However, they can act as patronage mechanisms as well and help politicians bring particularistic benefits to their constituencies.

Minimum wage guarantees and layoff restrictions provide employed workers with rents and job security. The job-security function does not necessarily entail rent for the workers because it could simply be a means of filling in for insurance-market failures. Nevertheless, the restrictions may cause distortion because they reduce the flexibility of firms and markets. The distortions would obviously be much larger if, in addition to job security, labour-market regulations grant rents to workers. However, there is some controversy about the size of the costs because either employers bypass the regulations somehow, or the insurance and coordination benefits that the regulations bring to the labour market counteract their harmful effects. Jurajda and Mitchell's survey of empirical work in chapter 4 of this volume suggests that on the whole the evidence supports the view that labour-market regulations have substantial negative impacts on the level of employment, especially for new entrants. A recent study by Blanchard and Wolfers (1999) further shows that institutions protecting employment significantly slow down labour-market adjustment to shocks. Therefore, restrictive labour policies appear to be costly in terms of growth and the direct bearers of the costs are firms and unemployed workers.

To understand why a government may pursue such costly interventions, it is useful to consider them in the context of other interventions that can achieve similar redistribution and insurance goals. Using tax/subsidy mechanisms to induce employers to fulfill the goal of the policy may seem less costly. However, as discussed earlier (p. 190), incomplete contracting may make such a solution very costly and make direct controls more attractive. The government, of course, may want to opt for full control of some firms (that is, public ownership) to make the implementation of its employment policy even easier. However, this usually has additional adverse effects on other aspects of enterprise activity, which may not achieve any policy goal. When this is the case, it makes sense to impose labour-market regulations but not public ownership, and to leave other production decisions to private managers to avoid further distortions.

An important implication of the above view is that extensive public ownership might be viewed as the only solution left if there are strong demands for redistribution but institutions are weak in the country. When institutions are somewhat stronger and/or redistribution demands are weaker, more efficient solutions can be devised, such as selected direct interventions in labour, product or other markets. When the country has strong institutions, interventions are likely to take a more efficient form, especially cash (tax or subsidy) transfers. The important implication for economic growth is that focusing on policy reform without improvements in institutions may not do any good. In fact, forcing the government to use market solutions that the institutions cannot support may cause greater tensions and prove costly to growth. This may explain why many less-developed countries that have gone along with policy reform of multilateral institutions have not seen better growth rates.

The above perspective on the motives behind market controls has many other implications as well. For example, it suggests that given institutional capabilities, the extent of government intervention should be positively related to the need for redistribution, say the extent of vulnerability of the economy to external shocks (terms of trade fluctuations and the degree of openness). Many other similar relationships are also worth considering. For example, given the significance of separation of powers in public-spending decisions, it is natural to ask how it is related to regulatory policies. Similarly, the degree of democracy and the extent of participation of the population in the political process are likely to raise the demand for more secure jobs, better pay, lower consumer prices and, hence, induce increased intervention. These are important effects that political economy country studies should carefully consider when they analyse policy choices.

Political-economy determinants of policy and institutional reform

To improve their performance, slow-growing countries ultimately need to adopt more efficient policies and institutions. If the country is endowed with good institutions, then reform is essentially a matter of identifying and implementing appropriate policies. However, when the country also suffers from institutional weaknesses, then the range of feasible policies is more limited and reforms must target institutions as well as policies.

How can a reform become feasible in a setting where some policies and institutions have been in place for some time and are supported by entrenched interest groups? Based on the discussion in section 2, the answer to this question must be sought in the changes in the political cost/benefit ratio of reform. Such changes come about in two ways: (1) when there are significant exogenous shocks – such as terms-of-trade movements and geological and climate changes – that alter the characteristics of various economic resources or interest groups; or (2) as a consequence of endogenous evolutions in resource endowments and interest-group characteristics (due to investment, technological innovation and population changes, which reshape income distribution and growth options). In either case, change in the economy's conditions alters the ratio of political costs to benefits of adopting new policies or institutions, which may trigger the appropriate reform.

When we focus on reforms, the most salient example we can think of is that of former communist countries. The systematic failures of central-planning rendered prohibitive the costs of maintaining it alive. Together with inner pressures from the population and stronger divisions inside the political elites, those heightened costs triggered the fall of the Berlin Wall and initiated the 'transition' of those countries to capitalism and democracy. However, the experience of those countries is extremely mixed. Both economic and political institutions were completely ill-adapted to democratic and free-market conditions, and few countries have managed a successful transition until now. Many countries of the former USSR even fell into some kind of underdevelopment trap, leading to a return of authoritarian regimes and/or a quasi-absence of reforms (for example Belarus, Turkmenistan or Uzbekistan). In terms of their economic success, the main dividing line between successful and unsuccessful countries is precisely drawn by the ability of the countries to develop strong-enough institutions to pursue reforms (Castanheira and Popov, 2000). For instance, Poland and the Czech Republic benefited from better social and political institutions and from a broad consensus in the population, which was pressing for democratization and a break up with communism. This forced political parties to become accountable to the population and advance with the reform programmes. By contrast, Belarus or Ukraine did not benefit from such strong pressures nor enjoy strong-enough institutions, and hence several reforms were stalled or even reversed. Inaction in Ukraine induced a shift towards rent-seeking activities and caused output to fall precipitously. Belarus fared better in the short run by maintaining many of the old policies and institutions intact and limiting the potential adverse effects of transition on output.[23] However, even in Belarus delayed reforms are damaging the country's prospects of growth in the coming decades. The important observation arising from these experiences is that although most countries viewed the adoption of Western institutions as the main means of achieving economic growth, there were substantial variations in their responses and the outcomes. The central question is how and when growth-oriented reforms can be initiated and made successful.

The empirical work on the conditions under which reforms can and should occur is in its infancy. The view that reform can be analysed as a cost/benefit matter (see our earlier discussion, p. 171–2) makes the task look deceptively simple. Part of the difficulty lies in the operationalization of this idea because political costs and benefits are not as tangible as economic costs and benefits and their determinants are not easy to identify. In the reform literature one often runs into studies that have tried to bypass these difficulties by coming up with *ad hoc* hypotheses and, sometimes, by taking the actions of politicians as *prima facie* indications of benefits exceeding costs. This approach has produced a host of hypotheses that are either unfalsifiable or fail to have predictive power. For example, the studies brought together in Williamson (1994) examine a variety of claims listed in Table 5.2, none of which eventually proves either necessary or sufficient for successful reform (Rodrik, 1996). Another example is World Bank (1995) that, among other things, identifies the exclusion of beneficiaries of the status quo from the leadership's base of support as a precondition for reform. This claim is hard to falsify because political leaders who make decisions against the interests of a particular group are presumably excluding that group from their base of support.[24] The choice obviously depends on the costs and benefits of excluding various groups, which themselves depend on the conditions in the country. Therefore, to arrive at testable hypotheses, research on reform should identify which country conditions matter for the political costs and benefits of a policy change, and come up with specific hypotheses about the relationship of such factors with reform outcomes.

An important issue in analysing the cost and benefit of reforms is the identification of the choices and constraints that various actors face in bringing about change. This task typically requires historical knowledge about the evolution of institutions and the role of specific actors in those evolutions (for example the role of Mao in the Chinese experience). As a result, one has to rely on case studies, which are time consuming and often depend on a qualitative assessment of the evidence rather than statistical corroboration. Alston, Eggertsson and North (1996) have brought together a number of such studies that cover a host of issues and use a variety of methods to build cases for their hypothesis. For example, Alston and Ferrie (1993) claim that welfare reform in the United States in the 1960s was a consequence of technological change that reduced the need for paternalistic relationships as a means of reducing transaction costs in US agriculture. To support this claim, they put together a body of evidence that ranges

Table 5.2   Hypotheses about reform

Policy reform emerges in response to crisis
Strong external support (aid) is an important condition for successful reform
Authoritarian regimes are best at carrying out reform
Policy reform is a right-wing programme
Reformers enjoy a 'honeymoon period' of support at the start of a new administration before opposition builds up
Reforms are difficult to sustain unless the government has a solid base of legislative support
A government may compensate for the lack of a strong base of support if the opposition is weak and fragmented
Social consensus is a powerful factor impelling reform
Visionary leadership is important
A coherent and united economic team is important
Successful reform requires economists in positions of political responsibility
Successful reform requires a comprehensive programme capable of rapid implementation
Reformers should mask their intentions to the general public
Reformers should make good use of the media
Reform becomes easier if the losers are compensated
Sustainability can be enhanced by accelerating the emergence of winners

Source: Williamson (1994), as summarized by Rodrik (1996).

from the history of paternalism in the US South following the abolition of slavery, to the details of voting records in US Congressional committees and the mechanism that placed Congressmen representing Southern landlords in agenda-setting positions. Another example is the pioneering work of Cheung (1975) on the rise and fall of rent controls in Hong Kong that shows how political forces motivated rent controls, and how the response of market participants eventually changed the economic and political conditions and led to abandonment of the ordinance.

Although individual case studies have been helpful in shedding light on crucial issues, the specificity of their methodologies often makes it difficult to replicate them across countries and reach more general results. In recent years, a number of projects have been initiated that largely resolve this problem by forming teams of researchers who use a common framework to carry out parallel case studies of many countries. This makes the evidence and analysis more comparable across countries and helps strengthen the results. It also offers possibilities for the development of replicable methodologies for documenting and analysing institutional data. A good example of such a project is the study of telecom reform conducted by Levy and Spiller (1996). The study documents a close connection between successful telecom reform and access to commitment mechanisms by the government, and further shows that the availability of more efficient commitment mechanisms and a more capable bureaucracy can enhance the post-reform performance of the telecom sector. Von Hagen and Harden (1994) offer another example with a comparative study of budget institutions in the European Union member countries. Their evidence makes a strong case for the positive role of *ex ante* agreements and delegation in bringing about fiscal discipline.[25] The current GRP project offers an opportunity for another application of a common-framework methodology in the study of the causes of economic growth and stagnation across countries in each region of the world.

While the case-study approach is yielding increasingly systematic information about the political economy of reform, some insights can be gained based on the relationship between policy changes and political and economic factors for which comparable data already exists. For example, some recent studies try to relate the probability of reform in a given situation to the economic and political characteristics that are believed to affect the efficiency gains from reform or the costs of negotiating and maintaining the new policies. An example of this approach is Campos and Esfahani (1996) who examine the problem of public enterprise (PE) reform in 15 countries since the early 1970s. They find that the probability of reform rises with the extent of existing inefficiency in the PE sector, the extent of industrialization, the capability of private entrepreneurs, and the openness of the economy, all of which tend to raise the benefits of more market-oriented PEs or reduce the costs of redistribution needed for the reforms. Li, Qiang and Xu (2000) carry out a much more extensive exercise of this kind focused on reform in the telecommunications sector. They also confirm that the probability of reform rises with initial inefficiency in the sector and higher demand for telecom services. In addition, they find that controlling for other factors   decentralization, democracy and strong rule of law – raises the chances of reform (perhaps reflecting stronger commitment capability), though checks and balances and constraints on executive discretion do the opposite. Also, reform becomes more likely with privatization in neighbouring countries, right-wing orientation of politicians, and foreign support (especially when it is targeted toward telecom privatization and the country is more democratic).

The above studies produce some evidence concerning the role of crises in motivating reform. Most case studies of reform suggest that major policy changes are preceded by a sense of crisis in the country, but the meaning of crisis is often left vague. Declining GDP and rising inflation are often the key measures used for this purpose when the concept is made more specific. Yet, even such measures are always interpreted in context. For example, when observers interpret a situation of rising inflation or falling GDP growth as a crisis, they are always aware that similar experiences elsewhere or at different times may not be necessarily viewed as crises. Because of this vagueness, as Rodrik (1996) observes, sometimes the association of crises with reforms resembles a tautology. In any event, there is some evidence that reforms are often associated with poor economic performance (especially negative GDP growth), though not all reforms follow economic downturns and certainly not all downturns lead to reform (Campos and Esfahani, 1996). In fact, there are occasions where crises trigger the reversal of reforms and the adoption of inefficient restrictive policies (Kelegama and Parikh, 2000; Rodríguez, 2000; Castanheira and Popov 2000). Another weakness of the existing evidence is that it offers no indication of how crises motivate reform. There are quite a few ideas floating around in this respect, but no empirical test of their relative importance.[26]

The issue whether economic reform becomes more feasible or less so with democratization is one that has received a great deal of attention in the literature (Haggard and Webb, 1994). There does not seem to be any simple relationship between democracy and growth other than the observation that variance of growth is smaller in democracies. This ambiguity seems to pervade a great deal of results in the reform literature as well (Williamson, 1994). A difficulty in past studies of this kind is that they often define democracy as a phenomenon that can be measured by a single indicator, when the reality is probably much more complex. There are a myriad of institutional elements that underlie a political-economy system and those elements may be combined in many different ways to form a particular system. These elements and the ways in which they combine have different effects on the extent to which the system reaches *representation, coordination* and *commitment*. For example, competitiveness of elections enhances representation; however, if the electoral and decision-making procedures give rise to fragmentation among policy-makers and excessive veto points, then coordination will be weak. These nuances are receiving increased attention in the recent literature. Indeed, Li, Qiang and Xu's (2000) finding that democracy facilitates reform when the elected executive faces fewer constraints in setting policy supports this perspective.

The above observation seems to be consistent with the assessment of the regional survey papers. Latin American countries have proceeded with reform more swiftly when the executive has faced less constraint, as in Mexico in the 1980s and Argentina in the early 1990s (Rodríguez, 2000). In East Asia, Krongkaew (2000) observes that democracy has been generally weak, but bureaucracy has played a major role in representing various interests, and reform has been more difficult when there have been rifts between politicians and bureaucrats. Kelegama and Parikh (2000) also suggest that in South Asian democracies, reform has proceeded faster when the executive has used greater discretion, though the speed has had a negative effect on the quality of new policies and on subsequent economic performance. Among African and Middle Eastern countries, democracies have been less common and the executives have generally faced fewer checks and balances, but this has not always helped reform (Bates and Devarajan, 2000; Esfahani, 2000a). The problem in these countries appears to be the weakness of commitment mechanisms. This phenomenon is rather evident in the difficulties that many resource-rich countries in these regions have had in removing highly distortionary mass subsidies (for example on food and energy). Replacing those subsidies with cash payments could have substantially improved resource allocation and released resources for investment and growth. However, attempts at removing the subsidies have often triggered strong reactions in the population, expressing concern that the cash payments would be soon diluted and the reallocated resources would be taken over by the elite rather being used for public benefit (Esfahani, 2001).

4   Conclusions

The theoretical framework and the empirical evidence reviewed in this chapter suggest that there are systematic approaches to the political economy of growth that can generate tangible insights into the process of growth and concrete implications for policy and institutional reforms. We have attempted to combine these approaches to a common methodology that can be used by country case studies.

At the heart of the methodology is the idea that suboptimal growth outcomes are the result of contracting problems among the players in an economy. Inefficiency may arise when policy-makers represent only narrow interests, cannot commit the government to constrained sets of future actions, or fail to coordinate themselves and the groups that they represent. The severity of these contracting problems varies across

202 The Political Economy of Growth

countries according to the institutions that structure interactions among individuals and groups. The resources over which socio-economic groups need to contract also matter in terms of the surpluses that they render and the deadweight losses that they generate in cases of redistribution. Therefore, the methodology implies that the analysis of the political-economy conditions for economic growth in a country should start with an accurate assessment of the political actors in the game, the institutions governing their interactions, and the nature of the resources over which they compete. Then one needs to examine policy interventions and seek explanations for their efficiency or inefficiency based on the nature of contracting failures among the political actors and the elasticity of the existing resources. If the observed inefficiencies cannot be connected to institutional weaknesses, the task is to highlight the contradiction and look for alternative explanations. This process can inform and enrich the methodology and lead us to better understanding of the connections between political economy factors and the process of growth. It could also help identify the fundamental problems that constrain growth and, thus, offer insights for the design of more effective reform programmes.

In implementing the methodology, it is important to keep several points in mind:

1 To understand both past and prospective growth, it is necessary to identify which factors can be taken as exogenous and which factors should be treated as endogenous. Some institutions (such as ethnic divisions or constitutions in most countries) are relatively stable and play a fundamental role in shaping policies and government interventions. These should be critically analysed and distinguished from other rules that may be manipulated more easily.

2 The proposed explanations for existing policies must include comparisons of those policies with alternative ones that seem more efficient. The comparisons should clarify why the alternatives have not been adopted. This is not to say that the outcomes should be treated as deterministic; the world is complex and there are many factors that one does not observe. There is also the possibility of multiple outcomes or differences in the applicability of the various policies. The issue is that gross misallocations cannot be systematically explained by unidentified factors.

3 The explanations should take account of the rationality of political actors and not be based on unfalsifiable statements that amount to

saying that those actors, 'don't know any better'. The explanations also should go beyond tautologies such as 'the status quo is preserved because the interest groups that benefit from it are more powerful than others'. One needs to show what is the source of greater power and identify the institutional factors that prevent policy-maker and interest groups from coming up with better deals.

4 It is important to analyse how government interventions actually work, see how market failures are addressed, and how they can be corrected. For instance, the case of FSU countries showed that privatizing firms does not work without proper institution-building. Country case studies should envision potential reforms in that way: should we immediately modify government intervention or is it necessary to improve institutions in the first place? If the latter holds true, how can it be done? For example, how to reduce corruption and/or make the government more trustworthy?

5 When there are policy reforms and institutional changes, it is crucial to examine how inefficiencies and costs of existing and alternative policies have changed over time. Are actual policy reforms a response to changes in the underlying resources and institutions? Do policies change in predictable ways (that is, in the direction predicted by the size of efficiency gains relative to the costs of change)?

Finally, in numerous occasions we have underlined the weaknesses and unknowns of the existing political-economy theories of growth. Studying concrete country cases with the present methodology can provide an opportunity to explore those areas and help fill in those hollows.

Notes

1 These papers examine the case of Africa (Bates and Devarajan, 2000), East Asia (Krongkaew, 2000), South Asia (Kelegama and Parikh, 2000), Latin America (Rodríguez, 2000), Middle East and North Africa (Esfahani, 2000a), and transition countries (Castanheira and Popov, 2000).

2 Following Krongkaew (2000), one could further subdivide these groups on a case-by-case basis, in order to account for the relative powers or the ranks of the officials (e.g. ministers vs civil servants, the dominant party vs the others) or the real power of different pressure groups (e.g. unions vs the army or other groups present in the country). We do not go this far. Our distinction here is meant to capture the *functional* differences in their access to power: voters have power at election times, and much less power when elections are away. Instead, pressure groups can maintain their influence (sometimes by monetary means, sometimes by demonstrations and strikes) on a more regular basis. Political elites, on their side, directly control the policy levers, favouring one or another group.

3 See Alesina and Rodrik (1994), Persson and Tabellini (1994), Bertola (1993), Benabou (1996), Perotti (1996a), Saint-Paul and Verdier (1996) or Desdoigts and Moizeau (2001) among others. Verdier (1994), Aghion and Howitt (1998, chs 4 and 9) and Persson and Tabellini (2000, chs 3, 6 and 14) provide a survey of this literature.

4 Combining the voting and interest-group approaches, which has come to be known as 'citizen-candidate' framework, was originated by Osborne and Slivinski (1996) and Besley and Coate (1997). More recent contributions to this line of research include Rivière (2000) and Morelli (2000).

5 Of course, the word 'rent' should be taken with a broad meaning. Most of the time, we would think of economic rents but we also mean political power or religious dominance among others.

6 The reason why deadweight losses matter is that extracting rents that do not benefit anyone is a waste that politicians try to avoid.

7 For an analysis of such an effect in the context of a multi-product firm, see Dixit and Stiglitz (1977).

8 Alternatively, the rich may want to ally themselves with the poor against the middle class. See Perotti (1992) for an analysis of such a model, and Desdoigts and Moizeau (2001) who analyse the dynamic interactions between growth and coalition formation across the process of development.

9 Interestingly, these effects do not change much when interest groups, rather than voters, influence policy choices in parliamentary versus presidential regimes (Helpman and Persson, 1998; Bennedsen and Feldmann, 1999).

10 Of course, putting in place such constraints needs coordination at some earlier stage, but that may be easier to achieve because at a rule-making stage each actor would be comparing the benefits of constraining others (and preventing the commons tragedy) with the costs of restricting his/her own future uncertain options.

11 For instance, a 'natural experiment' that is being widely analysed is the case of transition countries in Europe and Asia. Many of those countries used to suffer from similar problems and adopted apparently similar institutional arrangements. However, their relative performance – both in terms of their economic and political transformation – does not reflect this apparent similarity. In some cases, it even seems that attempting to mimic what is efficient in other countries has actually led some of these countries to complete disarray (Castanheira and Popov, 2000).

12 There is another important perspective on policy persistence formalized by Coate and Morris (1999). This view suggests that the actions undertaken by economic agents to benefit from existing policies involve sunk investments that increase the willingness of those agents to pay for the policy. This creates incentives in the political system to preserve existing policies. However, unlike the other two views summarized in the text, this one does not explain the persistence of inefficient policies, because maintained policies at each point in time are efficient given the nature of the existing assets. What this view can explain is the suboptimal use of policies that can be beneficial in the short run, but not in the long run. Polities may oppose such policies because they anticipate that they will not be reversed once adopted. Of course, this problem may not exist if the government could commit to the reversal of such policies.

13 See Roland (2000) for an insightful discussion on the relative merits of gradualism vs 'shock therapy'.

14 For detailed accounts of political developments in Malaysia, see Milne and Mauzy (1980), Means (1991) and Bowie (1991).
15 Proportionality of representation makes coordination more difficult because it allows smaller interest groups to join the policy-making process independently, whereas the use of plurality acts as a delegation mechanism whereby hosts of smaller interest groups have to line up behind the same candidate.
16 For instance, Barro (1991) underlines the positive association between educational attainments and investment rates.
17 However, the endogenous growth literature underlined that this convergence effect only occurs once human capital is controlled for.
18 Note that inequalities in the access to education may also overlap with those two dimensions.
19 Income Gini coefficients in Latin America are typically between 0.4 and 0.6 (data are from the World Income Inequality Database (WIID) of the United Nations Development Programme.)
20 Redistributions in Korea and Taiwan in the 1950s resulted in Gini coefficients of respectively 0.32 and 0.35 in the 1960s.
21 For a review of land-reform experiences and examples of disasters following such programmes, see de Janvry and Sadoulet (1989). More recently, Moldova also redistributed land but poor capital markets prevented individual farmers from maintaining their capital stock, which resulted in lowering yet further agricultural productivity and prospective growth in the sector. Additional steps to improve agricultural efficiency are being undertaken by the government.
22 Note however that there are no precise factors that allow for a clear distinction between 'public' and 'private' firms. For example, Shleifer and Vishny (1994) identify PEs as those that receive rents from the treasury in exchange for complying with employment or other government requirements. However, it is not clear why the government would not prefer to use private firms to implement the same transfers. Here again, as argues Esfahani (2000b), the fact that the government can more readily control the actions of a manager in a public firm may help explain the *correlation* between public ownership and those transfers.
23 Ukrainian GDP in 1999 approached 40 per cent of its 1991 level, while the Belarus figure represented about 80 per cent of its 1991 level.
24 For a further critique of World Bank (1995), see Ramamurti (1999) and Campos and Esfahani (2000).
25 See also Boeri, Börsch-Supan and Tabellini (2001) for a survey of voters' positions on welfare-state reforms.
26 One specific area for which there has been a test attempt is the rising cost of public funds idea proposed by Boycko, Shleifer and Vishny (1996) and Yarrow (1999). Li, Qiang and Xu (2000) find that reform probability tends to rise with budget deficits, but declines with inflation. Thus, the implications for the cost-of-funds hypothesis remain ambiguous.

References

Aghion, P. and P. Bolton (1990) 'Government Domestic Debt and the Risk of Default: A Political-Economic Model of the Strategic Role of Debt', in R.

Dornbusch and M. Draghi (eds), *Capital Markets and Debt Management* (Cambridge, Mass.: MIT Press).

Aghion, P. and P. Howitt (1998) *Endogenous Growth Theory* (Cambridge, Mass.: MIT Press).

Alesina, A. and A. Drazen (1991) 'Why Are Stabilizations Delayed?' *American Economic Review*, vol. 81, pp. 1170–88.

Alesina, A. and R. Perotti (1995) 'The Political Economy of Budget Deficits', *International Monetary Fund Staff Papers*, vol. 42(1), pp. 1–31.

Alesina, A. and R. Perotti (1996) 'Income Distribution, Political Instability and Investment', *European Economic Review*, vol. 40, pp. 1202–29.

Alesina, A. and R. Perotti (1999) 'Budget Deficits and Budget Procedures', in J. M. Poterba and J. von Hagen (eds), *Fiscal Institutions and Fiscal Performance* (Chicago: University of Chicago Press), pp. 13–57.

Alesina, A. and D. Rodrik (1994) 'Distributive Politics and Economic Growth', *Quarterly Journal of Economics*, vol. 109, pp. 465–90.

Alesina, A. and G. Tabellini (1990) 'Voting on the Budget Deficit', *American Economic Review*, vol. 80, pp. 37–49.

Alston, L. J. and J. P. Ferrie (1993) 'Paternalism in Agricultural Labour Contracts in the U.S. South: Implications for the Growth of the Welfare State', *American Economic Review*, vol. 83, pp. 852–76.

Alston, L. J., T. Eggertsson and D. C. North (eds) (1996) *Empirical Studies in Institutional Change* (Cambridge: Cambridge University Press).

Ayittey, G. B. N. (1995) 'Nigeria: The High Cost of Erratic Financial Policies', *Economic Reform Today*, vol. 1, pp. 15–20.

Banerjee, A. and E. Duflo (2000) 'Inequality and Growth: What Can the Data Say?' MIT mimeo, June.

Bardhan, P. and D. Mookherjee (2000) 'Corruption and Decentralization of Infrastructure Delivery in Developing Countries', IED Discussion Paper no. 104, Boston University.

Baron, D. P. (1994) 'Electoral Competition with Informed and Uninformed Voters', *American Political Science Review*, vol. 88, pp. 33–47.

Barro, R. (1991) 'Economic Growth in a Cross Section of Countries', *Quarterly Journal of Economics*, vol. 105, pp. 407–43.

Barro, R. J. (1997) *Determinants of Economic Growth* (Cambridge, MA: MIT Press).

Barro, R. (1999) 'Inequality, Growth and Investment', NBER Working Paper no. 7038.

Barro, R. and X. Sala-í-Martin (1995) *Economic Growth* (New York: McGraw Hill).

Bates, R. and S. Devarajan (2000) 'Framework Paper on the Political Economy of African Growth', manuscript.

Becker, G. (1983) 'A Theory of Competition among Pressure Groups for Political Influence', *Quarterly Journal of Economics*, vol. 98(3), pp. 371–400.

Becker, G. S., K. M. Murphy and R. Tamura (1990) 'Human Capital, Fertility, and Economic Growth', *Journal of Political Economy*, vol. 98(5), part 2, pp. S12–S37.

Benabou, R. (1996) 'Inequality and Growth', in B. Bernanke and J. Rotemberg (eds), *NBER Macroeconomics Annual 1996* (Cambridge, MA: MIT Press).

Bennedsen, M. and S. E. Feldmann (1999) 'Legislative Structure, Incentives, and Informational Lobbying', Harris School Working Paper, University of Chicago.

Bertola, G. (1993) 'Factor Shares and Savings in Endogenous Growth', *American Economic Review*, vol. 83(5), pp. 1184–98.

Besley, T. and S. Coate (1997) 'An Economic Model of Representative Democracy', *Quarterly Journal of Economics*, vol. 112, pp. 85–114.

Besley, T. and S. Coate (2001) 'Lobbying and Welfare in a Representative Democracy', *Review of Economic Studies*, vol. 68(1), pp. 67–81.

Binswanger, H. and K. Deininger (1997) 'Explaining Agricultural and Agrarian Policies in Developing Countries', *Journal of Economic Literature*, vol. 35(4), pp. 1958–2005.

Black, D. (1958) *The Theory of Committees and Elections* (Cambridge: Cambridge University Press).

Blanchard, O. and J. Wolfers (1999) 'The Role of Shocks and Institutions in the Rise of European Unemployment: The Aggregate Evidence', manuscript, MIT.

Boeri, T., A. Börsch-Supan and G. Tabellini (2001) 'Would You Like to Shrink the Welfare State? A Survey of European Citizens', *Economic Policy*, vol. 32, pp. 9–50.

Bourguignon, F. and T. Verdier (2000) 'Oligarchy, Democracy, Inequality and Growth', *Journal Development Economics*, vol. 62(2), pp. 285–313.

Bowie, A. (1991) *Crossing the Industrial Divide* (New York: Columbia University Press).

Boycko, M., A. Shleifer and R. W. Vishny (1996) 'A Theory of Privatization', *Economic Journal*, vol. 106, pp. 309–19.

Campos, J. E. and H. S. Esfahani (1996) 'Why and When Do Governments Initiate Public Enterprise Reform?' *World Bank Economic Review*, vol. 10(3), pp. 451–85.

Campos, J. E. and H. S. Esfahani (2000) 'Credible Commitment and Success with Public Enterprise Reform', *World Development*, vol. 28(2), pp. 221–44.

Campos, J. E. and H. Root (1996) *The Key to the East Asian Miracle: Making Shared Growth Credible* (Washington, DC: Brookings Institution).

Campos, N. F. and F. Coricelli (2000) 'Growth In Transition: What We Know, What We Don't, and What We Should', paper prepared for GDN Global Research Project on 'Explaining Growth'.

Castanheira, M. and V. Popov (2000) 'Framework Paper on the Political Economics of Growth in Transition Countries,' mimeo, Economics, Education and Research Consortium (EERC), Moscow.

Castanheira, M. and G. Roland (2000) 'The Optimal Speed of Transition: a General Equilibrium Analysis', *International Economic Review*, vol. 4(1), pp. 219–39.

Chari, V. V. and H. Cole (1993) 'A Contribution to the Theory of Pork Barrel Spending', *Staff Report* no. 156, Federal Reserve Bank of Minneapolis.

Chari, V. V. and P. Kehoe (1999) 'Optimal Fiscal and Monetary Policy', in John Taylor and Mike Woodford (eds), *Handbook of Macroeconomics* (Amsterdam: North Holland), pp. 1671–745.

Cheung, S. N. S. (1975) 'Roofs and Stars: The Stated Intentions and Actual Effects of a Rents Ordinance', *Economic Inquiry*, vol. 13, pp. 1–21.

Coate, S. and S. Morris (1999) 'Policy Persistence', *American Economic Review*, vol. 89(5), pp. 1327–36.

Collier, P. (1998) 'The Political Economy of Ethnicity', paper presented at the Annual World Bank Conference on Development Economics, Washington, DC, 20–21 April 1998.

Collier, P. and J. W. Gunning (2000) 'The Microeconomics of African Growth, 1950–2000', GDN Working Paper.

Dao, M. Q. and H. S. Esfahani (1995) 'A Competitive Model of Growth of Government', *Journal of Economic Studies*, vol. 22(2), pp. 4–20.

Dehajia, V. (1997) 'Optimal Restructuring under a Political Constraint', University of Michigan, Davidson Institute Working Paper no. 35.

de Janvry, A. and E. Sadoulet (1989) 'A Study in Resistance to Institutional Change: The Lost Game of Latin American Land Reform', *World Development*, vol. 17, pp. 1397–407.

Desdoigts, A. and F. Moizeau (2001) 'Multiple Politico-Economic Regimes, Inequality and Growth', Université d'Evry mimeo.

Dewatripont, M. and G. Roland (1992a) 'Economic Reform and Dynamic Political Constraints', *Review of Economic Studies*, vol. 59, pp. 703–30.

Dewatripont, M. and G. Roland (1992b) 'The Virtues of Gradualism and Legitimacy in the Transition to a Market Economy', *Economic Journal*, vol. 102, pp. 291–300.

Dewatripont, M. and G. Roland (1995) 'The Design of Reform Packages under Uncertainty', *American Economic Review*, vol. 83(5), pp. 1207–23.

Dewatripont, M. and G. Roland (1996) 'Transition as a Process of Large-Scale Institutional Change', *Economics of Transition*, vol. 4, pp. 1–30.

Dixit, A. and J. E. Stiglitz (1977) 'Monopolistic Competition and Optimum Product Diversity', *American Economic Review*, vol. 67, pp. 297–308.

Downs, A. (1957) *An Economic Theory of Democracy* (New York: Harper).

Drazen, A. and V. Grilli (1993) 'The Benefit of Crises for Economic Reform', *American Economic Review*, vol. 83, pp. 598–607.

Duflo, E. (2000) 'The Medium Run Effects of Educational Expansion: Evidence from a Large School Construction Program in Indonesia,' MIT mimeo.

Easterly, W. and R. Levine (1997) 'Africa's Growth Tragedy: Policies and Ethnic Divisions', *Quarterly Journal of Economics*, vol. 112(4), 1203–50.

Edwards, S. (1993) 'Openness, Trade Liberalization, and Growth in Developing Countries', *Journal of Economic Literature*, vol. 31(3), pp. 1358–93.

Esfahani, H. S. (2000a) 'Political Economy of Growth in MENA Countries: A Framework for Country Case Studies,' GDN Working Paper.

Esfahani, H. S. (2000b) 'Institutions and Government Controls', *Journal of Development Economics*, vol. 63(2), pp. 197–229.

Esfahani, H. S. (2001) 'A Political Economy Model of Resource Pricing with Evidence from the Fuel Market,' manuscript, University of Illinois.

Esfahani, H. S. and M. T. Ramírez (2001) 'Institutions, Infrastructure, and Economic Growth,' manuscript, University of Illinois.

Fernandez, R. and D. Rodrik (1991) 'Resistance to Reform: Status-Quo Bias in the Presence of Individual-Specific Uncertainty', *American Economic Review*, vol. 81, pp. 1146–55.

Figini, P. (1998) 'Inequality and Growth Revisited,' Trinity College, Dublin mimeo.

Forbes, K. J. (2000) 'A Reassessment of the Relationship between Inequality and Growth', *American Economic Review*, vol. 90(4), pp. 869–87.

Grossman, G. and E. Helpman (1994) 'Protection for Sale,' *American Economic Review*, vol. 84(4), pp. 833–50.

Haggard, S. and R. R. Kaufman (1992) 'Economic Adjustment and the Prospects for Democracy', in S. Haggard and R. Kaufman (eds), *The Politics of Economic Adjustment* (Princeton: Princeton University Press), pp. 319–500.

Haggard, S. and S. Webb (eds) (1994) *Voting for Reform* (Oxford: Oxford University Press).

Hart, O., A. Shleifer and R. W. Vishny (1997) 'The Proper Scope of Government: Theory and an Application to Prisons', *Quarterly Journal of Economics*, vol. 112, pp. 1127–61.

Helpman, E. and T. Persson (1998) 'Lobbying and Legislative Bargaining', NBER Working Paper no. 6589.

Hotelling, H. (1929) 'Stability in Competition', *Economic Journal*, vol. 39, pp. 41–57.

Hou, K. and D. Robinson (2000) 'Towards a Property Rights View of Government Ownership', manuscript, University of Chicago.

Inter-American Development Bank (IADB) (1998) *Economic and Social Progress Report 1998: Latin America after a Decade of Reforms* (Washington DC: Part III, chs 1 and 2).

Kelegama, S. and K. Parikh (2000) 'Political Economy of Growth and Reforms in South Asia', manuscript.

Knack, S.and P.Keefer (1995) 'The Effects of Institutions on Public Investment', preliminary draft of paper presented in American Economic Association Meeting, 1996, San Francisco.

Krongkaew, M. (2000) 'The Political Economy of Growth in Developing East Asia: A Thematic Paper', GDN Working Paper.

Krueger, A. O. (1974) 'The Political Economy of the Rent-Seeking Society', *American Economic Review*, vol. 6(3), vol. 291–303.

Kydland, L. and E. C. Prescott (1977) 'Rules Rather Than Discretion: The Inconsistency of Optimal Plans', *Journal of Political Economy*, vol. 85(3), pp. 473–91.

La Porta, R., F. Lopez-de-Silanes, A. Shleifer and R. Vishny (1999) 'The Quality of Government', *Journal of Law, Economics, and Organization*, vol. 15(1), pp. 222–79.

Leighley, J. and J. Nagler (1992) 'Socioeconomic Class Bias in Turnout, 1964–1988: The Voters Remain the Same', *American Political Science Review*, vol. 86(3), pp. 725–36.

Levy, B. and P. Spiller (eds) (1996) *Regulations, Institutions and Commitment: The Case of Telecommunications* (Cambridge: Cambridge University Press).

Li, W., C. Z.-W. Qiang and L. C. Xu (2000) 'The Political Economy of Telecommunications Reforms', manuscript, the World Bank.

Lim, H. (1998) *Korea's Growth and Industrial Transformation* (London, Macmillan – Palgrave).

Lindbeck, A. and J. Weibull (1987) 'Balanced Budget Redistribution as the Outcome of Political Competition', *Public Choice*, vol. 52, pp. 273–97.

Lucas, R. (1988) 'On the Mechanics of Economic Development', *Journal of Monetary Economics*, vol. 2(1), pp. 3–42.

McGuire, M. C. and M. Olson, Jr (1996) 'The Economics of Autocracy and Majority Rule: The Invisible Hand and the Use of Force', *Journal of Economic Literature*, vol. 34(1), pp. 72–96.

Means, G. P. (1991) *Malaysian Politics: The Second Generation* (Oxford: Oxford University Press).

Megginson, W. L. and J. M. Netter (2000) 'From State to Market: A Survey of Empirical Studies on Privatization', manuscript, University of Oklahoma.

Milne, R. S. and Mauzy, D. K. (1980) *Politics and Government in Malaysia* (Vancouver, Canada: University of British Columbia Press).

Morelli, M. (2000) 'Equilibrium party structure and policy outcomes under different political systems', Iowa State University mimeo.

North, D. C. (1990) *Institutions, Institutional Change, and Economic Performance* (Cambridge: Cambridge University Press).

Olson, M. (1965) *The Logic of Collective Action* (Cambridge, MA: Harvard University Press).

Olson, M. (1982) *The Rise and Decline of Nations* (New Haven: Yale University Press).

Osborne, M. J. and A. Slivinski (1996) 'A Model of Political Competition with Citizen-Candidates', *Quarterly Journal of Economics*, vol. 111, pp. 65–96.

Parente, S. L. and E. C. Prescott (2000) *Barriers to Riches* (Cambridge MA: MIT Press).

Pechman, J. A. (1985) *Who Paid the Taxes, 1966-85?* (Washington, DC: The Brookings Institution).

Perotti, R. (1992) 'Income Distribution, Politics, and Growth', *American Economic Review*, vol. 80(2), pp. 311–16.

Perotti, R. (1996a) 'Growth, Income Distribution and Democracy: What the Data Say', *Journal of Economic Growth*, vol. 1(2), pp. 149–87.

Perotti, R. (1996b) 'Redistribution and Non-consumption Smoothing in an Open Economy', *Review of Economic Studies*, vol. 63, pp. 411–33.

Perry, G. (2000) 'Reports on the Four Thematic Groups: Sources of Aggregate Growth', Global Development Network, Summary of Prague Workshop on Explaining Growth, June 2000.

Persson, T., G. Roland and G. Tabellini (1997) 'Separation of Powers and Political Accountability', *Quarterly Journal of Economics*, vol. 112(4), pp. 1163–202.

Persson, T., G. Roland and G. Tabellini (1998) 'Towards Micropolitical Foundations of Public Finance', *European Economic Review*, vol. 42, pp. 685–94.

Persson, T. and L. Svensson (1989) 'Why a Stubborn Conservative Would Run a Deficit: Policy with Time–consistent Preferences', *Quarterly Journal of Economics*, vol. 104, pp. 325–45.

Persson, T. and G. Tabellini (1994) 'Is Inequality Harmful for Growth?' *American Economic Review*, vol. 84, pp. 600–21.

Persson, T. and G. Tabellini (2000) *Political Economics: Explaining Economic Policy* (Cambridge, Mass.: MIT Press).

Persson, T., G. Tabellini and F. Trebbi (2001) 'Electoral rules and corruption', NBER Working Paper no. W8154.

Pritchett, L. (1999) 'Where Has All the Education Gone?', manuscript, the World Bank.

Rajan, R. and L. Zingales. (1998) 'Power in a Theory of the Firm', *Quarterly Journal of Economics*, vol. 113, pp. 387–432.

Ramamurti, R. (1999) 'Why Haven't Developing Countries Privatized Deeper and Faster?', *World Development*, vol. 22, pp. 137–55.

Rauch, J. E. and P. B. Evans (2000) 'Bureaucratic Structure and Bureaucratic Performance in Less Developed Countries', *Journal of Public Economics*, vol. 75(1), pp. 49–71.

Rhee J.-C. (1994) *The State and Industry in South Korea: the Limits of the Authoritarian State* (London and New York: Routledge).

Rivière, A. (2000) 'Citizen Candidacy, Party Formation and Duverger's Law', European Centre for Advanced Research in Economics (ECARES) mimeo.

Roberts, M. J. and J. R. Tybout (1995) 'An Empirical Model of Sunk Costs and the Decision to Export', World Bank Working Paper no. 1436.

Robinson, J. (1997) 'When Is the State Predatory?', manuscript, University of Southern California.

Rodríguez, F. (2000) 'The Political Economy of Latin American Economic Growth', manuscript, Global Development Network.

Rodrik, D. (1994) 'The Rush to Free Trade. Why so Late? Why Now? Will it Last?', in S. Haggard and S. Webb (eds), *Voting for Reform* (Oxford: Oxford University Press).

Rodrik, D. (1996) 'Understanding Economic Policy Reform', *Journal of Economic Literature*, vol. 34(1), pp. 9–41.

Rodrik, D. (1999) 'Where Did All the Growth Go? External Shocks, Growth Collapses and Social Conflict', *Journal of Economic Growth*, vol. 4, pp. 358–412.

Roemer, J. E. (1985) 'Rationalizing Revolutionary Ideology,' *Econometrica*, vol. 53, pp. 85–108.

Rogoff, K. (1985) 'The Optimal Degree of Commitment to an Intermediate Monetary Target', *Quarterly Journal of Economics*, vol. 100(4), pp. 1169–89.

Roland, G. (2000) *Transition and Economics. Politics, Markets and Firms* (Cambridge, Mass.: MIT Press).

Sachs, J. D. and A. Warner (1995) 'Natural Resource Abundance and Economic Growth', NBER Working Paper no. 5398.

Saint-Paul, G. and T. Verdier (1996) 'Inequality, Redistribution and Growth,' *European Economic Review*, vol. 40(3–5).

Schmidt-Hebbel, K. and L. Serven (2000) 'Does Income Inequality Raise Aggregate Saving?', *Journal of Development Economics*, vol. 6(2), pp. 417–46.

Shepsle, K. (1979) 'Institutional Arrangement and Equilibrium in Multidimensional Voting Models', *American Journal of Political Science*, vol. 23, pp. 27–60.

Shleifer, A. and R. W. Vishny (1994) 'Politicians and Firms', *Quarterly Journal of Economics*, vol. 109, pp. 995–1025.

Stein, E., E. Talvi and A. Grisanti (1998) 'Institutional Arrangements and Fiscal Performance: The Latin American Experience', NBER Working Paper no. 6358.

Svensson, J. (1997) 'Accountability, Polarization and Growth: Is More Democracy Better?' Washington, DC: The World Bank.

Tanzi, V. (1998) 'Corruption Around the World: Causes, Consequences, Scope, and Cures', *IMF Staff Papers*, vol. 4(4), pp. 559–94.

Topel, R. (1999) 'Labour Markets and Economic Growth', in Orley Ashenfelter and David Card (eds), *Handbook of Labour Economics*, vol. 3. Amsterdam: North Holland, pp. 2943–84.

Tornell, A. and P. Lane (1999) 'Growth and Voracity', *American Economic Review*, vol. 89(1), pp. 22–46.

Treisman, D. (2000) 'Decentralization and Inflation: Commitment, Collective Action, or Continuity?' *American Political Science Review*. vol. 94(4), pp. 837–58.

Velasco, A. (1999) 'A Model of Endogenous Fiscal Deficits and Delayed Fiscal Reforms', in J. M. Poterba and J. von Hagen (eds), *Fiscal Institutions and Fiscal Performance* (Chicago: University of Chicago Press), pp. 37–57.

Verdier, T. (1994) 'Models of Political Economy of Growth: A Short Survey', *European Economic Review*, vol. 38(3–4), pp. 757–63

von Hagen, J. (1992) 'Budgeting Procedures and Fiscal Performance in European Communities', manuscript, University of Mannheim.

von Hagen, J. and I. J. Harden (1994) 'National Budget Processes and Fiscal Performance', *European Economy, Reports and Studies*, vol. 3, pp. 311–418.

von Hagen, J. and I. J. Harden (1995) 'Budget Processes and Commitment to Fiscal Discipline', *European Economic Review*, vol. 39, pp. 771–9.

Waterbury, J. (1983) *The Egypt of Nasser and Sadat: The Political Economy of Two Regimes* (Princeton, NJ: Princeton University Press).

Waterbury, J. (1993) *Exposed to Innumerable Delusions: Public Enterprise and State Power in Egypt, India, Mexico, and Turkey* (Cambridge: Cambridge University Press).

Williamson, J. (1994) *The Political Economy of Policy Reform* (Washington, DC: Institute for International Economics).

World Bank (1995) *Bureaucrats in Business: The Economics and Politics of Government Ownership* (Washington, DC: The World Bank).

Yarrow, G. (1999) 'A Theory of Privatization, or Why Bureaucrats Are Still in Business?' *World Development*, vol. 22(1), pp. 157–68.

6
A Conclusion to Cross-National Growth Research: A Foreword 'To the Countries Themselves'

Lant Pritchett

1 Introduction

I am happy to write the conclusion to this volume because the approach to growth research that is reflected in this volume is promising. By taking seriously the experiences of regions, and next of individual countries, and by taking an integrated approach of macroeconomic, microeconomics, markets and political economy jointly this research can hope to capture the richness and texture of actual country experiences.

I am also happy to write this conclusion, because it is also a beginning of a further round of detailed examinations of individual countries. Meeting the theories and general regression empirics of growth with studies of individual countries should be a productive encounter.

Finally, I am also happy to conclude a volume opened by Robert Solow. As a graduate student I learned both macroeconomics and microeconomics from Professor Solow, and I remember learning two particularly important and sophisticated economic principles that have stuck with me. First, 'it's not what you don't know that kills you, it's what you *do* know that *ain't* so' and, second, 'Just because the tyre is flat does not mean the hole is on the bottom.'

There is an impressive range and quality of research that went into this volume – 24 papers (one for each of four topics in each of six regions). The findings from these are already aptly synthesized in the topical summaries here. I would do this research endeavour a disservice if I tried to further summarize the summaries – the richness of the individual studies and topics would be squeezed out leaving a dry rind of abstraction. As an alternative way of bringing this stage of the research to a conclusion and pointing forward to the future research in the country studies I want to ask two questions: 'what is it that we *know* about growth that maybe, just maybe, ain't so?', and 'why are we looking at the growth agenda only at the bottom of the flat tyre?' Building on each of these questions I want to point to possible ways forward as we move to the individual country studies.

2   Things we know that just possibly ain't so

Let me begin with four things that we 'know', in the sense that they are widely repeated and taken as conventional wisdom. These four propositions might possibly be right, and I am not sure they are wrong, but maybe, just maybe, they might not be so.

Education is a key to economic growth is a new truth that 'old' theories ignored

When the approach of the 'new growth' theories is applied to education, the old saying *what is true is not new and what is new is not true* is especially applicable. That education is important for economic growth and development is not something anyone who was paying attention to the development literature 'learned' recently. For instance the quote 'Deeper understanding of the forces affecting long-term economic and social progress is leading to recognition of the fact that investment in education is an indispensable prerequisite of future economic growth' – 2001? 1991? No. This is from the 1960s.[1] Although education was not part of the formal models of the first Solow vintage, no-one thinking about the issues doubted the key role of education in development.[2]

The first generation new growth theories tried to argue that education and knowledge were the things that could account for steady-state differences in growth rates because knowledge is non-rival and hence is not subject to diminishing returns.[3] In these theories education contributes even more to long-run growth than the observed wage returns would suggest because of these spillovers.

First, I think today everyone accepts that the first round of models in which the level of education or the level of knowledge has the effect of accelerating the proportionate rate of growth of technical progress are false. Charlie Jones (1995a,b) was the first to point out the obvious: one cannot maintain as even vaguely descriptive of the OECD experience a model with a steady-state relationship between growth *rates* – which had been steady for more than 100 years[4] – and the absolute level of education or knowledge or R&D effort which have, by any account, increased several-fold. A stationary variable simply cannot have a stable relationship with a non-stationary variable.

Secondly, in explaining recent experience of developing countries the intellectual challenge is exactly the opposite of finding a model that explains why growth has remained so high for so long. That is, one challenge is to understand why growth rates in OECD countries are still so high and have not converged to just the rate of growth of TFP as the Solow model predicts. Some might think education might have something to do with explaining why OECD growth has been surprisingly fast and persistent relative to existing theories. In many developing countries the problem is *exactly* the opposite.

Educational attainment has absolutely exploded in developing countries over the last 40 years for which we have data, and if there is one policy that has been pursued nearly everywhere, it is the rapid expansion of education. And yet growth is slow, even slower than in the OECD, and except for the two biggest countries and a mere handful of others, slowed even more in the 1980s and 1990s, just as people benefiting from the investments in an initial round of education investments were rapidly changing the educational composition of the labour force.

Thirdly, growth theories do not start from an empirical puzzle of why the impact of education has been demonstrably larger than the standard models expect and then create a theory to explain why. Rather, they started from the other end (puzzles about growth) and worked to a theory with the implication that the aggregate impact of education should be larger than the aggregated micro (for example Mincer wage regression) impacts. But no paper in the literature has ever demonstrated that the returns to education are significantly *larger* than would be expected from the micro data. That is, finding a relationship between the level of output and the level of education is hardly a surprise. After all, the association at the individual level between earnings and education is probably the second most well-established fact in economics. But the real puzzle with education and growth is explaining why education has not appeared to have even the growth impact the standard neoclassical growth model paired with the standard Mincer micro returns would have predicted. When the impact of the growth of schooling (or growth in human capital) on the growth of output is estimated in 'production function' specifications that include physical capital accumulation, researchers not only fail to find education is more important than expected, they rarely find even a statistically significant coefficient, and at times find coefficients that are precisely estimated to be near zero.

The 'experiment' of massive expansions in formal schooling has already been tried and the results are deeply puzzling. I would think that there is a *prima facie* case for an educational puzzle in countries where levels of schooling have increased substantially over time and real wages have fallen. If there were an upward-sloping wage–education profile, and this did reflect higher productivity of schooled workers, and this productivity was not just private with negative spillovers, then an increase in the average schooling of the labour force should increase average wages. Of course falling real wages could represent a falling capital stock or falling productivity for reasons exogenous to education, but education and the labour market at least deserve consideration. In those country cases in which these puzzles emerge, this suggests that the country studies need to dig more deeply into (a) the mechanics of schooling, (b) the occupations of the schooled, and (c) changes over time in the supply and demand for educated labour.

In Tanzania, students take the Primary School Leaving Exam after seven years of education. On the mathematics portion, 83 per cent of the students scored *less than 13 per cent*, and in language 80 per cent scored less than 13 per cent. In Nigeria in the secondary school leaving exams, of roughly half a million students taking the exams, 82.5 per cent received a 'flat failure' – the lowest possible score – in English and 63 per cent produced a 'flat failure' on the maths-general portion of the exam. In both these cases there is no evidence that four out of five students learned *anything* in all the years of schooling. In contrast, other developing countries top the list in internationally comparable examinations. At least some consideration of the learning outcomes is necessary before assessing the potential growth impact of 'more schooling'.

Even if the schooling is effective, in examining impacts in particular countries one needs to focus on what jobs the newly educated take up. In many developing countries, particularly in the aftermath of independence, huge portions of the educated and particularly the highly educated went into government and civil service. This is true of the excellent performers (Japan, Taiwan, Korea) as well as slow-growers (Côte d'Ivoire, Ghana). The growth impact depends on how effectively these newly-minted technocratic elites could use their education to promote development.

Even if schooling was effective, and even if most of the educated labour force were not absorbed by government, any investments made in a low-productivity policy environment will have low returns. An evaluation of language achievement of third-graders in 11 Latin

American countries found Cuba far and away the highest performing. The 25th percentile of achievement in Cuba was better than the *75th percentile of the next best country* (Argentina). These stellar educational achievements do not prevent Cuba from remaining an economic basket-case. The contribution of education to economic growth depends not only on the supply of educated labour, but also on an expanding demand for educated labour. Demand for educated labour depends on the evolution of technology (Foster and Rosenzweig, 1995, 1996) and the dynamism of the private economy (Birdsall *et al.*, 1995).

The country case studies need to go beyond 'education is good' to understand how quality of learning, demand for educated labour, and government policies (including hiring policies) interact to determine the impact of education on growth.

Except for the causality issue, the role of physical investment in growth is well-understood

Physical capital appears to be one of those areas where the empirical data kicks up the least fuss about being strapped into the theory. One thing the data seem to say clearly and unambiguously is that there is a relationship between physical capital and growth of about the magnitude one could expect, and that the relationship is robust to the variables used (Levine and Renelt, 1992). Cross-national regression results are in reasonable relationship to the microeconomic data about returns to firms, to aggregate results about capital shares in income, and are robust to whether one uses investment rates as a proxy or uses the growth of physical capital stocks. If one regresses growth on investment rates, there is a statistically significant coefficient of about the right magnitude (for example Africa – table 5.1.1, Latin America – table 6, East Asia table 6). Similarly, if one calculates a physical stock variable by cumulating the investment series, one also gets a coefficient on physical capital growth of roughly the 'right' magnitude (South Asia).

It might seem the only remaining question about this well-established partial association is whether it reflects cause and effect – whether investment and capital-stock growth cause economic growth, or whether capital-stock growth is driven by some other factor (for example technological change) that also causes economic growth seems to be the only remaining question in the growth-investment literature (Carroll and Weil, 1994; Blomstrom, Lipsey and Zejan, 1996).

However, I would like to point out one empirical puzzle about which I have not seen much discussion, much less a compelling resolution. The puzzle is that with both of the widely used data series the growth of physical capital is completely uncorrelated with the average investment shares. Countries with high ratios of investment to GDP are not more likely to be countries with a high growth of physical capital.

Of course the immediate regression consequence of the lack of correlation is that if one does what no-one would think of doing – putting both the investment rate and the growth of physical capital in the same growth regression – they get exactly the same 'reasonable' coefficients as if they were included separately. Table 6.1 does this as an illustration of doing the most naïve possible thing. The physical capital coefficient is not too different from capital shares estimated from national income data: 0.395. The average investment ratio gets a coefficient that is compatible with returns on investment: 0.086.

The puzzle is that if the two variables are included together – which makes *no* intuitive sense at all if investment is a proxy for capital-stock growth – they get *exactly* the same coefficients as when included singly.[5] This means at the very least that whatever role investment is playing in the growth regression, it cannot be simply as a proxy for physical capital accumulation, because even when one accounts for the role of investment in physical capital accumulation in the obvious way, this accounts for exactly *none* of the reason why investment shares are present in existing growth regressions.[6]

Table 6.1   Growth regressions with physical capital and investment

	Just capital	*Just investment*	*Both*
Constant	−.002 (.60)	.004 (1.04)	−.016 (3.53)
Growth rate of physical capital per worker (King–Levine)	.395 (7.01)		.389 (7.43)
Average share of investment to GDP (PWT5.6)		.086 (3.76)	.083 (4.37)
N	114	114	114
R-Squared	.305	.112	.408

This may be a minor puzzle, but I believe it brings out four points to consider in the country case studies when thinking about the role of capital and investment in growth:

(a) the role of relative price shifts in capital 'productivity' in value terms;
(b) the role of key bottlenecks;
(c) coordination of investment responses; and
(d) investment flows and maintenance and depreciation.

First, there is the deep question of valuation and revaluation of the capital stock and appropriate deflation. The reason people did (and do) one-sector growth models was explained by John Hicks (1965): intertemporally shifting relative prices makes the definition of, not to mention the analytics of, dynamic steady-state equilibria quite intractable. Solow's approach to one-sector models is eminently sensible: if what we mean by a steady state includes within it the restriction that relative prices do not shift, then we may as well aggregate into a single good. This is not to say relative prices are in fact stable: it is just that this is what we need to assume to make progress on a certain analytical tool that is useful for certain purposes. However, this limits the applicability of the tool to situations in which relative prices are in fact shifting, and it is entirely an open question as to how much ('all of' or even 'most of') the differences and changes in growth rates observed in the world are accounted for by differences in steady-state equilibria in which relative prices are fixed.

So what do we mean by a 'capital stock' in the real world where relative prices do shift? Particularly when assets are fixed, shifts in relative prices will change current market valuations. If one were to take the capital invested in any mine (copper, lead, nickel, tin) in the United States and compute 'value-added' in nominal terms (or 'real' terms where deflation was a general price deflator) over the cumulated, depreciated capital stock, I am sure one would find enormous fluctuations in capital productivity – the 'real' dollar value of goods and services produced per unit of 'real' capital might even go to zero as the mine is closed down. In many smaller countries a substantial portion of investment goes to a few industries (or is related to those industries). So, while in the USA relative price shifts might roughly cancel out and leave the value of the aggregate capital stock at new prices relative to historical prices roughly unchanged, they certainly do not in Zambia (copper) or Nigeria (oil) or Jamaica (bauxite) or Côte d'Ivoire (tree crops). In a case study one might want to pay attention to how much of investment flows went into capital whose value was dramatically reduced by changes in relative prices.

Secondly, forgive me for saying the obvious, but marginal is not average. Shifts in economic conditions may change dramatically the productivity of certain key investments, so in considering either slumps or take-offs in growth the intertemporal or cross-sectoral 'average' incremental capital–output ratio (ICOR) may not matter so much as having key investments happen at the right time. This is, for instance, true of investments in infrastructure. Highways built ahead of anticipated demand that fails to materialize may have no impact on growth, but the failure to expand a road or port may inhibit a key response to changed relative prices. Especially as prices and conditions fluctuate, the marginal product of the incremental investment – responding to new circumstances – may be incredibly higher than past investments.

Thirdly, in examining country cases, particularly cases in which countries after periods of stable or even rapid growth fall into a prolonged recession, the question of investment coordination could be very important (over and above its role in pure capital accumulation). That is, suppose there is a shock that creates both a slump in aggregate demand and a need for a sectoral shift (say, from sugar to textiles); models of multiple equilibria in which if sufficient investment occurs it is profitable for all but it is profitable for no investor singly could explain a sustained dearth of investment due to coordination problems – even when returns to investments, taken together, could be quite high.

Fourthly, in the country case studies one potentially important factor that is often overlooked in the aggregate studies of capital, investment and growth is the interaction of investment flows and depreciation. In the basic capital-stock accumulation function,

$$\Delta K^i_{t,t-1} = I^i_t - \delta K^i_{t-1}$$

depreciation is nearly always considered to be constant both across countries and across time; in particular, to be invariant with respect to any maintenance expenditures. Yet all who have travelled widely in developing countries have encountered instances of three types of excessive depreciation.

One source of excessive depreciation is the consequence of 'irrational exuberance' followed by a bust in cash flows so that capital assets are overdimensioned relative to the ability to maintain those assets – even to maintain adequate maintenance. A second source of depreciation is institutionally perverse undermaintenance of assets; one observer referred to many aid financed investments as 'capitalized foregone maintenance' because the incentives of donor and recipient implied that the preference is to buy new rather than maintain the old. A third source of excess depreciation is 'for the want of a nail' situations in which shortages of key recurrent inputs or spare parts (often controlled imports) cause huge capital assets to fall into disuse.

Growth can be usefully decomposed into 'accumulation' and 'productivity'

I realize this is a touchy subject to raise, as I am about to suggest that one of the four topics of this volume – growth decomposition – is something we 'know that ain't so'. Let me raise one empirical puzzle followed by three objections to the current practice in the literature (including all of the background contributions) and suggest how this might influence the country studies.

The puzzle is that nearly all of the estimates of TFP for developing countries are too low. How do I know they are too low? If one includes education in the factor accumulation, something like 40 per cent of developing countries have negative TFP growth over a 30-year period. Zero is too low to be a steady-state growth rate of TFP – an economy with that as a steady state has an equilibrium of zero output. Then there is another large set of developing countries that have TFP growth rates less than 1 per cent, which is the average growth in OECD countries. This implies that countries with low levels of TFP have slower rates of growth as well. While this could be true, there is a powerful intuition that countries that are behind can learn from the countries ahead. Now if there were compelling reasons to believe that TFP was precisely and correctly measured I would have to readjust my beliefs that the numbers were too low. But I think this puzzle suggests the possibility that current methods of computing capital-stock growth overstate, perhaps substantially, 'true' capital-stock growth. There are four ways in which using a cumulated, depreciated investment effort might overstate capital stocks in developing countries.

First, returning to the point above about capital stocks and shifts in relative prices, unless the deflation is done exactly right, relative price shifts can appear to be physical TFP (using the same machines to produce less widgets) when they are 'value total factor productivity' (using the same machines to produce the same widgets – but which sell for less). Nothing in my experience with economic statistics suggests that GDP measures are deflated exactly right.

Secondly, there is the question of the objective function of the investors. I was struck by a study (Jensen, 1993) that showed in the decade from 1980 to 1990 that General Motors spent $39.8 billion on R&D and $82 billion on capital expenditures. Net of capital depreciation the management of GM spent $62.8 billion on investments in the corporation. At the end of that period the equity value of the firm was $20.8 billion. By this study's account, GM's management lost their shareholders over *$100 billion dollars* relative to an alternative financial strategy of investing the money in benchmark assets outside the firm.[7] The author's point is that, at times, since the mechanisms for shareholder control over management are weak, firm managements often overinvest for reasons of pride, prestige, direct pecuniary interests of the management, and so forth.

However weak may be the control of GM shareholders over management, they at least have an exit option. The citizens' control over the efficiency and efficacy of capital investment in developing countries – think of Indonesia, India, Nigeria, Egypt – where they have weaker legal or political systems and do not have an 'exit' option for their tax revenues must be weaker by an order of magnitude. With GM, at least one can trade the shares so that you can know how much value GM has actually created with their investments. The theoretical point is that one can estimate 'capital' by cumulating investment at cost only under very tight conditions about the objective function for investors. These conditions are obviously and importantly false for nearly all investment in most developing countries.

Third, the cyclical adjustment of TFP numbers is a much more important issue in developing countries than in the OECD as the magnitude of the variability of output around its trend is several-fold larger. Since by construction physical and educational capital stocks evolve very smoothly – as they are not adjusted for either relative prices or capacity utilization – this imposes all of the cyclical fluctuation into the residual. This is fine as long as the residual is consistently called MOOI ('measure of our ignorance'), but when the residual is called TFP this calls to mind certain phenomena which are determinants of TFP in the long run (technical progress, operating efficiency) that simply cannot be the cause of large short-term and medium-term fluctuations in output.

What does it mean to say that TFP was negative 2.5 per cent per annum in Latin America in the 1980s? Anything meaningful? Andrés

Velasco tells of a Chilean industrialist who was admired for having weathered the macroeconomic storms of the 1980s. When asked of the secrets of his success at a business luncheon in his honour, he had a one-word answer: 'Plastics'. People pressed him, thinking this bold visionary had moved into the production of plastics. 'No', he replied, 'I bought some plastic sheets, shut all the factories down, draped the machines with plastics and waited for better times.' Is it useful to refer to the loss of production of machines 'in plastic' as a decline in TFP? Mechanically it is true – but the potential physical productivity is the same, the machines would not produce profitably, and the shut-down may have had nothing to do with the sector or distorted policies or investment mistakes or anything other than a contraction in aggregate demand.

What are the implications as we move into the country studies? First, I would think country-case authors would at the very least attempt to distinguish government investment from private-sector investment and make some attempt to adjust public-sector 'capital' for how much/many 'factors' had actually been created and were there versus what had been spent under the heading 'investment'. Second, in countries in which one or two single sectors were a dominant part of the economy, I would attempt to separate out capital stocks and output by sector ('oil and non-oil' or 'copper and non-copper'). Third, I would attempt to adjust the capital stocks and factors for utilization rates, or, alternatively, examine only cyclically-adjusted output. Fourth, I would attempt to produce capital stocks with more realistic depreciation rates, particularly if some reasonable estimates could be made about maintenance spending. One way of possibly examining all of these effects together in the public sector is to compare selling prices of privatized government firms versus 'book value' – I suspect that in many developing countries the capital value of an ongoing enterprise is a small fraction of the standard cumulated, depreciated investment. Only after making all of these adjustments could one reasonably begin to ask how much of growth was explained by 'factors', and how much was MOOI and how much of MOOI was gains in productive or economic efficiency.

East Asia is a growth success to be emulated

I cannot count how many papers I have read in which the country undergoing scrutiny is compared to East Asia to see how and where the country 'failed'. The working assumption is that everyone would be East Asia if they could, and not being a 'tiger' is a failure. There is another possibility: the rapid growth in East Asia was not entirely a desirable state of affairs: perhaps growth this rapid was pathologically high.

One implication of the extremely rapid growth, say of South Korea, is that there was a massive transfer of consumption from very, very poor people to quite rich people (in many cases the same people, just older). If we turn to Solow's 1970 exposition of growth theory to find the optimal rate of growth of consumption expenditures (c) then:

$$\frac{dc^*/dt}{c^*} = (r^* - a) / \sigma$$

This is the well-known condition that the rate of growth of consumption should be equal to the excess of the return on capital (r) over the rate of time preference (a) adjusted for the elasticity of substitution in consumption (σ) – where a high substitution coefficient implies marginal utility declines rapidly.

In Korea, real private consumption per capita grew at a 5.4 per cent per annum clip between 1969 and 1998, so that per capita consumption was 4.6 times higher in 1998 than in 1969 (three times the change in the USA). Taking a social discount rate of 1 per cent and a value of the consumption elasticity of 3 then the return to capital would have to be 15.2 per cent to justify this rate of growth as 'optimal'.

Obviously it is hard to pin down either of the parameters, but there are two observations. First, I find it hard to believe that someone currently 50 years old would not give up a few luxuries now for having had a bit more food when they were 20 in 1969 when real per capita consumption was only $700 (currently Bolivian private consumption per person is $780). This is just the interpersonal substitution, the intergenerational comparisons are even more stark – imagine how 70-year-olds feel about having sacrificed enormous amounts of consumption in their prime age in order that their grandchildren (and especially *other people's* grandchildren!) have the latest in electronic gadgets on which to amuse themselves zapping bad guys.

Second, the average real rate of interest on demand deposits over this period in Korea was only 2.4 per cent. Consumption sacrificed and invested in banks certainly was a welfare-reducing choice – and demand and time bank deposits were 39 per cent as large as private consumption in 1969.

Trying to resolve rapid growth, high savings and low interest rates within a strictly market equilibrium, optimal policy, framework is going to lead to contradictions. Maybe the return to capital was really,

really high – but, if so, why are returns on the 'risk-free' asset so low? Perhaps risk-aversion can explain the discrepancy between riskless assets and the return to capital – but to get risk-aversion high enough to explain a gap between a 2 per cent rate of interest and a 15 per cent return on capital one needs either enormous amounts of risk or high risk-aversion. The 'equity premium puzzle' in the USA is that in order to explain the gap between the return to a 'risk-free' asset and the US stockmarket requires coefficients of relative risk-aversion on the order of 50! (Mehra and Prescott, 1985). But the higher the consumer risk-aversion (σ) invoked to explain the risk premium, the higher the return of capital would need to be since risk-aversion and inequality-aversion are identical in the simple models. The magnitude of risk/inequality-aversion necessary to explain a risk premium that large then makes the rate of growth to make a person willing to save today even higher. One could invoke enormously high average returns to capital but with correspondingly enormous idiosyncratic risks, but then how did one generate such enormous investment levels if risks were so high?

One way out is to suggest consumers systematically underestimated growth and so were willing to save in 1969 because they did not know they would be so much richer in the future. This is logically tight, the growth rates were historically unprecedented, and perhaps it did take a long time for consumers really to believe they were permanent. But appealing to several decades of systematic forecast errors to explain behaviour is methodologically disappointing.

The out-of-the-box alternative is that these high rates of saving were neither optimal nor fully voluntary. It is not so hard to imagine that the governments, especially the first four Tigers, felt under threat. Three of them – South Korea, Taiwan, Hong Kong – were capitalist and Western allies perched on the periphery of a large, unstable, Communist empire. For these governments, rapid growth and industrialization was at least in part a military preparedness and regime survival issue on a number of fronts.

If this is the case, then the other countries are striving for the wrong objective by always comparing themselves to countries that were growing 'too fast'. Perhaps policy reform with an eye on East Asia is like launching into a fitness regime with pictures of Arnold Schwarzenegger (in his Mr Olympia days) on the mirror – greatly overshooting the optimal. The main implication for the country studies is to focus on how much lower growth was from the achievable, even perhaps optimal, growth.

3   Why we might be looking for the hole on the bottom of the flat tyre

The growth research reported in this volume is much richer and broader than the narrow agenda of the 'growth regression' type. One of the strengths of the overall project is expanding the range of concerns to try and bring a coherent approach that integrates growth regressions and decompositions with attention to politics and political economy, microeconomic behaviour of agents and, through the concern with factor markets especially, to institutions. Within this broader agenda I have four concerns about the general thrust of the research project, in which attention to places where the tyre is flat may detract from actually finding the hole:

- political economy without mistakes or ideas;
- institutional performance matters, but so do institutions;
- investigating policies as conditional rules about actions; and
- using 'growth' as a lens to look for levels.

Again, let me explain each concern and suggest how the next stage of the research, the country studies, might respond to these concerns.

Political economy with no mistakes or ideas

As I read through the framework paper and regional papers for political economy, I kept looking for the authors in the models and did not find them. I wanted to say: 'Political economist endogenize thyself!'

As it stands, the positive models of the determination of policies have no role for ideas of any type. Paradoxically this is a comfortable position for economists but is awkward for the policy-minded. After all, economists' *positive* models about consumer and firm behaviour either assume that they are perfectly well-informed, or extend the model and assume they are optimizing over the acquisition of information as well as other goods. Economists tend to look with disdain on those that actually give people 'self-help' advice either to corporeal or corporate persons (our theory of the firm has little use for management consultants). Economists are more comfortable with 'equalizing the objective function return across all activities' as a *description* rather than as a *prescription*.

But suppose the research agenda on political economy of growth begun here were pushed to conclusion, including the country studies, what would be the policy messages that would emerge? As it stands, there not only *would not* but *could not* be any policy *messages* emerging directly from this research on a logically consistent and intellectually honest level. That is, if one constructs an analytical model in which policies are completely determined by actors who are optimizing relative to their own interests and in which there is no formal, analytic role for 'policy messages' (or actors called 'policy message senders' or 'economic researchers') in affecting outcomes, one cannot then use this model to decide the appropriate policy messages. If the existing policies are an equilibrium in a Pareto sense, then it is not clear what one could expect the impact of a policy message of the type: 'change policy/institution X and the output will be Y' not its current value of Y.' Since presumably attempts to change the institutions were in the action set of the actors in the first place, this must also be in equilibrium. If sincere messages are those that increased the objective function of the recipient, it is not clear to whom this 'policy message' is a sincere message.

Moreover, without a model of policy messages' impact on policies, there is no rationale for sending a policy message like 'do this thing X that, if it were done, would improve everyone's welfare.' Since the models have no role for how actors respond to policy messages I could add to whatever model that emerges from this research an assumption that the 'policy-maker' (PM) regards the policy message sender (PMS) as an enemy and hence assumes that whatever message (M) is sent by PMS is not sincere, but is a trap. Hence the PM will interpret any new policy message received from the PMS source as the arrival of new information (which he did not previously have) about changes in fundamentals requiring adjustments in policies, and the adjustments in policies this message requires are *exactly the opposite* of what the PMS recommends. In this case a very complicated loop about the behaviour of the PMS and the policy-maker emerges – does the PMS know I am going to do the opposite and so is sending the opposite of what he really thinks, or is the PMS evil but naïve? – that may end up as a model of 'cheap talk'. Now, you may object that this is a particularly perverse model of response to policy messages – but it is at least as good as no model at all.

This is like the World Bank developing political-economy models of policy determination in order to better understand how to give its policy advice – while never endogenizing the impact of its policy advice. Either World Bank advice does, potentially, affect policy – in which case it has to be an element of a correctly specified model of policy determination, so a model without it is wrong and hence *prima facie* suspect – or it does not, even potentially, affect policy, in which case who cares?

The implications for the country studies of this are obvious. If there were in fact discrete episodes of policy reform that improved or worsened policy, then it would be interesting to know how those came about. Were they entirely the result of shifts of underlying fundamentals of the models, or did the arrival of new information (for example documented disappointing results, studies, performance of neighbours) change the ideas of leaders about the world and how it works. If new leaders came with different ideas, then what was the source of those ideas – pure self-interested rationalizations? Broad ideological beliefs from elsewhere?

Ideas could either matter because actors have wrong ideas and hence are not optimizing, or ideas could matter because ideas or information can change the relative powers of various actors inside the model. For instance, changes in the processes of decision-making so that inputs and outputs are more visible to stakeholders can, by itself, change patterns of accountability. The experience of Samuel Paul and his organization in Bangalore, India, in which the act of creating and publicizing a 'report card' of the performance of various public institutions has alone created a dynamic of change in at least some of the organizations.

I realize I am adding to an already impossible load of developing a completely general framework, but if any research (including this research) is to matter, then ideas must matter. Why not build them into the models?

Institutional performance matters, but do institutions?

Anyone who has worked in and around a developing country knows on one level that 'institutions matter'. When I returned from living in Indonesia a year ago, I had to buy a car and was pressed for time. I knew what type of car I wanted and I walked into a car dealership at 9:45 pm with nothing but a cheque-book – no insurance, no valid driver's licence and no car – drove off the lot at 10:30 pm with a brand new car. Rapid arms'-length market transactions are facilitated by well-functioning institutions. They could check my driving record and my credit record in real time, and the car dealership knew that if I defaulted on any aspect of the contract an array of institutions for enforcing contracts will kick-in in a predictable and reasonably efficacious matter. The similar process when I moved to Indonesia two years previously took nine weeks.

However, does this mean institutions matter or that institutional *performance* matters. That 'institutions matter' is not in fact obvious, and three commonsense facts suggest it is false, as successful countries have very different institutions and countries with exactly the same institutions have very different outcomes.

The first commonsense fact is that one set of countries – called the (non-expanded) OECD or 'Europe, areas of early European settlement (early to exclude Argentina) and Japan' – have all arrived at roughly similar levels of economic productivity and welfare. If 'institutions matter', then this set of countries should have similar sets of institutions, or at least institutions that are more like each other than they are like countries that have low levels of income. But it is hard to think how one could assert, either historically or contemporaneously, that 'institutions are alike' for the UK, France, Germany, Japan and the USA. They differ not just in laws but legal *systems*. Politically they have come to look more alike over time, but during their period of 'development' (1870 to 1950) they differed not just in politics (in the way that Massachusetts and Utah might be different) but in political *systems*. No one would venture to say that England's parliamentary democracy, Bismarck's Germany and Third Republic France had similar political institutions. Another area in which the institutional heterogeneity and performance similarity is striking is financial systems; crudely put, in Germany banks own firms, in Japan firms own banks, in the USA the two are at arms' length. Which is the 'best' system? If it matters, it can't be by much.

The second commonsense fact is that the 'four Tigers' have all had spectacular (perhaps too spectacular) performance. What is the relevant sense in which South Korea, Hong Kong, Taiwan and Singapore are 'institutionally' similar? One was, until recently, a British colony; one a break-off province of China not formally recognized as a country and ruled by a military government; while the United States had some influence, South Korea followed Japanese institutions in many respects; and Singapore was not a colony but in many ways followed British institutions.

The third commonsense fact is that most ex-colonies kept the institutional forms of their colonialists – but there have been very different outcomes across countries with *identical* political, legal, financial and economic institutions. The formal design of institutions must be much more alike between the UK, Jamaica, India and Kenya than UK institutions are like those of France. In many former colonies systems of law, education, finance and politics remain, on a formal level, *exactly* like their colonialist oppressor. However, while there might be some tendencies for some institutional systems to have outperformed others, in general these countries have neither 'converged' with their former colonists nor with other countries with similar institutional heritage.

One response is that institutional *form* does not matter, but 'institutions matter' because institutional *performance* does matter and institutional heterogeneity simply says that different institutional forms can be made to achieve roughly equivalent *performance*. This is probably right, but then the whole question has been begged; it is at least possible that 'institutional performance matters but *institutions* do not'.[8]

The country studies which examine how factor markets work and how institutions facilitate, or not, market transactions need to go beyond pointing out that institutional performance is poor and this is a detriment to economic welfare – that is obvious. They need to dig deeper into the question of *why* institutional performance is poor. Perhaps the answer is 'poorly designed institutions' – perhaps not. In De Soto's (2000) recent book *The Mystery of Capital* he points out that systems of property fail in Peru and many other developing countries so that wealth in real estate cannot be leveraged. But his more interesting observations come in his recognition that formal property systems in these countries are exactly like those in countries where they do work. In his examination of the development of property rights in the United States, he finds that it was not the case that good law created good transactions – rather, transactions carried on outside the ambit of the existing law – squatters, people using land 'illegally' – gathered the political power to change the law to accommodate the informal transactions.

Empirical investigation of policies as conditional rules about actions

One admirable thing about this research is the attempt to integrate the various pieces of the growth story to be sure it all fits together: how do empirical growth determinants at the cross-national level (sources of growth) fit with the microeconomic decisions of firms and households that make up those aggregates (microeconomics) as determined via interactions of governments, firms, and households (markets) and why does government choose the actions it does (political economy). However, a very weak link in this chain is that between the variables that float around on the right-hand side of growth regressions and actual decisions of governments. This partly a question of causation but also partly a question of identification and trying to solve causation problem in the usual econometric way may actually lead in the wrong direction.

Let me try and be more clear with a series of simple examples. Suppose we run a regression of growth on some variable X and find a positive relationship of magnitude ß. If a country could at no cost raise X we might be tempted to make a 'policy' recommendation: 'raise X'. At this point our academic colleagues would object saying that perhaps the partial association between growth and X is reverse so that higher growth causes more X, not vice versa. The usual econometric solution is to find some instrument that is associated with X and is not associated (either caused or caused by) growth and then estimate the same relationship and, if it comes out the same, feel at least modestly more reassured about our policy recommendation.

I think there are several problems that go deeper than that, however, and these problems are not so easily solved. The problems stem from the fact that in most instances a 'policy' is not an action and does not completely determine an outcome, but a *policy is a conditional rule, a mapping from states of the world to actions.* An insurance policy specifies pay-offs in response to states of the world, a store could have a policy of 'money back if not satisfied,' a company could have a policy of firing anyone late for work more than three times. Economic policies can be responsive to states of the world in several ways – all of which make growth regressions problematic.

As a first example, suppose that the true state of the world was that domestic production of 'widgets' is good for growth (so a protective tariff is good), and domestic production of 'woonsockets' is bad for growth (so a protective tariff is bad). Suppose the formula for growth over the relevant period was linear (each 10 percentage point change in the tariff raises or lowers growth by 10 percentage point):

$$g = \tau_{widgets} / 10 - \tau_{woonsockets} /10$$

Now suppose there were two each of four types of countries: countries of type A had a policy of 'free trade', B had a policy of promoting widgets, C had a 10 per cent tariff on both goods, and D has a policy of a whopping tariff of 40 per cent on woonsockets (which raises domestic production which is bad for growth) and a 10 per cent tariff on widgets. The growth outcomes will be as in Table 6.2. If one runs the OLS regression one finds that, as in Table 6.3 column 1, 'higher tariffs are associated with lower growth'.

Now I want to illustrate that the problem with this result is not in fact an econometric issue about direction of causation that can be fixed by better technique. Suppose that countries A and B were former

Table 6.2 Completely hypothetical example about tariffs and growth

Country	Tariff on woonsockets	Tariff on widgets	Average tariff	Tariff of colonial power	Growth rate
A	0	0	0	0	0
B	0	20	10	0	2
C	10	10	10	10	0
D	40	10	25	10	−3

colonies of a *laissez-faire* power, and countries C and D were former colonies of a protectionist power, so that A and C had the tariffs of the former colonial power and C and D retained the tariff on one of the two goods. I then do my very clever IV regression, knowing (suppose it is true, and it is by the simple formula) that a country's post-colonial growth did not influence the colonial power's tariff rates so using only that component of cross-national variation of tariffs that projects into the space of former colonialists tariffs (IV regression) will purge actual tariffs of any reverse causality. When I do that I get column 2 of Table 6.3 – which is just the same as column 1, and I am therefore home free on regression technique and still *completely wrong* about policy advice.

I am completely wrong because I am treating the *average* tariff as a complete summary statistic for tariff policy, when in fact it is not. A tariff *policy* is a rule that assigns tariffs to goods. The *policy* of free trade is clearly dominated by the *policy* of 'have a high tariff on the good on which it is growth-promoting to have a high tariff on', but is superior to a policy of 'have a high tariff on the good it is bad to have a high tariff on' and equal to a policy of 'equal tariff rates'. A tariff *policy* is a mapping from states of the world to tariffs, and so unless the variable included in the growth regression accurately captures difference in policies *as mappings* it creates an empirical fact about partial associations between summary statistics about *policy actions* and *outcomes* which is consistent with nearly any mapping between *policies* and *outcomes*.

Let me give a second example. Suppose that countries have normal times but at times they might have a temporary shock (such as a hurricane) or a permanent shock (commodity prices might fall). Table 6.4 gives the possible outcomes of the types of shocks and deficits so that running a deficit with no shock is bad, running a deficit to finance a temporary shock is good (reduces the negative impact of the shock), and running a deficit to finance a permanent shock is bad.

Table 6.3   Growth regressions to learn about policy impacts (dependent variable is always growth)

	Tariff regressions (based on hypothetical data in Table 6.2)		Budget deficit regressions (based on hypothetical data in Table 6.4)					
	OLS	IV	OLS	OLS	OLS	OLS	OLS	OLS
Average tariff	−.14 (2.31)	−.20 (2.17)						
Deficit			−.333	−.33	−1.28	−1.28 (2.94)	1	1 (1.97)
Hurricane				−1.5		−3.5 (5.51)		−3.5 (3.69)
Price shock				−3.5		−1.5 (1.83)		−1.5 (−2.04)
N	8	8	6	6	14	14	14	14
				One country of each type	One of each of A,B,C,D but five each of country type 'E' and 'F' (price shock)		One of each of A,B,C,D but five each of country type 'C' and 'D' (hurricane)	

Table 6.4   Possible outcomes of shock

Type of country	Permanent shock (commodity price)	Temporary shock (hurricane)	Budget deficit (yes/no)	Growth outcome (per cent per annum)
a	0	0	0	2
b	0	0	Yes	1
c	0	Yes	Yes	1
d	0	Yes	0	−1
e	Yes	0	Yes	−3
f	Yes	0	0	−1

What happens when you run regressions on this data-set? Is the 'policy variable' of budget deficits good or bad for growth? The econometric answer depends entirely on the distribution of countries in the sample. If there is one of each type, deficits look modestly bad.

If the sample is dominated by 'price shocks', countries' deficits look terrible. If the sample is populated with relatively more 'hurricane' countries, then deficits look good. 'Controlling for' hurricanes and price shocks doesn't change these results. But *none* of the regressions gives the right *policy* answer for *any* country. The right *deficit policy* is the conditional rule: 'observe the state of the world, if "no shock" do not run a deficit, if "hurricane" run a deficit, if "price shock" do not run a deficit'.

Of course the problem is even trickier than this in two ways: first, interactions of policies, and, second, going a step back and thinking about policies about making policies (institutions). In these examples I am still assuming one can assess the impact of policies without worry about what other, complementary, policies are doing. So, in the deficit example, how damaging a deficit will be depends on a number of features – can I borrow to finance this deficit or do I have to 'print money'? If I do 'print money', how quickly will this translate into inflation and how persistent will that inflation be? If I do print money, and I do create relatively persistent inflation, is that consistent with my exchange-rate policy? In other work I have argued that 'syndromes' of inconsistent policies end up being enormously bad for growth in ways that are hard to detect imagining each of them in isolation (Pritchett, 1998).

The second point is that one could imagine 'policy-making' as divided into three steps: a setting of an institutional 'rules of the game', the making of 'policy' (announcement of mapping from states of the world to policy actions), and 'policy implementation' in which some agent has to decide on which policy action to take, depending on their claim about which state of the world had been realized.

Let's go back to the tariff example. Countries A and C pre-committed to a tariff policy 'rules of the game' by retaining a customs union with their former colonialist power so they have no independent tariff policy. Countries B and D chose an institutional rules of the game of giving authority to a 'tariff commission to set tariffs'. In both instances the 'tariff commission' announced a tariff *policy* of 'placing high tariffs on goods the domestic production of which will promote the national welfare'. In implementation of that policy, the structure of agency relationships (incentives, accountability, and all that) was such that in country B those responsible for choosing policy *actions* made the right choices, and those in county D, for whatever reasons (corruption, incompetence, faulty computer programmes), chose policy *actions* that were wrong.

Is the superior tariff *policy* uniform or differentiated tariffs? The answer depends on the structure of implementation. If at the 'rules-of-the-game' stage one suspects that either policy or its implementation will be bad, then an institutional precommitment device that locks in non-optimal tariff structure (uniform tariffs) as the only policy will be preferred to a institutional environment in which the country has the possibility of choosing a superior tariff *policy* and tariff *policy actions* (actual tariffs) but will in fact choose lousy tariffs. Multilateral commitment devices can be seen as ways of sacrificing the potential gains of 'optimal' discretionary policy to avoid its potential losses.

The fact that many of the growth regressions variables are dramatically unstable over time in standard growth regressions – the coefficients switch *signs* across different periods for population growth (Kelley), trade (Clemens and Williamson) and social capital (Knack and Keefer, 1997) – and that the out-of-sample predictive power of many regressions is poor, suggests that the existing partial associations in growth regressions are not the final answer. Instability of coefficients *is* a model-specification test.

Of course the situation is even worse than this because many of the variables about which there is settling 'conventional wisdom' about the robustness of their partial associations with growth are not even as close to 'policies' as summary statistics of policy-action outcomes (like tariffs or budget deficits). Take a variable such as inequality: all acknowledge this is not a 'policy' variable, it is the *result* of a variety of past (accumulation) and present (demand for various factors) market outcomes plus a set of policies (about taxation, about transfers). There is absolutely no reason to believe that 'inequality' is a summary statistic for *any* policy or policy action. There are almost certainly policy actions that would improve inequality and growth, policy actions that would cause both inequality and growth to deteriorate, and policies that would move the two in different directions.

Take an accumulation variable like 'human capital'. Say we find a robust partial association between the level of years of schooling and the level of output.[9] That says nothing about schooling *policy*. Suppose you could even show this was causal from schooling to output; that still says nothing about *policy* – this is no more informative about policy than the 'finding' that there is a return to private physical-capital investment. Suppose you could show that the growth returns to schooling were higher than the individual returns – now at least there is some *potential* policy implication. But what is the *policy* because it is still the case that schooling is an outcome – which is an interaction of policies and private behaviours. Do all policies that increase schooling have the same impact on output? Suppose there are 10 children and I increase the average schooling of the labour force by one year in two different ways. One policy would be to test 10 children and then give the one for which the returns to schooling are the largest 10 years of schooling. The other policy would be to make all 10 children take one year of schooling. In both instances schooling has increased one year, but which do we expect to have the largest growth impact? These are something like real policy choices people face – do we devote more resources to improving the quality of higher secondary and tertiary schooling and hence retaining those who do enroll for longer – or do we devote the same resources to expanding access to basic education?

The implication for the country studies is that in deciding what went wrong in any given country, analysts must distinguish between the various levels of rules for policy-making, policies, and policy actions. Suppose that one can show in retrospect that Venezuela dramatically overexpanded domestic investment during the 'oil-boom' years. Was this because they pursued the wrong budget *policy* or because those responsible for policy implementation were factually wrong about the *state of the world* – anticipated the higher oil prices would last – and hence mapped to the wrong *policy action*?

Suppose in the country case study the analyst decides that protectionist tariffs in India did not promote economic growth. Is that because the *policy* of using tariffs to promote industries is necessarily wrong, or that the tariffs chosen just happened to be wrong, or because, given the sets of capabilities and accountabilities, decisions about particular policy actions within that policy were *bound* to be wrong? Even given the conclusion that trade-policy actions did not promote growth, these three different judgments about the source of that failure would have very different implications.

Looking for levels with growth rates

Before the emergence of the 'new-growth' literature, development economists were intellectually trapped between 'policy invariance' of the Solow model and the 'policy irrelevance' generated by the small size of the Harberger triangles. In the Solow model long-run per capita income growth depended only on TFP growth – but that was (by construction) exogenous and hence unaffected by policy. On the other hand, economists always believed that policies affected the *level* of output through efficiency gains. However, whenever the magnitude of those was calculated, one ran up against the problem that the magnitude of the gain seemed to be small. Arnold Harberger – no enemy of free trade – made famous the finding that the gains from reducing trade barriers were likely to be smallish fractions of GDP. His example of Chile in the 1970s suggested efficiency gains from trade reform of, at a maximum, 5 per cent of GDP.

But suppose one wanted to argue that any substantial fraction of the difference between the performance of India, chugging along at 2 per cent, and Korea, zooming along at 7 per cent, was due to trade policies. One might stick to level effects of trade reform and examine the growth-rate differences as transitional – but then the magnitude of the level effects had to be *orders of magnitude* larger than Harberger triangles. That is, suppose I want to explain growth rates that are higher by 5 percentage *points* for over a decade as a 'transition in levels' of microeconomic efficiency. Assuming that *all* of the transition happened in one decade, then the magnitude of the level effect necessary to explain the 5 per cent per annum growth differential as a transition between two levels had to be $(1.05)^{10}$ = 63 per cent of GDP. You can see the problem. Either only a small part of the observed growth differentials between high and low-growth performers was trade (and many other 'efficiency-gain' policy reforms had the same, or smaller, magnitudes), or the static model was wrong about the level effects by not just a little, but a lot.

One way to go about this was adding dynamic or non-competitive effects of various kinds into the models – so grafting onto the usual micro approaches to gains from trade theories of monopolization or imperfect competition, managerial slack, or to assume that the Solow 'A' was not available to everyone and trade had something to do with closing the gap between country A and world best practice A.

But then along came the policy equivalent of liberation theology – 'new-growth' models that suggested, with reasonably grounded models, there can be cross-national differences, not just in levels, but in growth rates of output. This intellectual innovation allowed everyone to just put growth over there on the left-hand side and start slapping stuff on the right-hand side and treat the equation as if it were well-specified (with usually some hand-waving appeal to a 'new-growth' model). Of course economists well-grounded in microeconomics always deplored this. Trade economists such as Bhagwati and Srinivasan – also no enemies of free trade – were always dubious about 'proving' trade reform was a good idea via growth regressions with specifications that seemed to imply steady-state growth gains from trade reform, which meant the growth gains were not a small per cent of GDP but *infinite*.

I think we are all now convinced that 'infinite' is not the right answer. At this stage the right answer has to be that policy reform can bring about level changes (not steady-state growth changes) but that these level changes are enormously larger that we would have guessed from the Harberger triangles or the Solow growth model. The question is: are we going to continue to make progress by thinking of 'growth' as what is to be explained, rather than 'levels' with growth modelled strictly as the transition between levels.

Looking for large level effects with growth regressions is possible, but one needs to be enormously careful about the modelling of the dynamics. That is, suppose we imagine changing a policy or institutional variable from 0 to 1 at time t, what is the output at future times $t + n$ over all n, and we are interested in both the 'long-run' impact and the adjustment path, the 'impulse response function'. Let me use the device of generating 'data' from a very simple model and then examining how various regressions would serve in identifying the 'true' coefficients and the true 'impulse response function'. Suppose the level 'potential' output is determined as a simple relationship between two variables (think of one as 'policies' and the other as 'institutions'):

$$Y_t^{P*} = P_{t,}, y_t^{I*} = I_t$$

The adjustment speeds for the two variables are allowed to be different. One can imagine very different time profiles of the output response functions with respect to a change in patent law versus a change in exchange-rate policy:

$$y_t^I = y_{t-1}^I + \theta^I * (y_t^{I*} - y_{t-1}^I), y_t^P = y_{t-1}^P + \theta^P * (y_t^{P*} - y_{t-1}^P)$$

Plus, we assume there are random shocks to output. The equation for output is:

$$y_t = y_t^I + y_t^P + Shock_t$$

I specify some process of exogenous policy or institutional reform where each happens each year with probability P of reform and the policy/institution either improves with an 80 per cent chance or gets worse with a 20 per cent chance. Now, suppose I want to estimate the long-run impact of policy or institutional reform on the level of output. There are five approaches common in the literature: (1) levels on levels, (2) growth on changes, (3) growth on levels, (4) growth on levels with lagged level of output to recover the growth impact, and (5) using 'panel' data to do fixed effects with growth on levels and lagged level:

(1) Levels on levels: $y_t^i = \alpha + \beta_I * I_t^i + \beta_p * P_t^i + \varepsilon 1_\tau^l$

(2) Growth on changes: $gr(y)_{t,t-n}^i = \alpha + \beta_I * \Delta I_{f(t,t-n)}^i + \beta_P * \Delta P_{f(t,t-n)}^i + \varepsilon 3_\tau^l$

(3) Growth on levels: $gr(y)_{t,t-n}^i = \alpha + \beta_I * I_{f(t,t-n)}^i + \beta_P * P_{f(t,t-n)}^i + \varepsilon 3_\tau^l$

(4) Growth on levels with lagged level:

$$gr(y)_{t,t-n}^i = \alpha + \lambda * y_{t-n}^i + \beta_I * I_{f(t,t-n)}^i + \beta_P * P_{f(t,t-n)}^i + e4_\tau^l$$

(5) Fixed effects with panel data (~ denotes deviation from country-specific means):

$$\tilde{g}r(y)_{t,t-n}^i = \lambda * \tilde{y}_{t-n}^i + \beta_I * \tilde{I}_{f(t,t-n)}^i + \beta_P * \tilde{P}_{f(t,t-n)}^i + e5_\tau^l$$

Even this collection of equations reveals several ways that the existing growth literature has been a little bit casual about how the specification of the dynamics will affect the usefulness of growth regressions to look for level effects. First, in the notation above I nuance the issue of whether the dependent variables of policies and institutions are specified as the beginning of period $(t - n)$, end of period (t), average over the period, average of end and beginning value, and so on. Because many variables are available only for a single cross-sectional observation or with only intermittent frequency (such as inequality or indicators of 'corruption' or tariff data), this issue is often 'nuanced' in the empirical work and choices are made on an entirely *ad hoc* basis. Second, it is often not made clear exactly what one is estimating. I could use any of the specifications to estimate the impact on the long-run (infinite horizon) *level* of output of a permanent change in policy/institutional variable from P to P' – but except in specification (1) this requires some calculations with the regression coefficients (and in specification (3) for any variable that the answer is not zero the answer will be absurd at sufficiently long forecast horizons). Third, all of these specifications assume the adjustment speed to disequilibria generated by a policy reform is the same for any and all reforms in policies and institutions.

There are pluses and minuses to the various regressions. The 'levels on levels' will get the long-run impulse response about right, but is silent on the dynamics and says nothing about growth rates that adjust to that long-run state. The 'growth on levels' regression will get the very long-run response very wrong (because it will be infinite at infinite horizons), and will get the growth rates also very wrong (because the initial burst of speed in response to reform will be missed). Any of the specifications that use the lagged level for dynamics will get both the dynamics and the long-run impulse response wrong because it imposes a very particular structure on the dynamics. In fact in this particular set-up the seemingly most econometrically 'sophisticated' (for example fixed-effect panel regressions) can be *the worst* (besides growth on levels) in estimating the level impact of institutional reform.[10]

This is not a new or particularly novel methodological point, because the econometrics of macroeconomic time series are well-known. The state of the art are VAR (vector auto-regressions) in which all variables are included with long and flexible lags and then this complex mix of parameters produces impulse-response functions – of which all the functional forms (1) to (5) are a special case.

But the real question is 'why?' – why use growth regressions at all? Suppose I want to know what the impact on output over the next 5 or 10 years in India would be of lowering average tariffs in *concertina* fashion by 20 percentage points. Suppose we all agree the output impact would not be zero and would not be infinite. Are there any circumstances in which a 'growth regression' is going to be the best methodology for addressing this question? Suppose I am recommending a subsidy to foreign direct investment, are there any circumstances in which a 'growth regression' is going to be the best methodology for estimating the impact? Suppose I want to know how much poorer Bolivia is because it is landlocked. Are there any circumstances in which 'growth regression' is going to be the best methodology to get the answer? All of these seem like 'level effects with transitional dynamics' questions to me. I regard as completely open the question as to whether a 'new' – or *any* single – growth model itself provides theoretical resolution to justify the necessary choice of parsimony between specifications (1) to (5).

Moreover, the big problem is that the level effects seem to be very much larger than we would have imagined if the extremely rapid growth rates observed are transitions across levels. Here the question is why 'Harberger triangle' answers might lead us astray and underestimate the long-run impacts of reform. But an overreaction to a 'new-growth' world in which all long-run impacts are infinite is not guaranteed to be the most fruitful methodology.

Of course, this last comment creates no new suggestions for the country studies, and in fact simply justifies the agenda of the growth-research project itself – moving beyond cross-national growth regressions to both country detail and moving beyond a strictly aggregated, macroeconomic approach to growth to try and understand complex phenomena of economic progress.

4 Conclusion

Much progress has been made in understanding economic growth, by the work reported on in this volume and elsewhere. But for all of the reasons above I look forward to the country studies. Not all studies will be able to do everything, but each will be able to do something that advances our knowledge. The study of the experiences of individual countries can be sufficiently fine-grained to provide the detail necessary for reliable policy guidance.

Notes

1 The idea that either the 'new' growth theory or the 'neo-classical revival' has 'discovered' the importance of human capital is belied by even a casual reading of Kuznets (1960), Lewis (1955), Schultz (1963) or Denison (1967). The quotation from Gunnar Myrdal's (1968) *Asian Drama*, written mostly in the late 1950s and early 1960s, shows he already treats the importance of human capital in development along with physical capital as the conventional wisdom.

2 There is a fair bit of *ex post* caricature of the early growth theorists as their actual thinking was much more sophisticated than that part of their thinking that was subsequently captured in formalization, and they get blamed for simplifications they never endorsed. For instance, Lewis (1955) is now attacked for having focused on raising savings rates, but in his book *The Theory of Economic Growth* the section on Capital is chapter V following chapters on the now fashionably 'new' topics of economic institutions, knowledge and culture.

3 Even here, Simon Kuznets' work in 1960 lays out succinctly the growth economics and implications of the non-rivalry of knowledge. What had not been done was to formalize these into models with equilibria and all that, which is a considerable and substantial contribution of the 'new-growth' economists, but the *idea* about non-rivalry of ideas was always there.

4 This is well-known and was one of Kaldor's six stylized facts that Solow (1970) tried to explain formally.

5 This finding is robust to the deletion of either influential observations or large regression residuals up to 10 per cent of the sample.

6 This implies that regressions with investment rate are not 'partialing out' the role of physical capital accumulation in growth at all (and vice versa, capital growth does not partial out investment) with a number of obvious implications about how growth regressions including either the investment or capital variable have been interpreted. That is, regressing growth on investment and some other policy (P) or institutional variables does not have the interpretation of 'impact of P on output conditional on accumulation'.

7 In perspective, total gross fixed capital formation in four developing countries – India, Indonesia, Nigeria and Egypt – with 1.1 billion people in 1990 was $125 billion (at market exchange rates).

8 *Order Without Law* (Ellickson, 1991) has a detailed study of dispute resolution in a particular area of California where ranching was a major industry and hence disputes often arose about livestock causing damage. One of the study's findings was that nearly all disputes were resolved successfully without recourse to the courts. That was not so surprising, as any economist could construct a negotiation model in which for the most part parties would settle conflicts roughly along the lines that they would get if they went to court, so that 'law mattered' even though few people went to court. But the really striking finding was that the resolutions people of roughly equal power reached voluntarily outside of court *had nothing to do with the law* in that the allocation of damages in informal settlements was not at all how liability was allocated in the relevant civil law or legal code. The book suggested to me that most people had an incentive to get along, and given that incentive would work out their disputes irrespective of the formal law.

9 You cannot find a robust association between the level of schooling and growth (except as part of some complicated co-integration relationship) because the two variables are of different orders of integration (Jones, 1995a) and you do not find a robust association between changes and changes (Pritchett, 2001).

10 This of course depends on the details of the simulation assumptions: for example relative magnitude of the shocks, the differences in adjustment speeds, and so on.

References

Birdsall, N., D. Ross and R. Sabot (1995) 'Inequalty and Growth Reconsidered: Lessons From East Asia', *World Bank Economic Review*, vol. 9(3), pp. 477–508.

Blomstrom, M., R. Lipsey and M. Zejan (1996) 'Is Fixed Investment the Key to Economic Growth?', *Quarterly Journal of Economics*, vol. 111(1), pp. 269–76.

Carroll, C. D and D. Weil (1994) 'Saving and Growth: A Reinterpretation'. *Carnegie-Rochester Conference Series on Public Policy*, vol. 40, pp. 133–92.

Chin H. H. and Jong-il Kim (2001) 'Sources of East Asian Growth: Some Evidence from Cross-country Studies', mimeo Global Development Network, Washington, DC.

Clemens, M. and J. Williamson (2001) 'Why the Tariff–Growth Correlation Changed after 1950', NBER Working Paper no. 8459.

Denison, E. (1967) *Why Growth Rates Differ: Postwar Experience in Nine Countries* (Washington, DC: Brookings Institution).

De Gregorio, J. and J.-W. Lee (1999) 'Economic Growth in Latin America: Sources and Prospects', mimeo Global Development Network, Washington, DC.

De Soto, H. (2000) *The Mystery of Capital: Why Capitalism Triumphs in the West and Fails Everywhere Else* (New York: Basic Books).

Ellickson, R. C. (1991) *Order Without Law: How Neighbors Settle Disputes* (Cambridge, Mass.: Harvard University Press).

Faisal B. and B. Guha-Khasnobis (2000) 'Sources of Growth in South Asian Countries', Global Development Network, November 2000.

Foster, A. and M. R. Rosenzweig (1996) 'Technical Change and Human-Capital Returns and Investments: Evidence from the Green Revolution'. *American Economic Review*, vol. 86(4), pp. 931–53.

Foster, A. and M. R. Rosenzweig (1995) 'Learning by Doing and Learning from Others: Human Capital and Technical Change in Agriculture', *Journal of Political Economy*, vol. 103(6), pp. 1176–209.

Hicks, J. (1965) *Capital and Growth* (Oxford: Clarendon Press).

Jensen, C. M. (1993) 'The Modern Industrial Revolution, Exit, and the Failure of Internal Control Systems', *Journal of Finance*, vol. 48, pp. 831–80.

Jones, C. I. (1995a) 'Time Series Tests of Endogenous Growth Models', *Quarterly Journal of Economics,* vol. 110, pp. 496–525.

Jones, C. I. (1995b) 'R&D-Based Models of Economic Growth', *Journal of Political Economy*, vol. 103, pp. 759–84.

Kelley, A. and R. Scmidt (1994) 'Population and Income Change: Recent Evidence', World Bank Working Papers, no. 249.

Knack, S. and P. Keefer (1997) 'Does Social Capital Have an Economic Payoff? A Cross-Country Investigation', *Quarterly Journal of Economics*, vol. 112, pp. 1251–88.

Kuznets, S. (1960) 'Population Change and Aggregate Output', reprinted as chapter 14 in J.L. Simon, *The Economics of Population: Key Modern Writings* (1997), vol. 1 (Cheltenham: Edward Elgar).

Levine, R. and D. Renelt (1992) 'A Sensitivity Analysis of Cross-Country Growth Regressions', *American Economic Review*, vol. 82, pp. 942–63.

Lewis, W.A. (1955) *The Theory of Economic Growth* (Homewood, Ill.: Irwin).

Mehra, R. and E. Prescott (1985) 'The Equity Premium: A Puzzle', *Journal of Monetary Economics*, vol. 15, pp. 145–61.

Myrdal, G. (1968) *Asian Drama: An Inquiry into the Poverty of Nations* (New York: Pantheon).

O'Connell, S. A. and B. J. Ndulu (1999) 'Governance and Growth in Sub-Saharan Africa', *Journal of Economic Perspectives*, vol. 13(3), pp. 41–66. (Corrections to tables 1 and 2 in this paper appeared in *JEP*, vol. 14(3), Summer 2000, pp. 241–2).

Pritchett, L. (1998) 'Our Dearly Departed Friend "Recent Growth Research"', Comments at American Economics Association meetings.

Pritchett, L. (2001) 'Where Has All the Education Gone?' *World Bank Economic Review,* 15(3), pp. 367–91.

Schultz, T. W. (1963*) The Economic Value of Education* (New York, NY: Columbia University Press).

Solow, R. M. (1970) *Growth Theory: An Exposition* (Oxford: Oxford University Press).

Index of Names

Subject Index

newly-industrialized economies
(NIEs) 36, 39
Nigeria 82t, 131, 149, 178, 180, 187,
192, 216, 219, 222, 242(n7)
Malaysia contrasted 175–6
non-policy variables 57–60
non-tariff barriers 65, 70, 73(n15),
112(n17)
Norway 178

oil 68, 126, 131, 143–4, 146, 147, 176,
178, 180, 223, 219, 236
old age 79, 80
openness to trade *see* trade openness
opposition (political) 162
organisation for Economic
Cooperation and Development
(OECD) 128
organized crime 8, 104, 128
overinvestment 87, 111(n7)
overregulation 103

Pakistan 12, 21, 23, 73(n17)
Papua New Guinea 23
Paraguay 23
parliamentary regimes 167, 169,
204(n9)
patents 133, 238
paternalism 197–8
patronage 194
Persian Gulf States 176
Peru 27, 29t, 103t, 230
PEs *see* public enterprises
Philippines 23, 82t, 103t, 187
physical capital xvi, xvii, 11–12, 18t,
33, 38–40, 44, 77, 82, 85,
151(n2), 183, 215, 241(n1)
growth regressions 218t, 241(n6)
initial 184–5
received wisdom challenged 217–21
see also alpha
piracy 173
plant size 81, 82t
plastics 223
Poland 104, 104t, 196
policy 33, 49, 55t, 56t, 60–5, 67, 68,
147, 171, 236, 238, 239
conditional rules about actions
230–6

empirical investigation 48, 230–6
inefficient 9
reason for non-adoption of alternative 202
status quo 203
policy actions 231, 232, 234–5, 236
policy choice 3, 28, 78, 154(n54), 241
policy failures 130, 131
policy impact: growth regressions
233t
policy implementation 103, 112(n14)
policy persistence 204(n12)
policy recommendations 9, 231
policy variables 17, 18–19t, 27
policy wedges 119, 122, 129, 133,
134, 148, 149, 153(n29–30)
policy-massage sender (PMS) 227
policy-making 5, 8, 66, 164, 168, 169,
179, 200, 201, 203, 227, 234, 236
political awareness 165
political economy xv, xix, 2–3, 66, 78,
126, 140, 144, 145, 146, 150,
159–212, 226–8, 230
application and empirical evidence
172–201
constraints 130, 137, 153(n32)
determinants of policy and institutional reform 195–201
exogenous uncertainty 178–81
government policies 189–95
natural resources 177–8
role of institutions 173–7
theories 160–72
transitory growth and role of initial
conditions 181–8
political power: unequal access 185
political stability 53t, 55t, 60, 142,
167, 174, 175, 181, 187
politicians 8, 160, 161, 162, 168, 172,
177, 197, 199
Portugal 185
poverty viii, xv, xvii, 32, 141, 165,
167, 178, 186, 187, 188, 204(n8),
224
poverty trap 184
presidential systems 168, 204(n9)
pressure groups 126, 130, 131, 145,
150, 159–60, 203(n2)
prices 220